DONALD CAMPBELL
BLUEBIRD AND THE
FINAL RECORD ATTEMPT

DONALD CAMPBELL
BLUEBIRD AND THE
FINAL RECORD ATTEMPT

NEIL SHEPPARD
FOREWORD BY GINA CAMPBELL QSO

For Sandra

First published in 2011
This paperback edition first published in 2012

The History Press
The Mill, Brimscombe Port
Stroud, Gloucestershire, GL5 2QG
www.thehistorypress.co.uk

© Neil Sheppard, 2011, 2012

The right of Neil Sheppard to be identified as the Author
of this work has been asserted in accordance with the
Copyrights, Designs and Patents Act 1988.

British Library Cataloguing in Publication Data.
A catalogue record for this book is available from the British
Library.

ISBN 978 0 7524 8258 3

Typesetting and origination by The History Press

Manufacturing Managed by Jellyfish Print Solutions ltd
Printed in Malta by Gutenberg Press.

CONTENTS

ACKNOWLEDGEMENTS

Donald Campbell, Bluebird and the Final Record Attempt represents a labour of love. It exists only as a direct result of the help I received from a group of quite extraordinary people, who provided the ingredients that make this book unique. I would like to thank them, for without their assistance the story you are just about to read would have been greatly diminished.

For introducing me to Donald Malcolm Campbell in the first place: my parents.

For their encouragement, permission and assistance, without which there would have been no book: my wife Sandra, Gina Campbell QSO, Tonia Bern-Campbell, Dr Keith Mitchell for his quite brilliant analysis chapter and Andrew Brealey.

For granting access to original engineering and analysis archives, as well as sharing their memories of events as they happened: Tony James, Bill Vanryne, Professor John Stollery, Clive Glynn, Ken Wheeler, the late Leo Villa and the late Ken Norris.

For providing the wonderful illustrations for use in this book, many of which had remained hidden for years: Eddie Whitham, Carl Rogerson, Norman Hurst, Paul Allonby, the late Geoff Hallawell, John Griffith, David De Lara, John Wardhaugh, Mike Ockenden, Mike Varndell, Don Wales, Stephen Darbishire, John Dart, Steve Wilding, Vicky Slowe of the Ruskin Museum, Joanne Burman of the BP Archive, David Scripps of Mirrorpix, Lucie Gregory of PA Photos, Catherine Theakston of Getty Images, Ben Smith of News International and Beatrice Donze of Longines.

For their recollections, memories and stories: Anthony 'Robbie' Robinson, the late Norman Luck, Geoffrey Mather, the late David Watt, the late Paul Evans and the late Ted Hamel (via his project diary).

For sharing their knowledge of all manner of things Campbell: Steve Holter, David Tremayne, Andy Griffin, Frederick Blois, Mark Longhurst, Geoff Holme and John Bullivant.

For their help with matters technical: Bill Smith, David Clarke and Dr Robert Englar.

For their help with matters creative and artistic: Stuart Biles, Michelle Tilling and Richard Leatherdale at The History Press, the late Chris Jackson and Manish Patel at Metro Imaging, Rona Innes, Joanne Craske and Rob Holding for their image retouching, Damien Burke, Sabrina Pennewiss, Howard Potter and Robert McCartney for their graphic design and artwork.

Finally, in addition to their contributions noted above, a special mention to Dr Keith Mitchell, Tony James, Professor John Stollery and Andrew Brealey, of E.P.A. Language Services who spent many hours reading and re-reading the manuscript before it was committed to print.

Thank you all.
Neil

ABOUT THE AUTHORS

Neil Sheppard M.Sc (Fin), pictured with Gina Campbell, is a structured investment product specialist living in London.

Neil is an acknowledged expert on Donald Campbell and has acted as historical consultant to The Bluebird Project and The Ruskin Museum.

He has contributed to a number of TV documentaries, magazine and newspaper articles, and has had a fascination with the life and works of Donald Campbell for over 30 years.

Dr Keith W. Mitchell B.Sc. (Hons), Ph.D., F.I.P.E.M., C.Sci. (Ret.) is a retired Consultant Medical Physicist, living in Northumberland.

His pastimes are the aerodynamics and design of giant radio-controlled model aircraft and the design and performance of hydroplanes, particularly Bluebird K7. He is a long-time admirer of Donald Campbell and his record-breaking achievements.

FOREWORD

I have been honoured to write the forewords to a few highly memorable books that have featured the trials, tribulations but above all the amazing achievements of my late father – Donald Malcolm Campbell. It is therefore extremely difficult to isolate one from another, and to say which is the most accurate, the most interesting, the most flattering!

I first met Neil Sheppard online, apparently this is the modern twenty-first-century way of doing these things. I quickly realised that Neil was not your ordinary enthusiast, as his knowledge and attention to detail on aspects of Donald Campbell and Bluebird were second to none, so he became known by me as 'The Learned One'.

This worked to identify that anything that came online written by him was simply sure to be accurate to the 'nth' degree; such was his attention to detail and his exacting attitude. When we met face to face, I was even more impressed by him as a person, and I am proud to call him a friend.

Neil did not earn these adulations lightly, and I therefore recommend everyone to purchase one of his books, maybe even two or three, as they will make a wonderful memorable gift for anyone, even if they have no particular interest in Donald Campbell and Bluebird. Neil's work will help ensure these two names will remain part of our heritage, in the realm of world land and water speeds, which still thrills the blood of the nation.

Gina D. Campbell QSO
Yorkshire, 2011

PREFACE
'THE OLD SEA OF FATE'

The basic facts are beyond doubt. On Wednesday 4 January 1967, Donald Malcolm Campbell was piloting his jet boat, Bluebird K7, across Coniston Water, in search of his eighth World Water Speed Record, when suddenly and inexplicably his boat took off. Bluebird climbed into the air and somersaulted before finally impacting the concrete like surface of the lake. It killed him.

This book covers all the possibilities and presents its own theories about the cause of Campbell's crash. But ultimately, the theories and explanations don't really matter. How he died was clear. The TV cameras captured the event for all to see. His death left behind a larger mystery. Not the mystery of why Bluebird took to the air on its return journey through the measured kilometre at 300mph, when success was just seconds away. The real mystery surrounds Campbell himself – why was he there in the middle of a particularly horrid winter, what was he trying to do, and what was the force that meant he could not turn back from his task.

Donald Campbell was unlike most other people. He *had* to be to break seven World Water Speed Records and, in 1964, become the only man in history to break the Land and Water Speed Records in the same year.

He was immensely brave. He was intensely patriotic. He was incredibly determined. He believed in God, not the churchgoing or public displays, but a basic belief in a spiritual sense. He also believed in fate. He loved life and lived it well. He was light of heart and optimistic of nature, but behind the public façade of the speed king lay a complex character – proud and vulnerable, anxious about his place in the world. He was also tired. He was disappointed at the lack of support for the new rocket car with which he dreamed of bringing the Land Speed Record back to Britain. He had been doing the impossible for more than fifteen years, carrying on his father's role in an age when logic told him everything was against it.

Within seven months of Sir Malcolm Campbell's death, Donald had stepped into Bluebird's cockpit and his father's legend. He never escaped. One has to admire the way he did it all, matching his father's achievements although the odds were increasing all the time. He overcame setbacks and disappointments his father never faced. His personal triumphs with the Water Speed Record led him to the record on land. His father had held both records – the son would do the same. Taking the risk and responsibility himself, backing it with the prestige he had built in his own right on water, he aimed to secure resounding success in a second golden age of record-breaking. He would have done it as well, had his Bluebird CN7 car not spun out of control and crashed at 350mph at Bonneville in 1960.

Nothing was quite the same after that.

Yes, the car was rebuilt; yes, he recovered from his injuries; yes, a new course was found, but the crash had shown him that his pursuit of speed could have lethal consequences. He never forgot it.

His subsequent ordeal and eventual success at Lake Eyre in 1964 demonstrated the true price he was willing to pay for the record. Everything ultimately depended on him and him alone. On *his* bravery – *his* courage. He held his nerve, his driving was supreme.

The pressure must have been unbearable. He was trapped between the legend of his father's achievements and the memory of the crash at Bonneville. All the time, he knew he would have to take a calculated risk with the odds stacked against him. In Australia, he won out – twice – but the double success of 1964 did not bring the public acclaim and recognition that it would have brought in Sir Malcolm's day. If it had, the disaster at Coniston would not have occurred. It was that lack of impact which caused Donald to re-engineer his faithful old warhorse, the iconic Bluebird K7, for one last joust with the unknown. This book tells the story of that joust – of *his* determination and *his* courage.

Donald Campbell will always be remembered for what he became at the point Bluebird left the surface of Coniston Water. *A legend . . .* He will always be a legend, his like will never be seen again but his legacy will endure.

Neil Sheppard
London, 2011

'We're all playing for the same team . . .'

I had better explain briefly where my interest in Donald Campbell came from . . .

Returning home from a day out with my parents, we were driving along the shoreline of Ullswater, prompting mum and dad's conversation to turn to a time when they had witnessed a man called Donald Campbell driving his jet-propelled boat, Bluebird, out on the lake. Having an interest in things that went fast, suddenly, I was paying attention.

They told the story of how in the summer of 1955, they had spent many an evening alongside the shore, with hundreds of other people, witnessing Campbell's high-speed trials in Bluebird K7, as a precursor to breaking his first World Water Speed Record. I was amazed that something so exciting could take place on my doorstep.

Within a few days, I was pestering mum to visit the local library to see if they had any Campbell books that would satisfy my curiosity. We picked up the biography *Donald Campbell CBE*. My parents didn't hear much of me for the rest of that evening, and the next or the one after that . . . I was totally engrossed and have been ever since . . . I hope when you have read this book, you will be too.

During the research for this book, I was very fortunate to speak to a number of Donald Campbell's former team members, his friends and members of the press who had been with him during the final record attempt. Their memories were still vivid after all these years, surely a mark of the effect that Donald Campbell and the events of the autumn and winter of 1966/67 had had on each of them. I wanted this book to capture their first-hand memories, not just to be my 'second-hand' interpretation – if you like, for their own individual voices to be heard.

Interspaced over the following nine chapters are the perspectives of seven eyewitnesses to the events you are about to read about, four people who were intimately involved in the engineering and operation of Bluebird K7, two members of the press, who covered the final attempt and finally, from a personal friend, 'Robbie' Robinson, who witnessed the final tragedy at close hand, and who, 34 years later, delivered the eulogy at Donald's funeral. 'Robbie' very kindly allowed me to use that personal tribute in this volume.

I hope you agree with me that what shines through is the very real impact Donald had on each individual, with stories of kindness, determination and loyalty, their testaments are truly the mark of the man.

The Key Players

Donald Malcolm Campbell CBE ('Skipper'): Born 1921. Bluebird pilot and team leader. Holder of the WSR seven times and the LSR once. Only person in history to break the LSR and WSR in the same year.

Tonia Bern-Campbell ('Fred'): Born 1934. Professional singer and cabaret performer. Donald's third wife, married 24 December 1958.

Leo Villa OBE ('Unc'): Born 1899. Chief engineer to Sir Malcolm and Donald Campbell, overseeing 21 world speed records on land and water from 1924 to 1964.

Maurice Parfitt ('Maurie'): Born 1916. Technical engineer to Donald Campbell since 1954.

Ken Norris B.Sc., A.C.G.I., F.I.Mech.E., F.R.Ae.S.: Born 1921. Co-designer of Bluebird K7 hydroplane and Bluebird CN7 car. Co-founder of Norris Brothers Ltd, consulting engineers.

Lewis Norris C.Eng., M.I.Mech.E. ('Lew'): Born 1924. Co-designer of Bluebird K7 hydroplane and Bluebird CN7 car. Co-founder of Norris Brothers Ltd, consulting engineers.

Tony James C.Eng., M.I.Mech.E.: Born 1933. Project Manager at Norris Brothers R&D Ltd. Manager for Bluebird K7's modifications and refit August – November 1966.

Louis Goossens: Born 1929. Donald Campbell's house manager since 1959. General team assistant.

Clive Glynn: Born 1944. Apprentice mechanic co-opted into Bluebird team in November 1966.

Anthony Robinson ('Robbie'): Born 1944. Team assistant and course boat pilot. Son of Connie Robinson, of the Sun Hotel, Bluebird team base in autumn/ winter of 1966/67.

Corporal Paul Evans: Royal Army Signals Corps. Responsible for team radio communications during Bluebird trials.

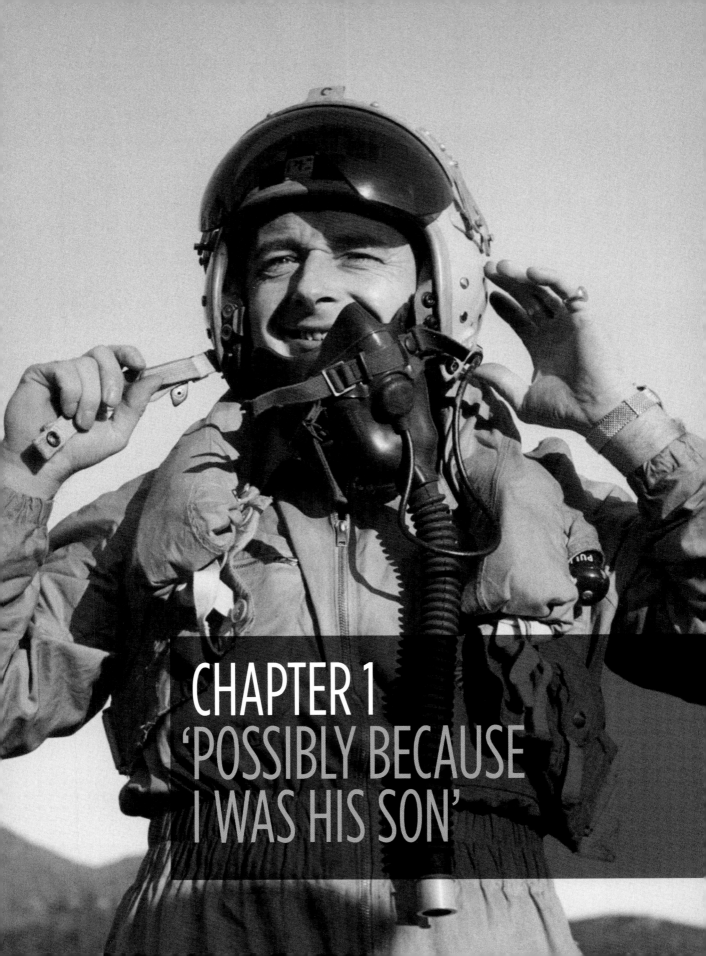

CHAPTER 1
'POSSIBLY BECAUSE I WAS HIS SON'

Donald Malcolm Campbell was born on 23 March 1921, the only son of the greatest speed record-breaker of the inter-war years, Sir Malcolm Campbell. This extraordinary background was to shape his entire character. In fact, Donald never truly escaped from his father's shadow.

Sir Malcolm and Donald Campbell with Bluebird K4 at Coniston in August 1939.
© Don Wales

Sir Malcolm Campbell set the World Land Speed Record (LSR) nine times and the World Water Speed Record (WSR) four times in his famous Blue Birds. Lionised by the press and fêted as a national hero, though often regarded as arrogant, he had little time for normal family life. Donald and his younger sister Jean took second place to their father's record-breaking activities. Nonetheless, Donald worshipped his rather distant father. But while Sir Malcolm was still alive, there would only be one record-breaker in the family and Donald was firmly discouraged from following in his father's career path. Sir Malcolm even speculated once that Donald would kill himself if he ever drove a speed boat.

> 'It was hell being Sir Malcolm Campbell's son, but I have to be at least as good as he was. Every time I go out in a speed boat, I realise more and more just how good my father was and how much he really knew about this game. There is far more to it than just sitting in a boat and putting your foot down.'
>
> **Donald Campbell in the *Evening Standard*, December 1966**

When Sir Malcolm died on 1 January 1949 as the result of a stroke, Donald, by now married and with a young daughter, Gina, found that neither the Blue Bird car nor the K4 hydroplane had been left to him. Instead, everything in Sir Malcolm's estate was to be auctioned and the proceeds placed in a trust for his grandchildren. It was a mean-spirited act designed to thwart Donald, but Sir Malcolm had not reckoned on something that Donald *had* inherited from his father – guts and dogged determination. Donald bought the two vehicles from the estate as keepsakes, little knowing what role they would play in his own future.

In early spring 1949, as his father's estate was being wound up, Donald received a visit from Goldie Gardner, Sir Malcolm's ex-project manager and a record-breaker in his own right. Gardner mentioned that Henry Kaiser, an American industrialist and builder of wartime Liberty ships, was working on a boat to be called 'Aluminium First' with the aim of making an attempt on the Water Speed Record.

After Gardner had left, Donald sat in his father's study thinking about what he had been told. At that moment, he made the decision to carry on with his father's work. Years later, he described his instinctive reaction to Kaiser as being 'to hell with you'.

He sought out Leo Villa, his father's faithful chief mechanic, who was clearing up Sir Malcolm's private garage. 'Leo, Henry Kaiser is going to take the old man's record back to America – we're going to do something about it. Are you with me?'

> 'The name passed from one car to another, from track racing to World Speed Records, from land to water, from father to son. In the passage of time, as world record succeeded world record, each became just one more milestone of human progress, a single word in the book of human endeavour, a book perhaps without an end. A book in which every man has something to write, of his struggles, successes and failures on his ascent of the mountain of progress. But each can only go so far since the mountain has no summit, for it leads to the stars. It has to be climbed for mankind cannot regress; he may pause momentarily, but there is no going back on the path of life. In bygone days, disease took a toll which progressing science is giving us the means to overcome; it is also giving us the means to totally destroy. With our faith in God, right has always triumphed over might. Life is an eternal challenge, a variant on Maeterlinck's theme perhaps, but man is given only two real sources of happiness; a happy marriage, which means a happy home, and the satisfaction of a job well done. If this be true, the theme and the variant are synonymous and inseparable, for one without the other is like a dish without flavour, a day without sunshine.'
>
> Donald Campbell, *The Eternal Challenge*, 1965

Villa looked at Donald, realised that he was deadly serious, and offered the following counsel: 'Before you do, think very carefully. If you once start, you'll never stop and no matter how long you're at it, you'll never get used to the atmosphere. It'll require a lot of thought and a lot of money, and like your dad, you'll keep on going faster and faster to keep ahead.' Donald retorted, 'I don't believe that, I just want to keep the old flag flying, get the record and call it a day.'

In later life, when he was firmly stuck on the record-breaker's treadmill, Donald admitted that Leo had been absolutely right. The die was cast.

In the summer of 1949, Donald returned to the scene of his father's last record-breaking success – Coniston Water in the English Lake District – but not before overcoming the first hurdle in his new career as a would-be record-breaker.

Sir Malcolm had converted his Blue Bird K4 hydroplane to jet power after the war, but the jet engine manufacturer would not countenance a novice like Donald taking over an unproven concept and demanded the engine back. Donald promptly sold the 1935 Blue Bird car in order to buy back a Rolls-Royce 'R' type piston engine and the V-drive, propeller shaft and other gear which Sir Malcolm had sold to a car dealer named Simpson along with the earlier Blue Bird K3 boat. With the equipment back in his possession, Donald had Blue Bird K4 converted to propeller drive again.

Donald and his new team were back at Coniston in late July. On the day of his first run, he was impatient to get going and in no mood to be held back by Leo Villa's caution. After his initial low-speed trial, he came back to the slipway and announced: 'Bloody marvellous Leo, it's a piece of cake, I don't know what you were worried about.'

During the next run, Donald pushed K4 a bit harder, got into a skid, and returned ashen-faced and suitably chastened, telling the assembled team: 'This job's bloody dangerous!' After more trials he was ready to have a go at the record. Two runs later, the second of which ended with him covered in hot gearbox oil, he was told he had exceeded his father's WSR. In the middle of lamenting that he had broken his old man's record, he was informed by the timekeepers that they had made a mistake and he was actually some 3mph short. The team would have to return south to repair the gearbox, so for now his challenge was over. Kaiser's boat came to nought, but Donald had the bug and was now determined to beat his father's old mark. Shortly after arriving back at Coniston in late summer 1950 for further trials, he received the news that another American, Stanley Sayers, had raised the record to 160.32mph in a boat called Slo-Mo-Shun IV. A long series of trials followed, without success. Although Blue Bird had sufficient power, the trim of the boat caused problems, so eventually the team returned south for a rethink.

By 1951, with the help of a young designer named Lewis Norris, K4 had been modified to make it a 'prop-rider' as opposed to her original immersed propeller configuration. This would greatly reduce hydrodynamic drag as the third planing point would now be the propeller hub, meaning one of the two propeller blades was always out of the water at high speed. She now sported two cockpits, the second one being for Leo Villa. The pair worked ceaselessly towards exceeding Sayers' record and also enjoyed a measure of success with K4 as a circuit racer, winning the Oltranza Cup in Italy in the spring of that year. Returning to Coniston in September, they finally got Bluebird up to 170mph after further trials. Above the roar of the engine, Donald shouted across to Leo: 'This is way above the record – good old Bluebird.' Seconds later, both were lucky to survive a horrific crash when a propellor shaft support strut failed and Bluebird's gearbox sheared its mountings, punching a large hole in the underside of the boat. K4 was wrecked.

Sayers raised the record the following year to 178.497mph in Slo-Mo-Shun IV. Alongside Donald Campbell, Britain's other potential contender for Water Speed Record honours was John Cobb. He had commissioned the world's first purpose-built jet boat, Crusader, with a target speed of over 200mph, and began trials on Loch Ness in autumn 1952. Cobb was killed during a subsequent attempt on the record, causing Donald's spirits to sink. The famous Campbell determination soon reasserted itself though, and he resolved to build a new Bluebird boat.

The necessary money was raised by selling Campbell's share in a thriving engineering business he had helped to establish. The decision to dedicate himself to record-breaking meant limited time and space for conventional family life. His first marriage was already behind him and he was now married for a second time. Donald would have been the first to admit that to succeed in his chosen career, it would be necessary to become extremely selfish and single-minded in pursuing his goal.

The money from the sale of the engineering business allowed him to commission Lewis Norris and brother Ken, who had set up as consulting engineers in Burgess Hill and Haywards Heath, West Sussex, to design and build an ultra-strong, all-metal, jet-powered craft – Bluebird K7. (The first Bluebird, Sir Malcolm's vehicles having always been designated Blue Bird). The boat was finished by the end of 1954 and taken to Ullswater in the Lake District in early 1955. After many months of unsuccessful trials and a major redesign, Donald finally broke the feared 'water barrier' with a speed of 202.32mph on 23 July 1955, having previously been forced to mortgage his house to raise sufficient funds.

K7 at Ullswater, July 1955.
© Ruskin Museum

He raised the record again to 216.2mph in November 1955 on Lake Mead in Nevada. It was now clear that he was hooked on record-breaking. The Lake Mead success brought further recognition with the award of a CBE in 1956. His reputation was never higher.

The Water Barrier

Donald Campbell often talked of the 'water barrier'.
What is it? It's probably better to describe what it is not.

The term supersonic is used to define a speed greater than the speed of sound (Mach 1), i.e. the sound barrier. It is not strictly speaking a barrier, just the speed at which an aircraft exceeds the speed of sound. In dry air at 20°C (68°F), the threshold value required for an object to be travelling at supersonic speed is approximately 343m/s (1,125ft/s, 768mph or 1,236km/h). In other words, 'sound barrier' is a label used to describe supersonic speed.

'Water barrier' does not refer to a speed, but rather to a phenomenon that affects hydroplanes.

Campbell was describing a situation where Bluebird began to pitch quite violently at up to six cycles per second, accompanied by significant vertical acceleration depending on water conditions. The existence of this pitching cycle had been observed in Cobb's boat, Crusader. It convinced Norris Brothers to build K7 as strongly as they possibly could, to withstand this severe buffeting.

In Donald's own words:

'In Bluebird, at 200mph, she will start a gentle pitch; at 210mph, the cycle will build up to between 4 and 6 cycles per second, accompanied by vertical acceleration of between +4 and +6g. At 215mph comes the edge of the barrier. Vision is severely affected by this violent vibration phase, with the instrument panel, nose of the boat, water and horizon becoming one vibrating, merging blur. The right foot, however tightly wedged against the throttle, goes out of control.'

Continuing to accelerate, over flat, calm water the pitching cycle tended to be damped out at the top of the barrier speed, which was around 250–260mph. Over disturbed water, the pitching cycle would tend to continue. It is this pitching cycle that Donald referred to in his comment 'I can't get over the top' on some of the fast runs in December 1966, and the final runs on 4 January, the complaint that it was difficult to see where he was on the course.

The term 'breaking the water barrier' was the convenient and dramatic way Donald chose to label Bluebird's behaviour at high speed, at a time in the 1950s when the sound barrier held a strong fascination for schoolboys and their fathers alike.

Campbell received significant financial backing for this and subsequent attempts, usually at Coniston, first from Mobil, and later in the 1950s from BP, as well as Dunlop, Smiths Industries and Lucas.

In addition, holiday camp magnate Sir Billy Butlin, who made a fortune during the post-war boom years, put up a large gold cup and an annual £5,000 prize for any Briton who broke the World Water Speed Record. Campbell used this prize money to boost his sponsorship income in the 1950s, deliberately nudging the record up little by little – 225.63mph in 1956, 239.07mph in 1957, 248.62mph in 1958 and finally 260.35mph in May 1959, all of these records being set on Coniston Water.

During the same period, Donald's personal life was in a state of flux – record-breaking and marriage do not necessarily mix – and his second marriage ended in June 1957. In December 1958, he was married for the third time, to a Belgian singer named Tonia Bern.

Bluebird K7 on the slipway at Coniston in September 1958.
© BP Archive

Donald with Bluebird K7 at Coniston in May 1959.
© BP Archive

In the eyes of the world, these achievements made Donald a great success, but Donald's thinking was still dominated by his father. He constantly sought Leo's opinion as to whether the old man would have approved. 'Do you think the old man would be proud?' he would ask. 'Of course he would,' Villa would reply, seemingly exasperated that Donald rated his own triumphs less highly than those of his father.

A PHOTOGRAPHER'S PERSPECTIVE
PAUL ALLONBY ON DONALD CAMPBELL

'I first met Donald Campbell on one of his earlier attempts at the world record on Coniston, either 1958 or '59. I was at that time training to be a photographer with Sanderson & Dixon of Ambleside and was with Reg Sanderson, who knew Donald quite well from earlier attempts and had photographed him on numerous occasions.

Donald and Reg introduced me to photographer Geoff Hallawell who was an old friend of theirs and now of mine. Later that day, DC came to the studio where I was drying the photographs we had taken earlier, he chatted freely and came over as a very friendly person. David Watt of Coniston was the photo printer at that time and a great fan of Donald's. Little did I know then the association I would have with the Campbell story! I am still amazed at the interest shown in DC by people all over the country and who are still to this day buying photographs I took of the 66/67 attempt.'

It was after the Lake Mead success in 1955 that the seeds of Donald's ambition to hold the Land Speed Record as well were planted. At a party in Las Vegas, he was asked why he had never gone after the LSR. He put the matter to Leo. 'What about it, Leo? We'll get the water record here at Lake Mead, then fly out to Utah and get the land record on the same day.' Leo replied that he did not think record-breaking was that easy, and with Donald's luck they did not stand a chance, but by this time Donald wasn't listening. 'We'll see what Ken and Lew have to say about this.'

The Norris brothers were even more enthusiastic about the car than the boat. Like all of his projects, Donald wanted Bluebird CN7, as the car became known, to be the best of its type, a showcase of British engineering skill. Over the next four years, while Donald broke the WSR a further four times, CN7 gradually took shape.

CN7 was powered by a specially modified Bristol Siddeley Proteus gas turbine engine driving all four wheels. The existing LSR had been set by John Cobb in 1947 and stood at 394.19mph. Bluebird CN7 was designed to achieve 475–500mph – more than enough to smash Cobb's long-standing record. In August 1960, when CN7 was shipped to Bonneville Salt Flats, Utah, the scene of Sir Malcolm Campbell's last LSR, the outcome was felt to be a foregone conclusion.

Bluebird CN7 at the Bonneville Salt Flats, Utah, in September 1960.
© Leo Villa's Film and Picture Archive

The only question was by how far Bluebird would exceed Cobb's record. On arrival, Campbell found that, unlike his father 25 years earlier, he did not have the luxury of the salt flats to himself. There were three rivals for LSR honours, ranging from backyard piston engine specials to a pure thrust jet car. His entourage, which included representatives from the firms that had helped build CN7, looked ostentatious to American eyes. Campbell was spooked and felt the pressure to get going. On the sixth run in CN7, he lost control at over 360mph and crashed. It was the car's enormous structural integrity that saved his life. He was hospitalised with a fractured skull and a burst eardrum, as well as sundry cuts and bruises. Almost immediately, Campbell announced he was determined to have another go. Sir Alfred Owen, whose Rubery Owen industrial group had built CN7, offered to rebuild it. That single decision was to have a profound influence on the rest of Donald Campbell's life. His original plan had been to break the LSR at over 400mph in 1960, return to Bonneville the following year to really bump up the speed to something near 500mph, get the WSR with K7 and then retire, secure in the knowledge that he was worthy of his father's legacy.

Now, Campbell chose not to go back to Utah. He felt the Bonneville course was too short and he disliked having to share it with the competition. His main sponsor, BP, offered to find another venue and eventually Lake Eyre, in South Australia, was chosen.

Bluebird CN7 transported past the 'guardians' to Lake Eyre in 1963.
© BP Archive

It hadn't rained there for nine years and the vast dry bed of the salt lake offered a course of up to 20 miles, compared to Bonneville's 11 miles. Bluebird CN7 was rebuilt by the summer of 1962, about nine months later than Donald had hoped. By the end of 1962, the car had been shipped out to Australia ready for the new attempt. No sooner had low-speed runs started than the heavens opened. The course was compromised and by May 1963 Lake Eyre was flooded to a depth of 3 inches, causing the attempt to be abandoned. Donald was fiercely criticised in the press for alleged mismanagement of the project, despite the fact that he could hardly be held responsible for the weather.

To make matters worse, American Craig Breedlove drove his Shell sponsored pure thrust jet car 'Spirit of America' to a speed of 407.45mph at Bonneville in July 1963. Although the 'car' did not conform to FIA (Fédération Internationale de l'Automobile) regulations that stipulated it had to be wheel-driven and have a minimum of four wheels, in the eyes of the world, Breedlove was now the fastest man on earth.

Campbell returned to Australia in March 1964, but the course failed to fulfil its early promise and there were further spells of rain. Splits also emerged in the team, with his Dunlop representative and reserve driver, Andrew Mustard, accusing him of being physically unfit and lacking the skill to drive the car to record speeds. BP had pulled out as his main sponsor in March when he refused their request to appoint a project manager. Subsequently, Donald secured backing from Australian oil company, Ampol, whom he had lined up to cover the possibility of BP's exit.

The Lake Eyre track never dried out properly and Campbell was forced to make do with the conditions and resources he had. Finally, in July 1964, he was able to post some speeds that approached the record. On the 17th of that month, he took advantage of a break in the weather and made two courageous runs along the shortened and still-damp track, posting a new LSR of 403.1mph. He was bitterly disappointed that he had not exceeded Breedlove's speed, and got closer to CN7's design potential of 475mph. He also resented the fact that it had all been so difficult. 'We've made it – we got the bastard at last,' was his reaction to his success.

Breedlove's speed had not been recognised by the FIA, so Donald's 403.1mph represented the official Land Speed Record.

On the return run, where Campbell had covered the last third of the mile at 429.5mph and exited the measured mile at 440mph, Bluebird's 52-inch wheels had punched 3-inch ruts in the salt surface as the track disintegrated. CN7 had been close to careering out of control, yet few commentators appreciated the scale of Campbell's achievement. Bluebird was still accelerating as it left the measured mile on both runs, and there cannot be the slightest doubt that with a longer, drier track, Campbell would have easily exceeded Breedlove's speed and set a wheel-driven LSR that would have been very tough to beat. In later years, this record was largely reassessed and the CN7 episode is today seen as a triumph over adversity.

Donald now planned to go after the Water Speed Record one more time, to do what he had aimed for so many years ago during the initial planning stages of CN7 – break both records in the same year. After more setbacks and frustrations with the weather, he got his seventh WSR by the skin of his teeth on the last day of 1964, when he took Bluebird K7 to 276.33mph on Lake Dumbleyung near Perth, Western Australia.

This was his finest achievement: he became the first (and, to this day, only) man in history to break both the Land and Water Speed Records in the same year, a feat unlikely ever to be repeated.

CN7 racing across Lake Eyre.
© BP Archive

Tonia (holding Mr Whoppit) and Donald at Lake Dumbleyung after completing the second half of the 1964 LSR and WSR double.
© G. Campbell

CHAPTER 2
'SUPERSONIC LEAPFROG'

The world around him changed dramatically while Donald Campbell was chasing the LSR in the USA in 1960 and then making his subsequent attempts in Australia in 1963 and 1964. At the start of the decade, man had still not been into space and although the sound barrier had been broken many years earlier, record-breaking on land and water still held some allure in the eyes of the public and potential sponsors. By the middle of the decade, the space race was well under way and featured plans to land on the moon. This was the new frontier that captured the public's imagination – the space age had replaced the jet age. Around the same time, the British motor industry turned its attention to motor racing. The country had become the dominant force in Formula One Grand Prix racing, providing oil companies, tyre makers and component manufacturers with an attractive new promotional outlet. British or Commonwealth drivers took every successive drivers' championship from 1962 through to 1969. Sports fans had new high-speed heroes to follow, with drivers such as Graham Hill, Jim Clark, John Surtees, Jack Brabham and Jackie Stewart becoming household names.

This was the new reality facing Donald Campbell when he returned from Australia in late spring 1965. His success in capturing the double, although newsworthy, had not made the same headlines as his exploits in the 1950s. Record-breaking defined him, 'Speed is my life', he had once said, but now he needed to take stock and consider his next step. Should he continue to tread what he called 'this rather stony path'?

Following the successful Lake Eyre attempt, Campbell had commissioned Ken Norris to investigate building a new Bluebird car. Norris had already

Design sketches by
Ken Norris for Bluebird
Mach 1.1.
© Author's Collection

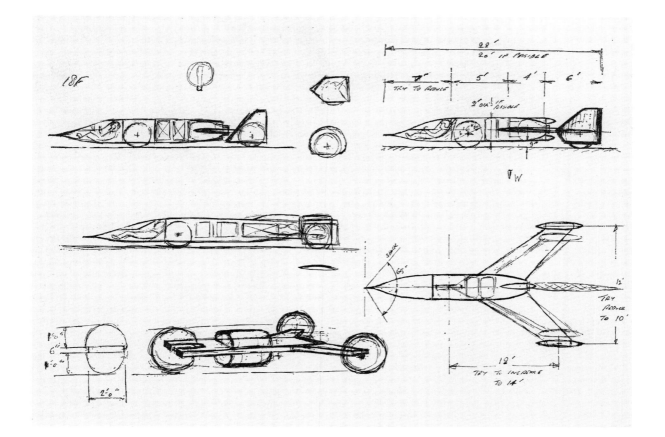

given thought to what the next Bluebird should be like and in 1963, after Craig Breedlove's unofficial record, had suggested a vehicle dubbed 'the amphibian' to break both records. It was to be powered by two Bristol Siddeley Orpheus jet engines and designed to work as a pure thrust jet car on land and, with its wheels removed, as a four-point hydroplane on water, with only minor modifications being required to enable transfer from one medium to the other.

The vehicle had a maximum design speed of 580mph for the LSR and 460mph for the record on water. This idea was presented to a number of potential backers in the autumn of 1964, after the LSR success, including BP and Dunlop, but met with zero interest. Shortly afterwards, Americans Craig Breedlove and Art Arfons both succeeded in taking the LSR beyond 500mph, effectively killing-off the Norris plan. The new amphibian would probably have been obsolete on completion and without the development potential to be a serious contender, at least for the LSR.

Donald decided that a massive jump in speed was called for. His vision was of a supersonic rocket car with a potential maximum speed of 840mph, referred to as Bluebird Mach 1.1. Norris Brothers were requested to undertake a design study.

After his WSR success, Donald and wife Tonia had stayed on in Australia to complete a film called *How Long A Mile*, which told the story of the Lake Eyre and Lake Dumbleyung trials and eventual success. While the film was being completed, back in the UK, Ken Norris made further progress with planning and design of the rocket car.

Donald, ever superstitious, chose a lucky date to hold a press conference at the Charing Cross Hotel on 7 July 1965 to announce his future record-breaking plans:

Donald and Tonia at the Charing Cross Hotel press conference.
© Press Association

'In terms of speed on the earth's surface, my next logical step must be to construct a Bluebird car that can reach Mach 1.1. The Americans are already making plans for such a vehicle and it would be tragic for the world image of British technology if we did not compete in this great contest and win. The nation whose technologies are first to seize the "faster than sound" record on land will be the nation whose industry will be seen to leapfrog into the 70s or 80s. We can have the car on the track within three years.'

Bluebird Mach 1.1 – was to be rocket-powered. Ken Norris had calculated that using rocket motors would result in a vehicle that had a very low frontal area, greater density and lighter weight than if he went down the jet engine route. Bluebird Mach 1.1 would also be a relatively compact and simple design. Norris specified two off-the-shelf Bristol Siddeley 605 rocket engines. The 605 had been developed as a take-off assist rocket engine for military aircraft and was fuelled with kerosene, using hydrogen peroxide as the fuel oxidant. Each engine was rated at 8,000lbs of thrust. In the Bluebird Mach 1.1 application, the combined thrust of 16,000lbs would be the equivalent of a staggering 36,000bhp at 840mph.

The compact size of the rocket motors enabled Ken Norris to design a vehicle with a very low cross-sectional area. A dart-like configuration was chosen, with two closely paired front wheels behind the nose-mounted cockpit and two rear wheels spaced 8 feet apart, faired into stabilising fins. The design was expected to be inherently stable in a straight line. The main structure of the car was both elegant and simple, yet it would ensure significant torsional strength and also allow separate storage of the two liquids, used as the propellant. The main chassis would be a steel box-like beam structure with internal rib strengthening, not unlike the main chassis members of Bluebird CN7. This would provide the frame to which were attached the rocket engines, one above and one below, as well as the propellant tanks – hydrogen peroxide on top, kerosene underneath. The frame would also house the torsion bar rear suspension. Clad in a slim pencil-shaped body with rear outrigger fins, the vehicle would feature a recumbent driving position. The wheels were to be machined from solid aluminium billets. As they were not required for propulsion, but merely to support the car, there would be no need for tyres.

Various dimensions were considered and eventually a full-scale mock-up of the car was built measuring 27 feet 8 inches long, 8 feet 6 inches wide at the rear wheels and with an overall height of just 3 feet 7 inches. Ground clearance was projected to be only 4.5 inches, giving Bluebird Mach 1.1 a very low centre of gravity and roll centre. The predicted weight was 1,660 kilograms including propellants. Bluebird Mach 1.1 would thus have a formidable power-to-weight ratio of 22,000bhp per tonne!

The initial announcement drew a muted response. Despite this disappointing lack of interest, progress on the rocket car continued. Donald Campbell was counting on the fact that it would cost much less than CN7, because it was a far simpler design. A business case for the project was put together, detailing Donald's previous successes with the Bluebird K7 hydroplane and Bluebird CN7 turbine car, plus the operating budget for the record attempts Campbell had made in the period from 1959 to 1964. The figures included receipts from sponsorship and all associated costs.

Additional income would also be expected from exhibitions, merchandising of models and from book rights related to the attempt. In his business plan, Donald indicated that he had received approaches from a large insurance group who were willing to insure the vehicle while it was running and pay a cash amount for the right to do so. The American Broadcasting Corporation had also expressed an interest in acquiring the exclusive television rights.

Campbell included the option of joining forces with a syndicate or single company willing to underwrite the cost of the attempt and handle the entire commercial management side, leaving Donald, his team and the Norris brothers to concentrate solely on engineering and operations. Full-scale construction was expected to begin in summer 1966 and take six months to complete.

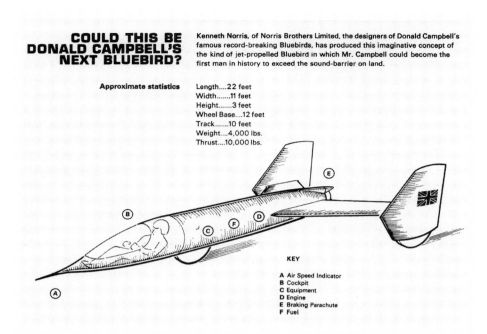

COULD THIS BE DONALD CAMPBELL'S NEXT BLUEBIRD?

Kenneth Norris, of Norris Brothers Limited, the designers of Donald Campbell's famous record-breaking Bluebirds, has produced this imaginative concept of the kind of jet-propelled Bluebird in which Mr. Campbell could become the first man in history to exceed the sound-barrier on land.

Approximate statistics

Length....22 feet
Width.......11 feet
Height.......3 feet
Wheel Base....12 feet
Track.......10 feet
Weight....4,000 lbs.
Thrust....10,000 lbs.

KEY

A Air Speed Indicator
B Cockpit
C Equipment
D Engine
E Braking Parachute
F Fuel

Donald's cost estimate for the new project was £125,000, the equivalent of £1,810,000 today (2011). The total was broken down as follows and provides a fascinating insight into the financial dimension of record-breaking:

£50,000 (2011 equivalent: £724,000) for detailed design and drawing, final supersonic wind-tunnel testing and construction of vehicle

£25,000 (2011 equivalent: £362,000) for administration, technical coordination, operational planning including maintenance and transport of operational team

£35,000 (2011 equivalent: £507,000) for high-speed trials and record attempt

£15,000 (2011 equivalent: £217,000) for contingencies

Against the estimated costs, he also set out the anticipated income from the record attempt:

£50,000 (2011 equivalent: £724,000) from sale of advertising rights to an oil company for fuel and lubricants

£15,000 (2011 equivalent: £217,000) from Joseph Lucas Limited for advertising rights relating to electrical and rocket control gear, suspension and braking components

£15,000 (2011 equivalent: £217,000) from basic material suppliers

£10,000 (2011 equivalent: £145,000) from insurance promotion

£25,000 (2011 equivalent: £362,000) from exclusive television rights

£10,000 (2011 equivalent: £145,000) from newspaper rights

Running trials and the record attempt were scheduled to commence on Lake Eyre in May 1967, but this depended, like so many aspects of the project, on the ability to find a backer or backers.

In early 1966, the Jamaican government showed interest in building a 12–14-mile strip of tarmac road for the attempt, which they hoped would subsequently be used by car manufacturers as a test facility. The absence of a main sponsor for the car meant that this proposal, and a similar one from Trinidad, never advanced beyond the planning stage.

In early spring 1966, the full-scale mock-up of Bluebird Mach 1.1 was displayed at Donald's home, Priors Ford in Leatherhead, alongside Bluebird CN7. Campbell invited his many contacts in the industrial and commercial world as well as the media to attend a presentation, but despite the progress made with the project, no firm backers were forthcoming, and interest in his new venture remained lukewarm at best. This reaction was a disappointment to Campbell, and the schedule he had laid out the previous summer was already doomed.

In order to drum up publicity, Donald investigated putting CN7 back into service. The car had been featured in the Lord Mayor's Show in London in November 1964, before going on display at the Montagu Motor Museum in the New Forest (now the National Motor Museum). In December 1965, Donald agreed to give a high-speed demonstration in CN7 at the Gala of Speed in aid of the RAF Benevolent Association and St John Ambulance the following summer. Campbell thought that in addition to supporting a good cause, the public would be interested in seeing Bluebird perform at high speed on British soil. He decided to give the car a thorough overhaul and set Leo and Maurice to work on this task. CN7 had never reached her true capability, so in

Donald Campbell, Jim Clark and Graham Hill at the Man of the Year Lunch at the Savoy Hotel, November 1965.
© Mirrorpix

order to raise interest in his rocket car project, Donald now made plans for an attempt on the World Standing Mile Record, held by the USA at 148mph. The attempt was scheduled to take place at Greenham Common air base, which had a 2.2-mile runway, in October 1966. If successful, CN7 would become the first car to hold both the flying and standing mile records.

To break the record, Campbell would be reliant on CN7's exceptional traction and acceleration – Bluebird would have to exit the measured mile at over 300mph. Dunlop were approached to provide twelve new tyres for the attempt, but refused to manufacture any more and were also unwilling to supply tyres left over from the 1964 attempt, citing deterioration suffered over the two-year storage period. Donald and Ken Norris vehemently denied that deterioration was an issue, but Dunlop would not budge. The simple truth was that they no longer wanted to be involved in record-breaking. Without the requisite tyres, the attempt was stymied.

Donald seemed to be encountering obstacles whichever way he turned. He was intensely patriotic. To him, a country's vitality could be measured by its willingness to push boundaries. He passionately wanted to keep Britain at the forefront of engineering endeavour, to show that Britain was not in terminal decline and also, on a personal level, to prove his detractors wrong. He visited America in early 1966. There he found his ideas and attitude greeted with enthusiasm. To try to break the sound barrier on land in a rocket car was still considered a pretty exciting thing to do.

His enthusiasm rekindled, the rocket car plans would continue in the background, but he needed a way of re-establishing his name in the public

The full-scale mock up of Bluebird Mach 1.1 at Priors Ford in spring 1966.
© Sound Stills

> …well a few months ago, I'd made up my mind to retire. We've had this design study going on now for the last 9 months, then we got to America a month ago and found this tremendous interest that is surrounding this endeavour, Three groups in America are going ahead hard now with the most tremendous backing of these giant American corporations. And suddenly I found that I couldn't retire…'
>
> **Donald Campbell, speaking in early 1966**

consciousness – a 'quick win' to show that 'Campbell was still popular'. With the CN7 route having been blocked, in May 1966 his thoughts turned back to Bluebird K7 and an eighth WSR, this time with the aim of exceeding 300mph. Quick success with K7 would, he felt sure, generate interest and enthusiasm for the rocket car.

Donald, Leo and Maurie with the full-scale mock up of Bluebird Mach 1.1 at Priors Ford in spring 1966.
© Sound Stills

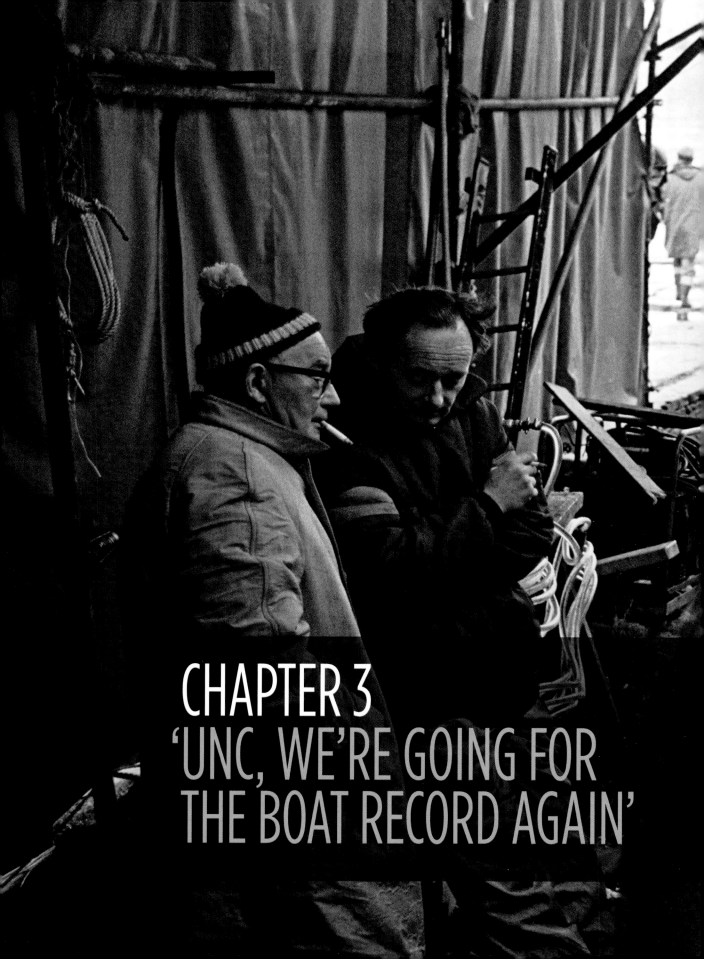

CHAPTER 3
'UNC, WE'RE GOING FOR THE BOAT RECORD AGAIN'

The origins of Donald's attempt to gain his eighth Water Speed Record lie in early May 1966. With the intended Bluebird CN7 bid for the standing mile record thwarted by Dunlop's unwillingness to supply tyres, Donald was forced to accept that the plan was effectively a non-starter, at least for the foreseeable future.

Tonia was not keen on the idea of another WSR attempt, but she could see Donald was determined and had been in a restless frame of mind for the previous couple of months. She had hoped he would throw all his energies into his insurance broking business.

In 1964, Campbell had discussed with Bristol Siddeley and the Air Ministry the loan of two Orpheus turbojet engines for the stillborn 'amphibian' project. He now resurrected these discussions, but with a different purpose in mind . . .

Talks with the Air Ministry about the use of an Orpheus jet in K7 began in early May. Donald had received a favourable response from Bristol Siddeley regarding their willingness to support him by helping to identify two Ministry-owned engines (one as a spare) that were 'time expired' and then providing technical assistance.

The reason for the engine change was twofold: the Metropolitan Vickers Beryl engine installed in Bluebird was underpowered for the contemplated speed (300mph) to be reached with a degree of safety, and it was effectively time expired. The Beryl was very advanced when first introduced in the late 1940s and had brought Donald seven WSRs since 1955, but by 1966 it was heavy, underpowered and over 15 years old. There was also grave concern that its compressor rotor blades were fatigued, with further use involving the risk of serious failure.

The Orpheus was similar in dimensions to the Beryl, but considerably lighter – 913lbs as opposed to 1,780lbs. It also developed 1,000lbs more thrust. This meant Bluebird would have a considerably higher power-to-weight ratio

Donald sweeps down the Swan River, past the BP building on Perth's waterfront, January 1965.
© Longines

and would accelerate to 300mph much more quickly. This was an important consideration given the confines of Coniston Water and Ullswater, the only two lakes in the UK that Donald considered suitable.

Ken Norris was enthusiastic, Lewis much less so. Initial feasibility discussions were held as to how the conversion could be carried out. Bluebird's hull was by now 12 years old. After her Dumbleyung record, she had been demonstrated in the salt water Swan River estuary in Perth, Western Australia. It was feared that the saline content of the water might have accelerated corrosion of her steel frame.

Ken and Lewis both recommended that a full ultrasonic investigation of Bluebird be carried out before proceeding with any new work. Subject to the hull being found satisfactory, the Norris brothers agreed that they would handle the conversion and refit.

> Any man that is going to succeed, and I don't care what walk of life he chooses, is going to have to be selfish. If you're going to succeed, you've got to put what you're trying to do first, way beyond your own comfort, way beyond your own pleasure and way before your own family considerations, now it doesn't matter whether it's business, or what have you, you have got to.'
>
> Donald Campbell, *The Price of a Record*, November 1966

On 19 May, Donald made contact with the Ultrasonoscope Company to request their assistance in carrying out ultrasonic tests on Bluebird's frame, who promptly agreed to carry out the work free of charge. Their proposal involved a combination of ultrasonic, X-ray and dye penetrant tests for fatigue cracks and to ascertain the extent of any corrosion. Ultrasonoscope also planned to enlist the help of the RAF's Controller of Non-Destructive Testing, such was the draw of the Campbell name.

Donald next had to broach the subject to Leo Villa.

'Unc, we're going for the boat record again.' Leo was far from keen on the idea, pointing out Bluebird's age and the fact that she had been gracefully retired after her Australian success. 'Don't worry, we'll have her properly X-rayed and I've arranged an Orpheus on loan,' Donald reassured him. 'And when do you have in mind for the attempt?' Leo enquired. 'Oh I don't know, end of August, beginning of September I expect.'

'Oh for heaven's sake, Donald, haven't we had enough of Coniston at that time of year?' Leo, ever loyal, was nonetheless won round.

Although the conversion and subsequent record attempt were expected to be achieved at relatively low cost, certainly compared to the Australian venture, Donald was still keen to enlist the help of as many potential backers as possible, particularly from the oil industry.

In addition to the 300mph WSR, Donald was giving serious consideration to attempting the world one-, three-, and six-hour endurance speed records, with Norman Buckley, a well-known endurance and class record-breaker, acting as co-pilot. While these plans were still in the formative stage, however, Buckley suffered a mild heart attack and shortly afterwards ruled himself out of further record attempts. Donald remained keen to attack the endurance records, believing they would have good TV coverage potential. He even considered training a female jet pilot as his co-driver. The goal was to take all three records at speeds close to 150mph. Donald began the search for a sponsor who would be willing to provide fuel and lubricants to be used in the attempt, as well as a financial contribution to be paid in two parts – £3,750 (equivalent to £54,000 nowadays) due upfront, with a further payment of the same amount after successfully breaking the outright record. The total cost was relatively small, given the promotional value involved, but Donald had his eye on the future.

Remember, the WSR was essentially a stepping-stone to fulfilling the greater ambition of building a rocket car to go after the speed of sound on land. Delivering success for a backer of the low-cost WSR venture would perhaps make it easier to obtain support for his longer-term goal.

By the end of May, the Air Ministry had authorised the free nine-month loan of two ex-development Orpheus 701 engines. This type gave 4,500lbs of thrust, limited only by fuel pump capacity. The engine serial numbers were 709 and 711, and both had at least 50 hours of remaining life, extendable for surface use. They would easily fulfil Donald's limited running needs. Engine 709, which was at British Aircraft Corporation premises in Luton, where it was acting as a test engine, was chosen as the primary engine because it would be in the team's hands first; 711 would be the spare. Norris Brothers had already started preliminary work on the modification plans.

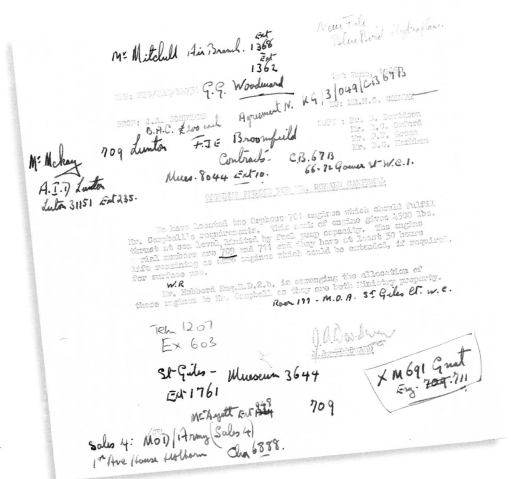

Bristol Siddeley/Air Ministry communication.
© G. Campbell

Towards the end of May, Donald turned his attention to the choice of venue for the attempt. Ullswater, England's second largest natural lake, would offer more room than his traditional venue, Coniston. Also, its three distinct reaches would allow a longer course to be plotted for the long-distance records.

In a letter dated 6 June, the Shell Oil Company was approached to provide sponsorship for the attempt. They had already provided extensive backing

BRISTOL SIDDELEY ORPHEUS 701 TURBOJET ENGINE

The Bristol Siddeley Orpheus 701 engine fitted to Bluebird in 1966 was a single-spool turbojet developed by Bristol Siddeley in the early 1950s for various light fighter/trainer applications.

The engine had its genesis in a 1952 request by aircraft manufacturer Folland for an engine with 5,000lbs of static thrust to power a new lightweight trainer/fighter they were developing – the Gnat. Stanley Hooker, Bristol Siddeley's engine design chief, led the development of the engine, which was his first completely original jet design. The Orpheus was a relatively simple engine and first flew in the Folland Gnat in 1955. The Gnat was subsequently used by the RAF Aerobatic Team, the Red Arrows, from 1964 to 1979.

Developing 4,500lbs of static thrust at sea level, the Orpheus 701 had a 7-stage axial compressor driven by a single-stage turbine.

Engine characteristics:
Length: 93.47in (2.374m) Diameter: 32.4in (0.823m) Dry weight: 975lbs
  (442kg)
Compressor: 7-stage axial compressor
Combustion chamber: Can-annular with 7 flame tubes
Turbine: Single-stage turbine
Fuel type: AVTUR aviation kerosene DERD 2494
Maximum thrust: 4,500lbs Thrust-to-weight ratio: 4.62lb/lb at 20°C intake
  temperature

The BS Orpheus 701 engine installed in Bluebird, serial number 711, was boosted to run at 110 per cent of stated maximum revs, for short sprint runs, by means of an enhanced fuel delivery system fitted in late December 1966. It was rated at 5,271.75lbs, corrected to 2°C intake inlet temperature.

to Craig Breedlove in the USA for his LSR attempts. Breedlove now held that record at 600.601mph, and Donald suggested that achieving a record of 300mph on water could be seen as a complementary fit that would appeal to Shell.

Donald was well aware that in the financially more straitened times of 1966 getting backing for his venture, however modest the sum involved, was going to be an uphill struggle. In a letter dated 13 June to John Davis, Director-General of the Confederation of British Industry, he wrote: 'I fear we are in for the inevitable struggle, which, by comparison, makes the endeavour seem simple, except possibly "á la moment critique".' As this example shows, the risks involved were never far from his mind.

At the end of 1965, Donald had agreed to demonstrate the newly overhauled Bluebird CN7 at Debden air station in Essex, at their Motor Sports Gala of Speed on 19 June, with proceeds going to the RAF Benevolent Association and St John Ambulance. He was feeling generally run down, so as a precaution he arranged for a friend, race and rally driver Peter Bolton, to be available as a reserve driver. The week before the event, Bolton was being given instructions with Donald at the helm on a very slow pass down the runway. At the far end, Bolton got into the driver's seat to take over. He was under strict instructions not to use the throttle – at idle, CN7 would do 150mph – but just to release the brakes and gently roll down the runway. Unfortunately, CN7 ran away with Bolton, left the track, ploughed through a hedge, literally flew over a minor road and ended up in a field. Bolton had put his braking foot on the brake and accelerator at the same time. CN7 sustained damage to her intake and rear suspension, causing Donald's spirits to plummet further. The demonstration run the following weekend was carried out at much lower speed than Donald had anticipated. CN7 would be out of commission for the foreseeable future and Campbell simply couldn't spare the money needed for the repair work.

By 20 June, Shell had written back saying that regretfully, after much consideration, they were unable to help with the WSR venture. BP were approached along similar lines and likewise declined to assist. These refusals did not dampen Donald's determination, however. He knew of at least three serious attempts being planned in America on his WSR. Lee Taylor had already survived a 250mph accident on Lake Havasu, Arizona, in April 1964, in his jet boat Hustler. He was now preparing for another attempt later that year. Craig Breedlove and Art Arfons, LSR rivals with their jet cars, now both had advanced plans, backed by corporate America, to mount WSR challenges. Donald wanted to bump the record beyond their reach before they got started.

On 23 June, he wrote to his solicitor, Victor Mishcon, outlining his plans and thoughts.

Debden air station, June 1966:

Top: Leo Villa standing in the cockpit of the damaged Bluebird CN7.
© Mirrorpix

Above: Donald and Tonia after the demonstration run. Tonia is holding Mr Whoppit, Campbell's teddy bear mascot.
© Mirrorpix

'*I believe passionately that this next attempt on the WSR will have considerable global impact, and, if it succeeds, will be a very good thing for Britain, both overseas and at home. Of course, it is going to be hazardous, probably more so than anything I have ever attempted. On the other hand, given patience, and good fortune, it has a very good chance of success, and I mean this in terms of the 300+mph mark.*'

He also acknowledged he was probably going to have to go it alone.

'*The future is difficult – our great problem is to find the £10,000 [today's equivalent: £144,000] to finance the modification and re-engineering of the hydroplane, the insurance and general operating costs.*'

Sunday 26 June found Donald, Leo, Ken Norris and Maurice Parfitt (Campbell's other full-time employee alongside Leo Villa, Parfitt had been part of the Bluebird team since 1954) at the premises of his friend Bill Coley, an

aviation metals dealer, in Hounslow, West London, where K7 was being stored. Orpheus engine number 709 had been delivered and Donald had arranged a photo opportunity. The Beryl engine was hoisted out of Bluebird's hull in preparation for the boat's 75-mile journey to Norris Brothers at Haywards Heath, East Sussex, where the conversion was to be carried out.

The move to Norris Brothers was scheduled to take place by the end of the second week of July, once a suitable workshop had been cleared and prepared. So with plans for the initial preparatory work already agreed and the Orpheus engine delivered, Donald took the opportunity to have a couple of weeks' holiday in the south of France.

He returned to England in mid-July and was disappointed to find that work on K7 was not progressing as quickly as he had hoped. The boat was still at Bill Coley's. To date, the Beryl and its fittings had been removed, and planning and design of the installation was in hand. Donald was now offered the opportunity to purchase the spare Orpheus engine, number 711, and the Gnat airframe that contained it, outright. This would allow him to have an engine beyond the nine-month loan period. Given the ludicrously cheap price of £200 (today's equivalent: £2,900), he jumped at the chance. The Gnat would also be a useful source of controls and engine pickup brackets for the refit. The formal agreement to purchase the Gnat, XM691, which was located at Dunsfold air station, was made on 20 July. Even though Orpheus 711 would now shortly be available to the team, it was decided to install 709 in the hull of K7 as planned, despite the fact that 711, having less hours on it, was the preferred engine.

A meeting was held at Bill Coley's on 21 July, where the main decisions regarding the installation were to be made. Leo and Maurice represented Donald, while Ken Norris, Ken Wheeler and Ted Ravenhill attended from Norris Brothers. Aeronautics expert Professor John Stollery from Imperial College, was also present. He would need to understand the new configuration so he could carry out further calculations for the trim. Bristol Siddeley, Smiths Industries and Lucas were also represented. Target completion date for the work was by the end of August ideally, and mid-September at the latest.

K7 and the Bristol Siddeley Orpheus number 709 were transferred to Norris Brothers the following week.

Above left: Left to right Maurie, Leo, Donald and Ken looking at the refit plans.
© Getty Images

Above right: Donald examines Bristol Siddeley Orpheus 709 at Bill Coley's.
© Getty Images

Bristol Siddeley were giving extensive technical assistance to the project and had assigned Ken Pearson to advise on the installation. At a meeting in early August, he made three recommendations regarding Bluebird's air intakes, intake ramps and spray deflectors. The intake lip should be given a thicker 'bull

AN AERODYNAMICIST'S PERSPECTIVE
PROFESSOR JOHN STOLLERY ON DONALD CAMPBELL

'I only met Donald Campbell twice so can hardly pretend that I knew him well. The first time was when we were doing the initial wind tunnel tests on the Bluebird Car CN7. Donald had arranged a press conference to be held in the laboratory at 11 a.m. About 10.30 the 'gentlemen of the Press' began to arrive. They showed little interest in either us or the models we were testing. In fact, most of them expressed acute disappointment that there was no food and nothing alcoholic to drink.

Sharp at 11 a.m., Donald appeared and the mood was transformed. He explained what was being done and why the aerodynamic loads were important. It was crucial to find a car body shape that at 400mph did not lift upwards so reducing the wheel loads and causing them to spin; or press downwards increasing the wheel loads so that the rubber tyres might break.

Donald then answered a barrage of questions, many of which I thought either irrelevant, insulting or personal. However, Donald remained calm, urbane and unruffled by all this chaos. He posed for innumerable pictures and answered nearly all the questions with candour and good humour. Only once did he suggest to a very young reporter, who asked a particularly inane question, that he should do his homework before venturing out into the wide, wide world.

Having exhausted the questions, Donald left and most of the press dwindled away. A couple did ask about our work and how the measurements were being made. The reports the next day naturally centered on Donald. I recall being horrified to read in the popular papers about 'blocks of wood' being tested in a wind tunnel.

The second and last time I met Donald was when he came to Imperial College on the last day of the tests to say thank you. There was no need to do this, Ken Norris and I had been undergraduates together at Imperial and the Head of the Aeronautics Dept (Prof H.B. Squire) had agreed we could test the Norris design. A research student and myself were happy to be involved and there was no question of payment (what a contrast to the present day – a bevy of accountants, insurance agents and health and safety officers would make such an initiative impossible). Donald spent a long time with us discussing the results and thanking us profusely for our efforts. To us it had been a serious exercise but also a lot of fun. As he left he handed each of us a white envelope. At most, we expected a handwritten note of thanks, but there was also a cheque. Mine was for £100 and to me, a young lecturer, at that time (1959), this was a fortune. Never has a present given me more pleasure. He was a kind and generous man.'

Orpheus 709 is lowered
into the stripped hull of K7.
© M. Ockenden

nose' radius to aid low-speed airflow as opposed to their present tighter radius.
The intake ramps should have their step blended in alongside the cockpit,
and the spray deflectors should be cut down to reduce their masking effect
on the intake. Pearson produced a sketch of the modified spray deflectors to
demonstrate the configuration he was trying to achieve. Ken Norris expressed
doubt as to how important these recommendations were, and was minded not
to carry them out if they would significantly delay completion of the refit or
involve substantial additional cost. As always, money was tight.

At least some backing for the attempt now came from an unlikely source.
Four Companies Television, a consortium comprising the Border, Grampian,
Westward and Ulster ITV companies, agreed to produce a 45-minute colour
documentary about the attempt, to be called *The Price of a Record*. This
programme was to be produced by Douglas Hurn and directed by Edward
Joffe. The script was written by John Pearson, Campbell's collaborator in
Bluebird and the Dead Lake, the story of his Lake Eyre exploits, and John Pett,
who also acted as interviewer for the programme. The documentary brought
in £500 (today's equivalent: £7,200) of much-needed money up front, plus a
cut of the profits when the programme was sold for air. Donald hoped that it
would be released for worldwide distribution.

Meanwhile, the plan to run on Ullswater had come to nothing. Since 1955,
when Campbell had first broken the WSR there, ownership of the lake bed had
passed to the National Trust. Ullswater Navigation Company, who owned the
launch site by Glenridding Pier, would have been very happy to accommodate
Bluebird, but the National Trust at that time was strongly opposed to the lake
being used for any record attempts. So Coniston it would have to be.

On the weekend of 13/14 August, Donald and Tonia paid a visit to the Lakes,
and to Coniston in particular. He was keen to start making arrangements for
the attempt to take place in the early autumn. Since 1959, the slipway at Pier

Cottage, that both he and his father had used, had changed hands, and he now sought the new owner's permission to use the site as his base. He was still concerned about the length of the lake, at only just over 5 miles. With the speeds being contemplated, he judged it was right on the edge of safety – to the point where he investigated the erection of arrester nets at the foot of the lake, similar to those employed on aircraft carriers.

He had also come to pay a visit to his oldest friend in Coniston, Connie Robinson, who ran the Sun Hotel, and her son Anthony, or 'Robbie' as he was known. Connie had looked after Donald on all his visits to Coniston, first at the Black Bull Inn and now here at the Sun. He arranged to rent her newly built bungalow for the duration of their stay for the very reasonable sum of £15 per week. It would allow him to have a home from home in Coniston throughout the attempt. Mrs Robinson would also act as unofficial agent, ensuring that accommodation would be found elsewhere in the village for team members and associates if the Sun became full.

Permission was requested from F.G. Riding, chairman of Coniston Parish Council, to make the attempt on Coniston Water. It was duly granted with great enthusiasm and the minimum of fuss.

Back at Haywards Heath, Tony James, a Norris Brothers' project manager, had returned from a two-week summer holiday with his family. Prior to his departure, he had been working with Imperial College, London, on the installation of a hypersonic wind tunnel. Now he was asked by Ken Norris to take care of the Bluebird refit and get it moving. The conversion was in good hands.

On Friday 26 August, a meeting was held at Haywards Heath between the Norris Brothers and Bristol Siddeley (BS) teams. The Gnat was now in the process of being stripped of useful components. The spare Orpheus, number 711, had been removed and put into store. The compressed-air start system, manufactured by Rotax, which had been donated by an Orpheus equipped experimental Hunting H126 aircraft, had been delivered, and during the meeting, the BS team of Jack Lavis and Ken Pearson made a number of recommendations regarding modifications to the boat, as well as installation details. It was again suggested that in order to satisfy the Orpheus's greater thirst for air, the air intake lip be modified to give it a more rounded profile. Also, moving the spray baffles further away from the body would ensure that they did not impede airflow at low speeds. BS recommended a static installation test of the engine before the boat was transported to Coniston, which they would be happy to conduct.

Assisting Tony James with the conversion were Ted Ravenhill, Mike Ockenden, Ken Wheeler and Stan Taylor as design engineers, with Bill Izatt, Peter Pateman and Ted Simmonds as engineering fitters. As ever, Leo Villa and Maurice Parfitt were there to advise and assist from Donald's side. Rotax would later assign Bill Vanryne to work on the air start system installation.

The Ultrasonoscope tests on Bluebird's hull commenced on 3 September. In addition to frame access through the empty engine compartment, the fairings around the rear spar and sponsons had also been removed. Testing of Bluebird's structure was completed on 5 September, later than Donald would have liked, causing the project timeline to slip by a number of weeks. Campbell had originally intended to be at Coniston by the middle of September.

AN ENGINEER'S PERSPECTIVE
TONY JAMES ON DONALD CAMPBELL

'To those of us who were privileged to contribute to Donald's attempt to raise the WSR in 1966, that year will always remain in our consciousness. Mere mention of the date acts as a trigger to bring back a wealth of memories.

I was a project manager at Norris Brothers Ltd and had worked for them since 1957 – too late to be involved in K7 originally. I was brought in at the end of the summer of 1966 to manage the refurbishment and re-engineering of Bluebird. Time was short and before long, autumn would soon be upon us with winter weather not far behind.

Donald Campbell was, to me, a legendary figure, a patriot and upholder of British endeavours in the world of engineering and record-breaking. At that time, I had only had brief contact with him through my work on improvements to the water jet driven boat Jetstar which arose out of Donald's involvement as a director of Dowty Marine.

The wooden shed at the back of Norris Brothers offices, where we carried out the work, was only just big enough to house Bluebird and every time we needed to lift the engine or move the craft outside we had to remove the end of the building. If I thought these conditions were primitive, they were bliss compared to working at Coniston on the slipway or in the makeshift workshop alongside, often in freezing conditions.

Donald, Leo and Maurie were often in attendance at Haywards Heath and took a vital interest in our work on the boat. I found Donald appreciative and every bit as passionate about record-breaking on behalf of Britain as I expected him to be, and keen to push the record out of the reach of the Americans.

For my part, I admired Donald tremendously and we all did our utmost to get the boat ready as soon as possible after refurbishing the hull, replacing the old Beryl engine with the 'new' Orpheus, fitting the Gnat stabilising fin, adding a water brake and a hundred and one other alterations and additions necessitated by the engine change. The mere mention that we were working on Bluebird would result in companies offering equipment and expertise – all at no cost. It was their way of contributing to a worthwhile endeavour with Donald at the helm. One of my abiding memories is how much the British companies and engineers were prepared to give of themselves in their own way, when the national interest was at stake.'

Ken and Lewis Norris had observed the tests and a few days later were in receipt of the Ultrasonoscope report. The bottom inner tube of Bluebird's space frame showed light corrosion, having lost some 0.030in from a total thickness of 0.220in. The main corrosion was around the stern area, where it was assumed water was more likely to collect. There was light corrosion to the planing shoes, and elsewhere, but the frame had stood up remarkably well to some 11+ years of high-stress use.

Lewis Norris produced an interpretation report for Donald where he estimated the loss in strength in the frame due to the corrosion. He put

The stripped hull of K7 ready for the Ultrasonoscope tests.
© M. Ockenden

this at 25 per cent in parts of the bottom frame member and 10 per cent elsewhere. This would reduce the ultimate 'g' loading capability from 27 g to 20 g. Given that K7 very rarely exceeded 6 g when running at high speed, the strength of the frame still gave Donald a very healthy reserve.

Lewis concluded the report with an oblique warning. He made a strong suggestion in the form of an assumption that no other high-speed running would be contemplated after this attempt and that Bluebird would be retired, stating that the hull had already exceeded its design limit and citing the fact that the frame would continue to deteriorate, albeit slowly, over time.

Shortly after the Ultrasonoscope tests had been completed, Donald and Tonia paid a visit to the Longines factory in St-Imier, Switzerland, to arrange for a Longines team to be sent to Coniston once the refit was complete to act as timekeepers for the attempt. They had provided this service at Coniston in the late 1950s and in Australia for the 1964 double. He also used the visit to say thank you and pay tribute to the company for their work in Australia.

On the engineering front, Norris Brothers had developed a hydraulic ram water brake for Bluebird to be deployed after each run through the measured distance. It would provide a significant deceleration effect, as well as creating considerable downward pressure around the bows when Bluebird was decelerating with the power of the engine switched off. The thrust line of the engine was slightly above the centre of gravity. This meant that when the engine was under full load the bows were forced down. Conversely, when the engine was spooled down at the end of each run there was an opposite effect. In her previous configuration, Bluebird had displayed a tendency to become very light at the bows when decelerating from very high speed as the downward pressure provided by the jet thrust was removed. Most important of all though, Donald would be able to accelerate and decelerate safely after each run within the space available at Coniston, allowing full use of the increased power of the Orpheus.

On 3 October, Donald wrote to John Pearson, biographer of his Lake Eyre LSR attempt and co-scriptwriter for the documentary *The Price of a Record* being made about the latest attempt. He professed himself to be 'shaking in my boots at the prospect of another attempt'.

Donald made another visit to the Lakes on the weekend of 8/9 October to sort out further details of the forthcoming attempt. He asked Norman Buckley to appoint a local firm to resurvey the measured kilometre and submit the survey details, so that a course certificate could then be issued by the Royal Yachting Association, the UK sanctioning body for UIM rules (Union Internationale Motonautique). George Lewthwaite, a Kendal building contractor, agreed to erect a tubular scaffolding structure, to be covered

Press release from the visit to the Longines factory, 9 September 1966.
© Longines

Caption S / 35 / A
For immediate publication

DONALD CAMPBELL AT THE LONGINES FACTORY

The celebrated Donald Campbell, holder of the world speed records on land – 648.565 km/h – and water – 444.615 km/h. – performances registered in Australia in 1964, has visited the Longines Watch Company's works.

Campbell is to make a new attempt on water in England this autumn, when he hopes to reach a speed of 500 km/h. He hopes to reach a speed of 500 km/h. He has arranged for Longines apparatus to be used for timing his future exploits. In 1964 already, the fabulous performances of the British pilot were timed by the Longines Chronociné-gines.

St. Imier, 9nd September 1966
FAB/gz-316

with heavy-duty blue ICI Plastolene plastic sheeting, over the slipway at Pier Cottage to act as a temporary boat shed to house Bluebird during her stay at Coniston.

The timetable continued to slip. The expected start date for trials was now Friday 21 October. Longines confirmed that they would have a team and their equipment at Coniston by 27 October. The timing apparatus consisted of a duplicate system of chronographs, certified to one-hundredth of a second, a camera system incorporating telescopes, and a course watch certified to one-thousandth of a second.

Given that it now looked like the attempt would be made in late autumn/ early winter, rather than late summer/early autumn, Bristol Siddeley took the precaution of issuing a warning about operating the engine at low ambient air temperatures and the risk of intake icing, which could cause significant damage to the turbine.

On 13 October, Donald made a final approach to BP to see if they would change their mind about being associated with the attempt. No longer hoping for financial sponsorship, he asked if they would be willing to supply fuel and lubricants for use in Bluebird, and indicated that they could make whatever promotional use they wanted of their involvement. He left to them the question of payment of a success fee. Given what had been achieved at Coniston seven and eight years before with the company's help, it must have been a soul-destroying letter to write. BP wrote back saying they saw no reason to change their earlier decision, but wished him good luck with the attempt. There were certainly factions in BP, at a senior level, which felt Donald was driven by private demons and would never give up the dangerous pursuit of record-breaking until he was killed.

The Royal Yachting Association issued its provisional sanction for the attempt on 17 October, pending completion of an application form. Lancashire police, within whose jurisdiction Coniston lay, agreed to provide an element of security and control at Pier Cottage, with Chief Constable Eric St Johnston communicating as much to Donald personally.

The unfinished tail fin from the scrapped Gnat fixed in place on K7's rear fairing.
© M. Ockenden

Styling the team 'Clanger and Company', Donald wrote to his old friend and supporter Bill Coley to tell him how things were progressing. The timetable had slipped a little further, and Bluebird was now scheduled to leave for Coniston on 24 October. Campbell was at least able to give one piece of good news – the *Daily Sketch* newspaper had agreed to provide some backing in return for exclusive story rights. Bill was asked if his company would make available a 'splendid' lorry to transport 'Uncle Villa's' tools, clobber and their little Jetstar ski-boat up to Coniston. Arthur Wilson, owner of the slipway, was told of the revised arrangements and asked jokingly to 'arrange some really splendid weather'. Connie Robinson received a similar weather request in a letter to her.

Meanwhile, Bluebird was at Bourners of Lancing having her bodywork prepared and resprayed her usual sapphire blue. This would then be finished off with the 'K7 infinity' symbol on each sponson, the Bluebird roundels on her rear flanks and nose, two Union flags painted centrally on each side of the tail fin, and a crossed Union Jack crest – signifying a British boat attempting a record on British waters – on her nose.

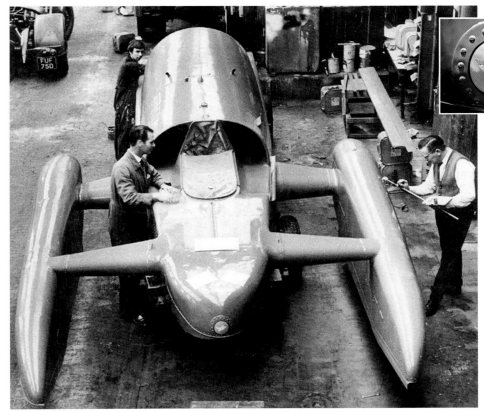

The hand-painted Bluebird symbol on K7's nose.
© J. Dart

Bluebird after her respray at Bourners. Note the signwriter completing K7's Lloyds unlimited registration symbol on her port sponson.
© Author's Collection

The freshly painted, engine-less hull returned to Norris Brothers for final installation of the Orpheus and its ancillaries in the week beginning 24 October. Handling the Orpheus refit involved Norris Brothers in carrying out extensive calculations to arrive at a new configuration for her trim, assisted by John Stollery at Imperial College. They aimed to meet the following key requirements:

Installation of Bristol Siddeley Orpheus with on-board starting capability to allow six starts before recharging
Record speed of 300mph plus
Maximum speed of 325mph plus
Turnover speed no lower than existing
Course length 4.5 miles maximum
Maintain safety factors re-centre of gravity in order to preserve high-speed stability, with planing state to be reached with no more difficulty than existing
Incorporate hydraulic ram water brake unit and actuation assembly
Incorporate 21lb polystyrene foam below sponson fairings and plastic airbags in main hull and nose compartment to provide additional buoyancy
Fit vertical aerodynamic stabilising fin adapted from Folland Gnat airframe incorporating airspeed pitot head
Install 4-gallon capacity low pressure fuel tank and pump into fuel line downstream of main fuel tank; sufficient fuel capacity to allow a run each way without refuelling
Target completion date 31 August, commence trials 14 September
Budget for installation £1,000 (today's equivalent: £14,500)

Above, from top:
Maurice and Leo discuss
K7's cockpit refit.
© M. Ockenden

Donald and Leo
contemplate the rebuilt
Bluebird K7.
© M. Ockenden

Donald back in
K7's cockpit.
© M. Ockenden

In addition to these key requirements, modifications were made to the positioning of the spray baffles to move them away from the bodywork to ensure they did not impede airflow into the air intakes at low speed. The stabilising fins, or planing blades, attached to the trailing edge root of each sponson were sharpened to ensure that each leading edge had a razor-like profile. The same work was carried out to the rudder and fixed rear fin, which also had 1in removed from its base, thereby reducing its drag slightly. The sharpening of the fins ensured that water adhered to the sides of each blade, rather than a blunt leading edge forming a bubble behind it and reducing blade effectiveness. The rear fixed fin was moved from its central position behind the rear planing shoe to a starboard position on the transom, equidistant from the centreline to the rudder on the port side of the transom. This change was needed to make way for the water brake.

The upper rear fairing had two square holes cut out to act as cooling ducts for the rear jet-pipe. These could be plugged as necessary, and in fact at Coniston the boat ran with the port side vent covered. A stiff rubber seal was fabricated and installed between the jet-pipe shroud and jet-pipe opening of the rear fairing, closing the lower half of the opening to prevent water ingress into the engine compartment. The upper half was left open to allow jet-pipe cooling airflow.

The Orpheus was mounted on two trunnions located either side of the of the engine compartment and attached to the engine just behind the axial compressor. At the front, on the starboard side of the lower half of the engine, was an adjustable steel turnbuckle used to align the axis of the engine in the boat. This allowed a small downward angle in the thrust line to help generate downward pressure on the front planing surfaces. The engine was mated to the rear of the bifurcated air intake by means of light alloy trunking that allowed for an element of movement to accommodate heat expansion.

The compressed air starting system, designed and manufactured by Rotax Ltd for the Orpheus engine in the Hunting H126 and Folland Gnat aircraft, was adapted for use in Bluebird. The system comprised two spherical air bottles containing 39lbs of dehumidified air, compressed to over 3,000psi. The bottles were attached to an A-frame over the front of the engine, with high-pressure pipes connecting them to a non-return valve and external 'plug-in' adapter. They were charged by means of a high-pressure, three-stage compressor, complete with air-drying and cleaning facility, housed in a specially adapted Land Rover vehicle.

The starting cycle was initiated by a switch in the cockpit, causing a solenoid-operated stop valve to open, thereby allowing high-pressure air to flow into a reducing valve, the pressure being lowered at the outlet to 300psi. The emerging air was fed to the starter motor inlet via a flexible pipe to power the starter turbine, which drove the engine through a gear reduction box. Bill Vanryne of London-based Rotax was drafted into the project to advise on and oversee installation and testing, as well as providing Donald and Leo with an operation procedure.

The installation of the Orpheus and its ancillaries, plus the other modifications such as the water brake and larger aerodynamic stabilising fin, meant that new calculations would have to be made to ascertain the effect of the refit on Bluebird's centre of gravity relative to the transom.

Given the nature of a hydroplane, which rides above the water with only a very small area of the hull in contact with the surface, and its potential to 'fly' if the critical pitch angle is exceeded, the key consideration during the refit was that the safe operating envelope for the Orpheus-powered boat should be no worse than with the Beryl, and if possible better. The static weight of K7 and the thrust of its jet engine exerted a moment about the centre of gravity, creating downward pressure on its forward planing points. Airflow over the boat from front to back created upward pressure below the hull, while suction-type lift on the upper surfaces pulled the nose up. Hydrodynamic lift was created via the angle of attack of K7's planing surfaces. Exhaustive wind tunnel tests were carried out on the hull throughout the 1950s as the boat's design was gradually refined. The effect of the 1966 modifications was incorporated into these findings, based on the aerodynamics work carried out by John Stollery of Imperial College.

For any given speed, the angle of incidence to the water surface could be calculated. K7 should not exceed a critical upper value called the upper pitching incidence limit, otherwise the boat would become airborne and flip over backwards. The Orpheus installation was calculated to have a 6° operating envelope at 300mph. This was determined using the craft's dry weight of 5,040lb, which produces a balancing moment to the lift moment the boat creates when in forward motion. A full 54-gallon load of fuel *plus the pilot* increases the all-up weight to 5,620lb. Jet thrust at full power also produces an additional nose-down moment. The centre of gravity of the Orpheus-equipped boat was calculated to be 145in from the transom, as opposed to 141in for the Beryl. The Orpheus-engined boat was lighter (5,620lb) than the Beryl (5,930lb), with an increase in load over the front planes of 50lb and a reduction on the rear plane of 360lb. The aim of maintaining the operating envelope had thus been met.

Bluebird's new hydraulic braking system was devised in October 1966 following a meeting between Donald, Ken Norris and Ken Wheeler from Norris Brothers. Once the general concept had been outlined, Wheeler was given responsibility for its design.

He came up with a simple but elegant solution. A steel box-section unit of approximately 12in x 4in x 4in housed a hydraulic jack which actuated a solid steel cylindrical rod some 2 inches in diameter, with operation being via a solenoid from a switch in the cockpit. When the switch was depressed, the hydraulic mechanism would slowly lower the steel rod about 4 inches below the transom, behind the rear planing shoe. This would cause very significant drag, and hence deceleration, when actuated above 200mph. Pressing the button a second time would raise the ram again when Bluebird had slowed enough.

Below, from top:
Tony James, Donald and Ken Norris discuss last-minute details of Bluebirds refit.
© M. Ockenden

The team work on K7 in the shed.
© A.E. James

Tony James in Bluebird's cockpit.
© A.E. James

The brake was designed to be applied some time after Bluebird had exited the measured distance, at a speed of below 250mph. The brake would dissipate a substantial amount of kinetic energy before being raised when the boat's speed had dropped to about 100mph.

The Gnat stabilising fin was incorporated in the refit for two reasons: it would provide significantly enhanced yaw stability and make Bluebird more liable to track in a straight line at very high speeds. Importantly, it would also give Bluebird a distinctive new appearance. In conjunction with her freshly repainted bodywork, complete with crossed Union flags on the nose and one on each side of the tail fin, K7 resembled a new boat. She certainly looked very different to the boat that had been launched 11 years earlier on Ullswater. This was crucial to Donald, who saw this attempt not only as a way to push the record beyond 300mph and out of the Americans' reach, but also as a generator of positive publicity for his rocket car and commercial ski boat plans.

By 28 October, Bluebird's refit was almost complete. BS had sent their two Orpheus specialists, Lavis and Pearson, to supervise the final installation. Rotax had detailed Bill Vanryne to assist in operation of the air start system. Residents living close to Norris Brothers' Burrell Road works had been warned that a series of jet engine tests would take place towards the end of the week.

Rollout on the 29 October 1966.
© M. Ockenden

Unfortunately, the BS engineers were called away by their head office at the last minute. The static test pencilled in for Saturday 29 October was to have been conducted by Jack Lavis. Bill Vanryne stepped into the breach, telling Leo that he could get the engine running if required. Bluebird was tethered to her wheel-chocked cradle in the early afternoon, nose pointed towards the Norris Brothers main building and jet-pipe into the empty car park lest she should break free and career off down the road. With everything secure, Leo gave Bill the instruction to climb into the cockpit. At 4.30 p.m., Bluebird experienced her first start with the Orpheus engine, with idle speed being maintained for a couple of minutes and the engine then shut down. The air start bottles were recharged and a few small adjustments made. At 5.25 p.m., the engine was run up again and left at idle for 1½ minutes. On switch-off, the rundown time was recorded at 35 seconds. A third start was made, with instrument readings meticulously recorded by Vanryne so Donald and Leo had a baseline for operation at Coniston. Six starts were made in all, with a typical crank time of only 3 seconds, jet-pipe temperature of 500°C, and a rundown time of 30 seconds. Tony and Leo, on behalf of Donald, pronounced themselves well satisfied. The next day, a Sunday, was a much-needed day off.

Left: K7 ready for her bodywork.
© A.E. James

Below from left:
Maurie working in the cockpit.
© A.E. James

Donald inspects his 'office'.
© C. Glynn

Donald watches Maurie make a few last-minute cockpit adjustments.
© M. Ockenden

An icon renewed.
© A.E. James

AN ENGINEERS PERSPECTIVE
BILL VANRYNE ON DONALD CAMPBELL

'In late October 1966, Donald Campbell requested I be sent to work with him on behalf of my company, Rotax Ltd. As a development engineer involved in rapid starting systems for jet aircraft, I initially worked on Bluebird at Norris Brothers' premises in Haywards Heath, assisting in the installation of the onboard, self-contained, air-driven start system for the Bristol Siddeley Orpheus.

On completion of this installation work, Leo Villa asked me to carry out a series of preliminary engine tests sitting in Bluebird's cockpit, i.e. start and run up Bluebird's engine, to test the compressed air starting system. I performed this six times, during the afternoon of that last Saturday of October, with the engine throttle set to engine idling speed to limit the power.

If maximum power had been inadvertently selected, a thought occurred that Bluebird sitting firmly on its wheeled trailer, might have broken loose and subsequently been seen travelling rapidly through the streets of Haywards Heath!'

Monday
31 October

Weather:
Dry but overcast

A few last-minute adjustments were made to K7, and then her fairings were screwed into position. Ken Norris had arranged something of a photo call as the completed K7 was rolled out.

In the late afternoon, K7, carefully swathed in blue Plastolene sheeting, left the Norris Brothers' premises in Haywards Heath to begin her journey to Coniston. She was, as usual, in the hands of Surrey-based haulage contractors Graham Adams and today would travel only as far as their depot for an overnight stay.

Top left:
Almost finished.
© M. Ockenden

Top right: Team photo at Burrell Road. Left to right: Maurice Parfitt, Tony James, Ken Norris, Donald, Leo, Peter Pateman and Bill Izatt.
© M. Ockenden

Bottom left: Donald with project manager Tony James.
© M. Ockenden

Bottom right: Bluebird ready to be packed off to Coniston.
© A.E. James

Bluebird on the back of
the Graham Adams truck.
© A E James

The female staff of Norris
Brothers assemble for a
photo call with K7.
© M. Ockenden

Project correspondence.
© G. Campbell

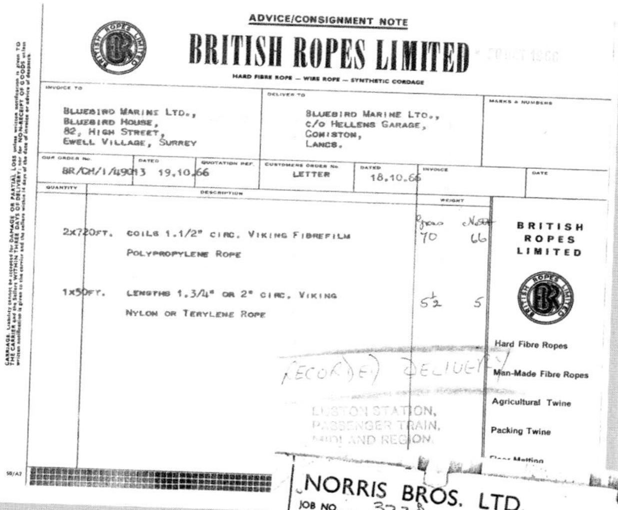

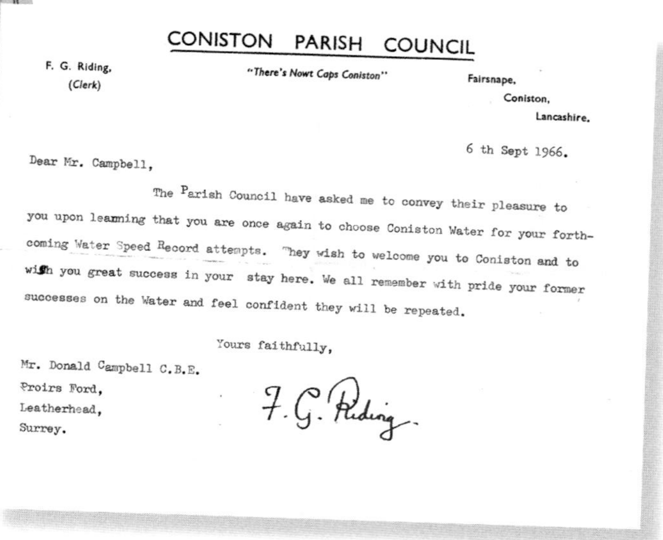

CONISTON PARISH COUNCIL

F. G. Riding,
(Clerk)

"There's Nowt Caps Coniston"

Fairsnape,
Coniston,
Lancashire.

6 th Sept 1966.

Dear Mr. Campbell,

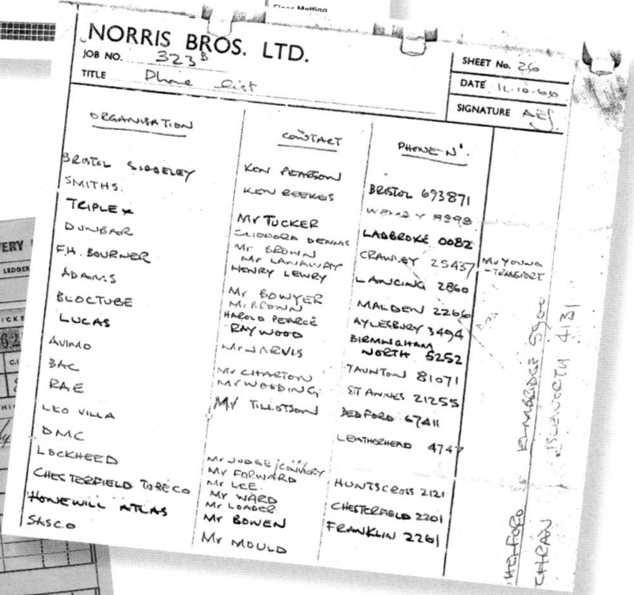

    The Parish Council have asked me to convey their pleasure to you upon learning that you are once again to choose Coniston Water for your forth-coming Water Speed Record attempts. They wish to welcome you to Coniston and to wish you great success in your stay here. We all remember with pride your former successes on the Water and feel confident they will be repeated.

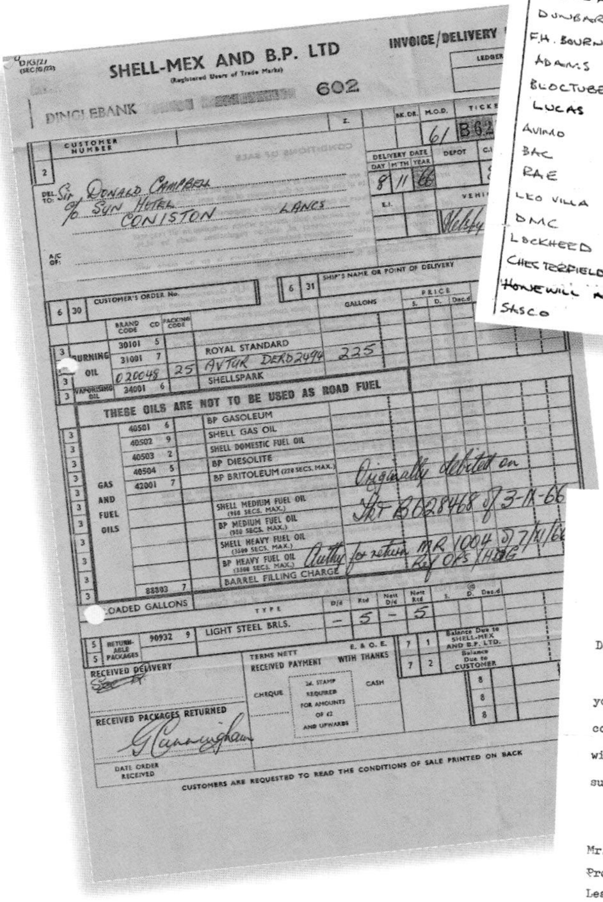

    Yours faithfully,

Mr. Donald Campbell C.B.E.
Proirs Ford,
Leatherhead,
Surrey.

F. G. Riding.

CHAPTER 4
'THERE IS NO FORM OF RECORD-BREAKING WHERE YOU GET IT SMOOTH'

Tuesday
1 November

Weather:
Dry and sunny

K7 left the Graham Adams depot to start her journey to Coniston in the early morning. She travelled on her wheeled cradle on the back of an articulated low-loader, protected by Plastolene sheeting. The route involved the M1, A5 and M6, with an overnight stop at Garstang, north of Preston (around 60 miles from the final destination). As the boat was making her journey northwards, Donald Campbell spent the day speaking to a reporter from the Daily Sketch at his Priors Ford home in Leatherhead, Surrey, about the forthcoming attempt. Walking at the bottom of his garden, he stopped to pick up a twig and throw it into the River Mole, which flowed through the grounds. 'A ripple like that could cause disaster for Bluebird,' he told the reporter. 'This is when the nerves get to me, a time when everything is under control but nothing is quite ready.'

Wednesday
2 November

Weather:
Dry and sunny

After leaving Garstang early that morning, Bluebird finished her journey via the A6, turning left at Levens Bridge to continue on the A595 to Greenodd, where the truck made a right turn to reach the narrow road leading to Torver and then Coniston village, arriving just after midday.

Bluebird had a police escort for the last few miles, her width and the narrowness of the roads making such a precaution necessary. She travelled through the centre of the village, turning right at the humpbacked bridge, past St Andrew's Church and the village green on the right, and over a second bridge spanning Yewdale Beck. A few hundred yards further on, the transporter carrying Bluebird turned right again to commence its journey down the track leading to Pier Cottage and the slipway.

Since the last visit in May 1959, the trees alongside the track had grown and Bluebird was now equipped with a much larger tail fin that increased overall height by some 4 feet. In order to avoid an overhanging branch, the driver of the transporter decided to take to the fields, where he got his vehicle well and truly stuck in the mud.

Leo Villa and Maurie Parfitt arrived just after midday to find Bluebird unable to complete the final few hundred yards of the journey to the slipway. Under Leo's direction, local farmers were called-on to assist with tractors and eventually heavy moving gear. It was some time before the truck was finally put back onto the track and down to the boathouse.

Bluebird was to be housed for what was hoped to be a short stay under a structure of tubular scaffolding erected by George Lewthwaite, a local building contractor, at the head of the railed slipway. The 'shed' was some 36 feet long, 18 feet wide and 11 feet 6 inches

Above from top:
K7 passing through Greenodd on her way to Coniston.
© P. Allonby

Stuck in mud on the way to Pier Cottage.
© G. Hallawell

high and was covered with the same type of heavy-duty blue plastic sheeting as was used to protect Bluebird on her journey to Coniston.

Leo and Maurie set up a workshop in the double garage across the yard from the slipway. It was a makeshift base, but one which would be adequate for a stay that was not expected to last longer than two to three weeks. Alongside Leo and Maurie, representatives from Bristol Siddeley had also travelled to Coniston to assist with testing Bluebird's new engine installation.

The transporter was parked in the yard and Leo, Maurie and the others repaired to their accommodation in the village. Donald Campbell had travelled from Leatherhead to Coniston in his E-Type Jaguar, arriving there in the early evening. The Bluebird team were staying at the Sun Hotel, run by Connie Robinson, who had always looked after the Campbell équipe, first at the Black Bull Inn and then at the Sun, during the successful Coniston attempts in the 1950s. Donald and Tonia, together with Louis and Julia Goossens, their house manager and housekeeper respectively, took over Connie's modern bungalow as their quarters, just down the road from the Sun.

PAUL ALLONBY ON DONALD CAMPBELL

'By 1966 I was running my own photographic business and was retained by the Lancashire Evening Post (LEP) to take news pictures in the Kendal/Ambleside areas. Although news was not my thing, I needed to take whatever work came along. It was for the LEP that in early November 1966 I photographed Bluebird at Greenodd en route to Coniston, where over the next 9 weeks, I and others spent many hours recording the preparations and modifications to Bluebird ready for the attempt at the world record.

During those 9 weeks, whenever I could, I would trundle along to Coniston each day when the conditions at first light were suitable to photograph any action until it was decided that there would be no run that day. I was then able to continue with my work as everyone else was stood down. It was always a bit of a dilemma for me, where I should position myself during any run. I wanted to be down the east side of the lake to record Bluebird at high speed, but if the record was broken, I would need to be back at Waterhead to photograph the celebrations and as it would take about 10mins to return, I would miss the arrival of DC at the jetty!'

Amid pleasant autumn sunshine, the team spent the day setting-up base. Bluebird was unloaded from the transporter and the rubber-tyred wheels removed from her cradle, to be replaced by railway wheels for use on the slipway. Shell-Mex and BP Ltd delivered 225 gallons of Avtur aviation kerosene in 45-gallon drums. Subsequent deliveries were made to Hadwin's garage in Torver, who then supplied full barrels to the slipway and picked-up the empties.

Thursday
3 November

Weather:
Dry with warm sunshine

One of the Land Rovers that had accompanied the Bluebird team to Australia in 1964 was positioned between the rails at the end of the slipway to allow its winch to be used for launching and recovering Bluebird. The vehicle was extensively equipped with compressors and battery-charging equipment and would be used to recharge Bluebird's air starting system and keep her batteries charged.

A caravan made by a company called Bluebird (!) and loaned to the project by Border Caravans Limited stood at the entrance to the yard. It served as an office, briefing room and coffee bar. The facilities included two telephones, one for use by Donald and Bluebird personnel, the other for the press.

Evidence of what little sponsorship Donald had been able to raise was to be found in the form of *Daily Sketch* banners hung around the site. There was none of the slick organisation that had existed in the 1950s, when Campbell's record attempts had been supported by the likes of Mobil, BP and Dunlop. In an effort to keep costs down, the record attempt itself was not even covered by any event insurance policy, Donald having decided that the £2,500 premium he had been quoted (equivalent to £35,500 today) was simply too expensive.

Lancashire police made available a police constable, Jim Sherdley, to look after security, and he was joined by Bill Jordan from the RAC. The Army advised on communications equipment between the base, Bluebird itself and the various course positions out on the lake, eventually sending a Signals Corps party to look after the whole communications system.

Leo and Maurie had been a fixture of all Donald's previous record attempts with K7. Assisting them was Louis, who as well as being Donald's house manager seemed to be able to turn his hand to any task and was described by Donald as his '*homme à tout faire*' (jack of all trades). Clive Glynn was a young apprentice mechanic who had become a temporary member of the Campbell team earlier that week. He was the son of a garage owner who was an acquaintance of Ken Norris, Bluebird's designer. This was to be his first taste of record-breaking.

A TEAM MEMBER'S PERSPECTIVE
CLIVE GLYNN ON DONALD CAMPBELL

'On Saturday 29 October I went over to Norris Brothers at Haywards Heath to see Bluebird K7 rolled out after her refit for the new record attempt. My father knew Ken Norris, and had been told that Donald was looking for an extra helper or two to go up to Coniston for a few weeks to assist with the trials and record attempt. Ken asked if I would be interested.

I went over to see Donald the following Monday at his offices in Bluebird House, Ewell. Campbell said that he hoped the work would suit me, he would like to have me on the team and that we would be away for two to three weeks at the most. I had got the job.

The next morning, I drove over to Donald's house, Priors Ford in Leatherhead, parked my MG in his garage, and was introduced to Louis Goossens. I was told we would be driving up in convoy, me in a Land Rover, Louis in a Morris Traveller. We stopped mid-way through the 7-hour journey and swapped vehicles. We arrived at the Sun Hotel in Coniston in the late afternoon. Accommodation had been arranged for me in Connie Robinson's brother's bungalow. 3 November dawned bright and clear. The daily ritual of an early rise and then of walking up to the Sun for breakfast began. Leo, Maurie and Louis were already there, and after we had finished, we went down to the lakeside to get Bluebird unloaded and on to the slipway. Donald arrived mid-morning. The crowd grew bigger as the day went on, and in the afternoon we pushed Bluebird down the slipway and into the water, so the press and TV could get a good look. Donald appeared keen to get on with the job.'

A number of support boats had been put at the team's disposal for whenever Bluebird was afloat. These consisted of an unsinkable Dory, which acted as the refuelling tender at the southern end of the lake, two Fairline 19ft cruisers lent by Oundle Marina in Peterborough, and a third cruiser provided for film camera crews from the BBC and the Canadian Broadcasting Company. As his personal runabout, Donald would be using the prototype of a 'Jetstar' ski-boat he was developing with Norris Brothers, via their company, Bluebird Marine, of which Donald was chairman. Campbell had high hopes of displaying it at the Boat Show in early 1967.

Clive and Louis working on K7 in the unfinished boat house. Note: left to right on Bluebird's transom, rudder, water brake and stabilising fin.
© C. Glynn

Once K7 was safely installed on the slipway in her temporary boathouse, Donald wasted no time in getting her afloat. Maurie, Louis and other willing helpers were drafted in to push Bluebird down the slipway and into Coniston's waters for the first time since 14 May 1959. The sun was shining and the assembled photographers and TV crews were able to get all the pictures they wanted. Donald was keen to maximise Bluebird's exposure. A large crowd of locals augmented the pressmen, photographers and camera crews standing by to watch Campbell's latest record attempt get under way.

Donald did not expect to be at Coniston for much more than two to three weeks, given favourable weather conditions. A number of trials would be conducted before wrapping-up with the actual attempt. He was accompanied this time by Tonia, who added a touch of 'showbiz' glamour and sparkle to the scene. She had brought her poodle Coco along, and for a short while the serious business of record-breaking was pushed to one side as she greeted old friends and posed for a few of the press photographers. Among the many who came to Coniston to watch and report on this new record attempt were David Benson and Norman Luck from the *Daily Express*, together with their photographer John Wardhaugh; Brian Boss of the *Daily Sketch* with his photographers Harvey Mann and Brian Taylor; and Keith Harrison and Eric Shaw from the Press Association. The BBC sent a film crew from their *Look North* programme, while John Pett and Dougie Hurn were there to make

Below left: K7 is winched down the slipway as Donald looks on
© Brian Millin collection

Below centre and right: In the late afternoon sun, Bluebird is lowered gently into the water for the first time.
© G. Hallawell

a film for Four Companies Television. Rediffusion sent a crew with a large mobile editing van, and Pathé and Movietone sent newsreel camera crews. From overseas, the Canadian Broadcasting Company was represented with a camera crew. Reporters and photographers from local newspapers made up the rest of the press corps.

BILL VANRYNE ON DONALD CAMPBELL

'The following Wednesday, 2nd November, back at the lab, my chief engineer came in and told me that I had been invited to join Donald's team at Coniston to assist with the initial trials of Bluebird, and make sure the start system worked in the field. This seemed to me to be almost unbelievable.

Donald was very pleased with the system; it proved to be of considerable use under the difficult initial operating conditions that were experienced at Coniston, throughout November, as it eliminated the reliance on a separate service boat for engine starting, a necessary feature with the Beryl engine installation.

My first impression of Donald was when he strode briskly into the cold, temporary boat shed where Bluebird was housed, along with the Land Rover support vehicle and the other equipment. He smiled at us cheerfully, greeting the team with enthusiasm, and then set to work alongside us in preparation of the immediate tasks in hand.'

Friday
4 November

Weather:
Misty, dull
and overcast

Below from left: Preparing to tow Bluebird away from the jetty.
© P. Allonby

Donald directing operations from the cockpit.
© P. Allonby

As dusk falls, K7 is towed out for her first low-speed run.
© Mirrorpix

With the base established, discussions were held with the Army Signals Corps as to the best form of communication between Bluebird, the jetty, the timekeepers and the course boats.

Towards the end of the day, with the light failing, Donald decided to get Bluebird afloat and cruise around the bay off the jetty just to get the feel of her again. K7 was launched in front of a large crowd of interested onlookers, but she appeared to be nose-heavy as she pottered around at low speed. Eventually, after about 15 minutes, Donald called for one of the course boats to tow Bluebird back in. Leo Villa later described the activity surrounding the recovery of Bluebird in a letter to his wife, Joan: 'We were fiddling about in the semi-dark, trying to get Bluebird back into the boathouse. Everything went wrong, what a bloody circus. I felt quite embarrassed, so much for trying to do things in a hurry.'

With Bluebird safely back on shore, Donald and his engineers had a debriefing session. He complained that he was unable to get anywhere near maximum revs and it was decided that the Bristol Siddeley (BS) engineers would make

a quick examination of the engine to see if any fault could be found. Ken Pearson, one of the BS specialists, who had arrived on the morning of the 4th, initially suspected that the fuel filter might be too fine, thereby restricting fuel flow. If this was the case, the problem would be easy to fix. When the fuel filter was checked and found to be of the correct specification, Jack Lavis, the other BS expert, who had only reached Coniston just before the run, suggested a more thorough examination of the engine. The jet engine compressor cover top plates were removed and light score marks found on the compressor blades. Lavis suspected that something solid might have been sucked into the intakes during the afternoon's running. The cover plates were replaced and a plan was made to give the engine a full-bore static test on the slipway the next morning. A new and unusual problem was also discovered – three nail holes were found in the lower hull, presumed to be a legacy of the boat's unsupervised travels around Australia in 1965. The holes were duly sealed and made watertight. Donald and his team finally left for their accommodation late in the evening, glad that they had at least begun to tackle the inevitable problems that would arise during the course of the attempt.

A REPORTER'S PERSPECTIVE
NORMAN LUCK ON DONALD CAMPBELL

Norman Luck was on the *Daily Express* from 1964 to 1996 as a staff reporter, foreign correspondent and latterly Chief Investigative reporter.
'On a cold November morning in 1966, I drove to Coniston, where I was told I would be witnessing history – a daring attempt by Donald Campbell to break his own world water speed record.

Journalists from around the world were assembled in whatever hotels, pub's and bed and breakfast establishments they could find. I was booked into the Railway Hotel, a tiny village pub less than two minutes from the boathouse on Coniston Water – the focal point of the action that was to unfold – where I was to spend many hours waiting as Donald Campbell fought the elements to achieve his dream.'

The morning was spent preparing K7 for her static test and consulting with the Signals Corps about a radio telephone system for boat-to-shore contact. Ken Norris, Bluebird's designer, and his colleague Tony James, who had been in charge of the refit of K7 at Haywards Heath, had joined the team temporarily together with Bill Vanryne from Rotax and Ken Reaks from Smiths. They were working alongside Leo and Maurie. The press and TV crews were out in force filming the team's preparations. Bluebird was lowered part-way down the slipway and Donald climbed into the cockpit to give an interview to John Pett of Four Companies TV.

Saturday
5 November

Weather:
Dry, bright, with a strengthening south-easterly breeze

Bluebird's 'base'.
© A.E. James

Above from left: Leo unfastens Bluebird's engine cover.
© A.E. James

Bluebird in her 'boathouse'.
© C. Glynn

Leo submits to a TV interview.
© W. Vanryne

Preparing for the static test.
© W. Vanryne

Below from left Bluebird's cockpit.

Bristol Siddeley Orpheus 709 before the static test.

When that was finished, the boat was drawn back towards the boat shed and the engine cover removed. It was now Leo's turn to be interviewed, while he worked on the boat. He talked about his time with Donald's father, Sir Malcolm, and Donald's initial record-breaking exploits in the 1950s. The various TV crews then set their equipment up to film the static test. In order to secure K7, heavy iron chains were attached to two towing eyes on the stern of the boat, which in turn were fastened by a frogman to the slipway itself. K7 was shackled to her cradle via the main spar, and with the winch cable on the front drawn taut, the boat was effectively immobilised. By lunchtime, Bluebird was ready for the test and a large crowd had gathered to watch the spectacle. They were warned to stand well clear of the air intakes for fear of anything being sucked in while the engine was under full load, and also well away from the jet stream caused by the 4,500lb of thrust developed by the Orpheus engine on full throttle (corrected to 4,792.5lb at 2°C intake inlet temperature).

Jack Lavis was to conduct the test, with other team members observing from the jetty or the boathouse, all equipped with cotton earplugs. Lavis climbed into the cockpit, drew the cover over his head and started the engine using Bluebird's on-board compressed air system. Slowly, revs were applied and the engine then throttled-back. This test was conducted a number of times. The final time, the crescendo was enormous, with the jet sending a large stream of

water across the lake. It was a truly spectacular sight and sound for all who witnessed it. As Lavis throttled back preparatory to shutdown, 'expensive' grinding noises were heard from the engine.

Emerging from the cockpit, Lavis stated that he too had been unable to reach maximum revs and that fuel pressure was low. It was obvious that a more thorough investigation was required to pinpoint the problem with the engine. If it could not operate at maximum power, Donald would be unable to chase his 300mph goal. A prolonged, closer inspection of the engine revealed deep score marks in the turbine compressor blades. The air intake was then examined, and the inner skin found to be severely buckled. The welding along one of the seams had split and a number of rivets had been torn out. This damage had been caused by the enormously increased air demands of the more powerful Orpheus engine, which led to increased *negative* pressure within the air-intake duct.

The inner panelling of the air-intakes formed the wall of the void behind the cockpit seat, this void being at atmospheric pressure. Hence the pressure differential in the intake duct – relative to atmospheric pressure – caused the inner wall to be sucked outwards into the duct, tearing it along the upper rivet line, the resultant debris being ingested by the compressor.

Preparing for the static test.
© W. Vanryne

Above from left: Left to right: Leo, Bill Vanryne, Jack Lavis and Ken Reaks in the boathouse.

Leo examines Bluebird's air starter instrumentation while Donald and Dougie Hurn look on.

Below from left: Tonia and Mr Whoppit.

Tony James and Bill Vanryne with K7.

Left to right: Tony James, Ken Pearson, Ken Norris, Jack Lavis and Bill Vanryne prepare for the static test.

Donald called a meeting in the caravan to decide what to do. Alongside Donald himself, Ken, Leo, Maurie, Lavis and Pearson from BS, Ken Reaks from Smith Industries and Tony James from Norris Brothers were present. It was decided to carry out a complete engine and air-intake examination to ascertain if the engine was a write-off.

Donald and Ken made their way up to the Sun Hotel to contact Norris Brothers headquarters and make plans for overcoming the technical woes. The intakes would at the very least have to be reinforced, perhaps even redesigned.

Leo, Maurie, Tony and the BS specialists worked long into the evening, removing the top casing from the turbine to try to establish the full extent of the problem. Donald worked alongside them. They found significant damage to many of the compressor blades; parts of the intake fastenings had obviously been sucked right through into the engine. The bitter truth was that this engine, Orpheus 709, was effectively ruined.

During the investigation that evening, Donald was interviewed by John Pett for the Four Companies documentary while the engineers continued with their work in the background. Obviously very much focused on how to overcome this setback, Campbell's answers were defensive.

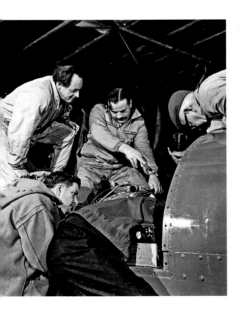

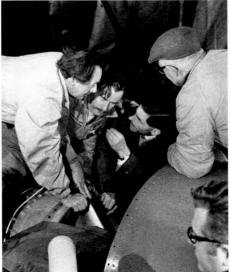

DC: 'Sorry, I can't buy this Campbell disaster bad luck what have you; there is no form of advanced engineering, no form of record-breaking where you get it smooth . . . it just doesn't happen, it wouldn't be record-breaking if it did happen that way. Records would be broken every week. World records today are broken but very seldom, and this is probably one of the reasons why . . . you don't get away with them easily.'

JP: 'Could you have foreseen this in any way?'

DC: 'No. This is one of the misfortunes that befall you if you decide to try and follow this rather stony path and it doesn't matter really whether you're playing with a world record-breaking car . . . err . . . high-speed aircraft . . . high-speed boat, or any form of advanced engineering . . . rocketry or what have you.'

JP: 'What is it going to mean to you in terms of time because this time it's your own money really?'

DC: 'Well it always has been.'

JP: 'But you haven't got as many backers this time.'

DC: 'Well we haven't got any backers at all . . . we've had associates through the years, but in terms of time? . . . About a week I suppose . . .'

JP: 'And money delay?'

DC: 'Well, you know the old meter is ticking over the whole time.'

JP: 'How long can you afford to go on if there is another delay?'

DC: 'This is the terrible part about trying to break a record. You see once you start, you're past the point of no return.'

JP: 'So you've got to go on?'

DC: 'You've got to go on . . . there is no going back in life, you start something, you've got to finish it.'

Donald Campbell speaking to John Pett for *The Price of a Record*,
5 November 1966

John Pett interviews Donald as the team work on K7.
© Mirrorpix

The air-intakes would clearly have to be repaired and reinforced. There were no facilities at Coniston to accomplish this, so the team set about removing them, which was no small task in the draughty and ill-suited temporary boathouse. To help make the job a little easier, the TV crews left the very bright film lights *in situ* while the engineers worked into the night.

> DC: 'Mr Pearson's got the engine well in hand, the worst problem we're going to have is exactly what technique to use to stiffen those intakes – the right way to go about it of course would be to make an entirely new intake structure. This would take about three months.'
>
> BB: 'Yes, how are you going to improvise then?'
>
> DC: 'That's just the point. This is where the British I think are probably the world's masters.'
>
> BB: 'Ha . . . Do you have any ideas about how you're going to set about it?'
>
> DC: 'Yes we do . . .'
>
> **Donald Campbell talking to Brian Boss of the *Daily Sketch*,**
> **5 November 1966**

Explaining the engine problems to Brian Boss of the *Daily Sketch*.
© Mirrorpix, G. Hallawell

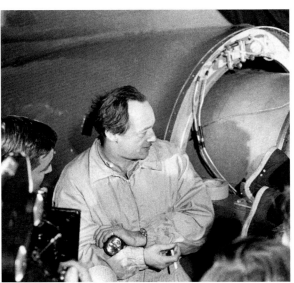

CLIVE GLYNN ON DONALD CAMPBELL

'The Saturday brought the engine static test. I got to work properly on Bluebird for the first time, helping ensure she was fastened securely to the slipway and her launch cradle. After the air intakes collapsed, it was chaos, as arrangements were made to get the spare engine to Coniston and the intakes back down south to be rebuilt. Ken Norris asked me to go back to Hayward's Heath with Frank Read in Bill Coley's truck to pick up the spare engine. I had one night at home, then it was back to Norris Brothers premises, where the engine was loaded on the truck for the journey back to Coniston.'

TONY JAMES ON DONALD CAMPBELL

'*Bluebird was finally finished on 31 October and she was transported to Coniston for the trials and the subsequent attempt. After K7 arrived at Coniston, the whole enterprise was supported by people who volunteered their services. We felt it was a British endeavour headed by the one man in the country who could do it and who was prepared to go all out to achieve a new record.*

Record-breaking is never easy. Donald knew that better than anyone. He had, in effect, a new boat with changed characteristics, which would only come to light when he and Bluebird attempted to go faster than any other boat had gone before. This time too, the attempt was made on a financial shoestring and time was pressing – the weather was closing in. All these factors must have worried Donald, but he always put on a brave face – especially with the press, who didn't understand the pressure they were putting him under for the sake of a good story.'

Details of the required modifications were worked out by Ken Norris and the BS engineers. They were then phoned through to Norris Brothers in Haywards Heath so they could begin preparations to carry out the modifications. Work carried on throughout the night, involving removal of the fuel tank and cutting through Bluebird's wiring loom. At 4.00 a.m., Bill Coley's truck, with Clive Glynn on board, was sent south to Haywards Heath to collect the spare Orpheus engine from the Gnat trainer Donald had bought that summer.

The morning was spent preparing for removal of the wrecked Orpheus engine, which entailed stripping away all the upper bodywork. In the early afternoon, Ken Norris and Tony James set off for Haywards Heath to start work on the drawings for the modified intakes.

Sunday
6 November

Weather:
Dry and overcast

At about 2.00 p.m., the damaged intakes themselves were put on the back of Peter Morris's Land Rover pick-up to begin their 350-mile journey south. The press and TV crews had assumed that the engine failure meant the end of the project, but Donald had other ideas. In an interview, he described the position that the project found itself in. 'These are not ordinary circumstances, we have neither the time nor the money to do this, but we are up here for a purpose. Somehow we have to devise a way of dealing with this matter in the field, as opposed to in the workshop. It is by no means the ideal way of doing it, but that is how it has to be.'

Later in the day, Donald and Tonia left Coniston to drive back to Surrey. Donald was keen that work on modifying the intakes should take no longer than necessary and felt that his presence would help lend an added sense of urgency to the task in hand. The air-intakes finally arrived at Haywards Heath early on Monday morning. In the meantime, travelling in the opposite direction, Bill Coley's Bedford truck carrying the spare Orpheus, number 711, was making its way towards Coniston, arriving early on Monday morning.

Monday
7 November

Weather:
Overcast but calm

Local firm Seymour Crane Hire was brought in to provide lifting equipment to unload the spare engine from Coley's truck and remove the damaged Orpheus from K7. The spare engine was lifted onto a purpose-built trolley and wheeled into the workshop.

The large yellow mobile crane was then positioned alongside the slipway. Leo, Maurie, Louis and Clive had disconnected all the auxiliaries from the damaged engine and undone the engine mounts. A special lifting rig had been bolted to the engine and hooked to the crane. The engine was then lifted out and moved to the workshop to have many of its accessories removed ready for fitting to the spare Orpheus. The temporary nature of the boathouse with its plastic sheeting stretched over a framework of tubular scaffolding made for unpleasantly draughty and cold working conditions. At least the rain held off, but it was dispiriting work. Considerable effort had been put into the Orpheus installation and external appearance of the boat. Bluebird now looked a sorry sight devoid of all her upper superstructure.

Right: Preparing to remove 709.
© C. Glynn

Far right: The intakes have already been removed as 709 is lifted from the hull.
© Leo Villa's Film and Picture Archive

Below: Orpheus 709 is hoisted out of K7.
© Leo Villa's Film and Picture Archive

BILL VANRYNE ON DONALD CAMPBELL

'There were times when Donald was under great stress. The initial engine was damaged beyond repair during the first full-power static test. To add to this difficulty, he was determined to put on a brave face for the press, who were always there, keen to get a story.

In answer to this, the following Monday, 7 November, a bold headline appeared in the Daily Sketch, who were backing the attempt, which read; 'We WILL Win by Guts and Skill'.

This was typical of his determination to win at any cost; where many others would have probably thrown in the towel, he persevered; 'Once you start something, you've got to finish it'. In the interview, he went on to describe how he was expecting this setback not to be the last they would encounter before reaching the magic figure of 300mph.

Everyone rallied round, working tirelessly to dismantle components for the removal of the engine. A crane was brought in to lift the engine out of Bluebird and into the nearby workshop, where it could be examined. To combat the freezing draughty conditions by the lakeside, we all wore layers of warm clothing under duffel coats; Donald was spotted wearing a blue woolly knitted hat with a bobble on the top, which earned him the title of 'Noddy'. Pretty soon, everybody was wearing a similar sort of knitted hat.'

Tuesday
8 November

*Weather:
Overcast, cold
but dry*

Donald was still in the south of England, overseeing the modifications to the air intakes with Tony James. Ken Norris had contracted Bourners of Lancing to carry out the work, at the suggestion of Clive Glynn's father. They were familiar with Bluebird from having worked on her bodywork during the refit.

It was not simply a case of strengthening the intakes. Bristol Siddeley had raised a number of important issues during the refit, which had not been addressed in the earlier modifications, but which now needed considering. Using the cross sectional area of the intakes (337.1 square inches), Ken Pearson calculated the negative pressure in the duct and recommended strengthening it, reshaping the outer lips to have a greater radius of curvature and – most importantly – subjecting the assembly to pressure depression tests. Modifications were completed by replacing the rivets that had been torn out and reinforcing the inner intake structure.

A light U-shaped aluminium lip was fitted around the leading edge of the intake, extending about 4 inches inside and outside each intake and making the leading edge more rounded and blunt. This feature was designed to give the air intakes a higher contraction ratio, and hence make them more efficient. In the upper quadrant on each side, the lip extended about 14 inches into the intake. This section was blended-in and firmly fixed in place, providing the necessary extra stiffness and strength to the intake mouth.

Back at Coniston, Jack Lavis and Ken Pearson from Bristol Siddeley had arrived to work on the replacement engine. Tony James had suggested to Donald that they patch up 709 so that it could be reinstalled in the boat to test the modified and reinforced intakes. This approach would minimise any risk of suffering problems with the replacement Orpheus. When this was suggested to Leo, he was not pleased. It would involve significant extra work, to repair the engine and then reinstall it in the hull, for one engine test. Leo Villa recalls: 'We had to locate each damaged compressor blade, then file it by hand. Those compressor blades that were beyond repair were removed. The corresponding blades on the compressor were also removed to ensure that the engine remained in balance.'

This was a time-consuming and laborious job, but it ensured that Orpheus 709 would be able to run again to allow testing of the modifications and reinforcement made to the intakes. In record-breaking terms, the unit was no longer a viable option, though.

The weather now took a turn for the worse, with strong winds and heavy rain arriving after the calm of the previous three days. Working conditions deteriorated accordingly, with the boathouse being buckled and strained by the wind and very nearly collapsing. Louis and Clive spent the day bailing water from the roof and reinforcing the structure where they could. The tarpaulin at the lake end of the boathouse took the brunt of the gale-force winds. At least at this stage they had a respite from late nights!

Meanwhile, Donald allowed himself an evening off to celebrate Tonia's birthday, taking her out to dinner at a restaurant near his Surrey home.

Wednesday
9 November to
Friday
11 November

Weather:
Wet and windy

Saturday
12 November to
Tuesday
15 November

Weather:
Wet and windy

Work continued on getting the damaged Orpheus ready as the elements battered the site. The replacement engine was stripped, cleaned and checked so that it could be fitted to K7 as soon as the reinforced intakes had been tested. The Union flag on the starboard side of Bluebird's tail fin was repainted by Ted Hamel, a friend of Sir Malcolm, who was staying in Coniston at Donald's invitation and had offered his assistance with the record bid. It had been painted on upside down – a sign of distress in nautical circles.

The 'Boathouse' with the garage-come-workshop behind.
© C. Glynn

The work needed on engine 709 for testing the revised intakes was finished, and the unit refitted to the hull to await Donald's return with the intakes. On the 14th and 15th, gale-force winds threatened to destroy the boathouse and further reinforcement was carried out. The transparent plastic 'curtains' which had formed the front and rear of the boathouse had been replaced by a heavy green tarpaulin at each end, but the one at the lake end was being shredded by the wind. The boat shed and workshop were kept warm by paraffin-fuelled space heaters that each consumed 10 gallons of fuel a day but did produce prodigious amounts of heat. Ted Hamel had been asked by Donald to repair the severed wiring loom by means of heavy-duty connecting strip. Leo was keen for this work to be completed before the modified air intakes arrived. The Army came back to install the radio communication system in Bluebird and the support boats. This equipment and team comprised a truck full of radio gear, a Land Rover, two officers, and four other ranks. Over the next few days, they would finally come up with an effective solution.

In the meantime, the water level of the lake had risen some 3 feet, restricting the amount of room available to work on K7 on the slipway outside the boat shed – a crucial space with all the heavy lifting to come.

Later that afternoon, the Sun began to get busy. Jack Lavis and Ken Pearson returned from BS, Tony James from Norris Brothers, and Bill Vanryne from Rotax. At about 6.00 p.m., Donald and Tonia also arrived back at Coniston. The project was under way again.

CLIVE GLYNN ON DONALD CAMPBELL

'The next few days we worked on Bluebird and both jet engines. The weather was miserable, but we wanted to get everything prepared for when the rebuilt air intakes came back. Louis and I spent part of the time baling water off the boathouse roof, and making the structure more secure. That seemed to be one of my main tasks as the weeks rolled by. That boat shed was cold and draughty and not built for winter weather.'

Wednesday
16 November

Weather:
Overcast, showers

Donald's arrival back at Coniston the previous evening preceded the air intakes, which were travelling up the M6 on the back of Bill Coley's truck. The truck finally arrived around mid-morning and Donald was there to greet it. The fuel tank and intake structure was hastily refitted to K7, and in the late afternoon Orpheus 709 ran for the last time. The Bristol Siddeley experts conducted the static test. The hills around Coniston reverberated to the sound of a jet engine at full bore as spray lashed across the lake. The test showed that the revised and reinforced intakes were a success. Donald and the team called it a day at about 7.00 p.m. and retired to the Sun for dinner.

Top left: The intakes arrive back at Coniston.
© Norman Hurst

Top right: Louis and Donald unload the rebuilt intakes from Bill Coley's truck.
© Norman Hurst

Bottom: Ken Pearson and Donald watch Jack Lavis working on 709.
© Norman Hurst

BILL VANRYNE ON DONALD CAMPBELL

'Donald's prediction about more problems proved to be true about 10 days later, when Bluebird, now fitted with the spare Orpheus engine, failed to achieve the planing position in subsequent trials. This problem too was one we just plugged away at until it was solved. On several occasions during these trying times, Donald's wife, Tonia, came down to the boathouse to give her support and to chat with us, to keep herself informed.

One important quality which Donald showed was kindness and a deep appreciation to all those who were taking an active part throughout the record attempts. It was never 'I' with Donald, always 'We'. As an example of this, one evening after sending 'Unc' back to his hotel to have a well-deserved early night, after a long hard day, Tony James and I were left to help Donald clear up and shut up shop for the evening. Donald turned to us, as we were about to depart and invited us both back to the bungalow where Tonia was preparing a meal. We spent a great evening with them both. Near the end of the night, he came back into the room with a set of the prestigious Bluebird overalls, complete with Union Jack crest, which he presented to Tony in recognition of his project management of the refit at Haywards Heath, and also for his contribution to the work at Coniston. He then told us that he had made us both members of the K7 Club in recognition of our help and assistance to him and the Bluebird team. These gestures were typical of his generous spirit.'

'I can't even take a pee in peace'. Donald returning from a call of nature!
© Norman Hurst

Left: Donald and his
E-Type at the jetty.
© Norman Hurst

Bottom left: Bill Jordan,
Donald and Ted Hamel
discuss the spare Orpheus
with Ken Pearson.
© Norman Hurst

Bottom right:
Leo checks his mail.
© A.E. James

In the morning, the damaged engine was hoisted out of the boat and work commenced on removing its auxiliary fittings for transfer to Orpheus 711. Lavis and Pearson then fitted the fuel system components to 711 and made a final examination of the unit to ensure that everything was in order. Installation of 711 was completed by the two Bristol Siddeley engineers, together with Tony James from Norris Brothers and Bill Vanryne from Rotax, by early afternoon. Donald assisted and kept everyone happy by providing those who smoked with a copious supply of cigarettes from the glove compartment of his car.

Despite the pressures, the team had already established a daily routine that kept them fed and watered. Every day around mid-morning, Robbie would drive down to the boathouse with hot coffee and a tin of biscuits. Everyone looked forward to this as the coffee was laced with brandy and of better quality than anyone could manage with the kettle and jar of instant in the caravan.

At lunchtime, depending on the programme for the day, team members would either troop-off into the village to find lunch, usually at the Sun or the Lakeland Snack Bar, or if time was short they would cram into the caravan or whatever shelter they could find and eat soup and steak and kidney pie brought down from the Sun. At around 4.30 in the afternoon, the morning ritual of coffee and biscuits was repeated, sometimes combined with tea and cake. When work on Bluebird was finished for the day, normal practice was for everyone to gather in the bar at the Sun. Donald was usually the last to arrive, having stopped off at the bungalow to update Tonia. The events of the day would usually dictate the mood. If all had gone well the gatherings would

Thursday
17 November

Weather:
Overcast, windy
but dry

Orpheus 709 is lifted
from K7's hull.
© W. Vanryne

Right: Jack Lavis,
Ken Pearson and Tony
James strip 709 of its fuel
system while Leo keeps
Tonia in the picture.
© W. Vanryne

Orpheus 711 is lowered
into Bluebird's hull.
© W. Vanryne

be light-hearted and sociable, with games of darts arranged between opposing teams. If things had not proceeded as planned, the atmosphere would be sombre and it would more often than not mean an early night.

With the engine installation work completed, all that remained was to replace the tail section and engine cover. In fact, this was no small job, with each section requiring four men to lift it into position. The tail section was fitted first, then it was the turn of the engine cover. Some 250 Dzus fasteners had to be tightened before both panels were secure, so it was a case of everyone mucking-in to get the job finished. After lunch on the 17th, with engine 711 now fitted to K7, Donald decided to conduct a further static test to check that all systems were functioning correctly. All was well and everyone retired to the village for supper. Later, Donald enjoyed an evening with the Bristol Siddeley engineers and some of the press boys in the bar of the Crown by way of saying thank-you for all their hard work and perseverance.

Above left: Preparing for the static test of Orpheus 711.
© C. Glynn

Above right: Spray is blasted across the lake as '711' is run up.
© C. Glynn

Left to right: Tony James, Jack Lavis, Bill Vanryne, Ken Pearson, Donald and Leo. Maurie must have taken the picture!
© A.E. James & W. Vanryne

Unwinding in the bar at the Crown Hotel, Coniston. © Norman Hurst

CHAPTER 5
'WE'RE ON OUR WAY...'

Friday
18 November

Weather:
Bright, breeze
dying down

The storm of the previous few days had finally blown itself out and Donald was impatient to get the project back on track. Everyone was up early that morning at the Sun, keen to get down to the slipway and get going. One aspect of the modified intakes that displeased Donald was the slightly darker shade of blue used by Bourners, which undermined the effort spent by them on Bluebird's bodywork in October.

The Bristol Siddeley engine team, together with Tony James and Bill Vanryne, were still on hand to assist in the event of further engine trouble.

By early afternoon the breeze had dropped. Although the lake was far from calm, Donald decided to launch Bluebird to see if he could get her up to planing speed. Word soon spread around Coniston and the press, photographers and TV camera crews all made their way down

The Sun Hotel.
© A.E. James

to the boathouse. Some more optimistic photographers drove round to the eastern side of the lake to the timing points, hoping to secure their first shots of Bluebird at high speed.

The pre-arranged launching drill was put into operation: Leo and Robbie manned the Fairline, ready to pull Bluebird out to the middle of the lake, Maurice took the controls of the Land Rover winch, and a line was attached to Bluebird's stern. On Donald's signal, Bluebird rolled slowly down the track into the water. She floated off her cradle and was pulled gently towards the end of the jetty. From there, Leo took the rope in the Fairline and towed her out into the lake. Donald put on his leather flying helmet, which contained his earphones, and the face mask that carried the radio-telephone mic. The line was released from the Fairline, and Campbell drew the canopy shut over his head and started the engine. Slowly, K7 moved away. He applied the throttle and Bluebird gathered pace, reaching perhaps 30mph. Huge waves of water poured over her sponsons and the spars linking them to the main hull, while clouds of spray formed by the jet stream billowed out behind her. The assembled audience waited for her to rise up into the planing position, expecting her hull to 'unstick' and Bluebird to tear off down the lake at high speed. The boat was not cooperating, however. She continued to wallow in the water and dipped her nose as more power was applied, flooding the engine. Four times Donald attempted to get Bluebird onto her planing points and four times the engine was flooded and brought to a halt. Finally, after about 20 minutes and with the water now very disturbed, Donald brought her back to the jetty. He called Leo over the intercom: 'The water is putting the bloody fire out, Unc.' Leo radioed back: 'Bring her in Skipper, bring her in.'

Top: Preparing Bluebird for launch.
© C. Glynn

Left: K7 still nose-heavy and failing to plane.
© Press Association

Bottom: Bluebird is positioned back on her cradle.
© A.E. James

Winching Bluebird back in.
© W. Vanryne & © A.E. James

As Bluebird was winched ashore, Donald was asked a somewhat tactless
question by a watching journalist – 'Anything wrong?' Donald snapped back,
'If you throw a bucket of water onto a fire it goes out, doesn't it? Well that's
what's bloody wrong, old friend.' It was not clear at that moment whether the
problem lay with K7 or the fact that conditions that afternoon were far from
suitable. The hydroplane was given the benefit of the doubt for that evening.
At least K7 now had a functioning engine and the intake modifications had
proved successful.

A meeting was held in the boathouse to try to identify the fault. Bluebird
featured two perspex spray guards, curved to match the shape of the air intakes,
one on each side of the cockpit. They were designed to deflect water thrown
up by the main rear spar at low speeds and had proved effective once their
design had been finalised in 1956. The spray baffles themselves had not been
modified since then, and K7 had achieved five records with them in this form.
However, Bristol Siddeley had suggested repositioning them further forwards
to try to give the air intakes more protection, and this change had been carried
out the previous day. The greater thrust of the Orpheus engine was forcing the
bow of the boat down into the water, creating a wave that overwhelmed the
baffles and entered the intakes, causing the engine to flame out as it ingested
the water. It would be a case of trial and error until the correct configuration
was found.

Saturday
19 November

Weather:
Sunny and calm

Louis was on standby duty and by 7.00 a.m. had already been down to the lakeside to assess conditions. He made his way back to the village, calling first at the bungalow to alert Donald and then at the Sun to rouse Leo, Maurice and the rest. Things looked good, was the word.

Coffee and toast were quickly consumed in the kitchen and then a convoy of cars set off for the lakeside. Donald had already arrived, but by now the breeze had started. They would have to wait, with Bluebird poised on the slipway ready for a quick launch.

In the early afternoon, the breeze died down. Bluebird was duly launched and towed towards the middle of the lake, taking great care to avoid disturbing the water. With better water conditions than the day before, the team was

optimistic that K7 could be persuaded to show a turn of speed. As Donald prepared for the run, Leo Villa decided to observe events from the Fairline while travelling alongside Bluebird as she accelerated. The results were disappointing: despite repeated attempts at planing, Bluebird again failed to respond correctly.

From Leo's vantage point, it seemed that the spray baffles had no chance of coping with the amount of water thrown up by the rear spar. As Bluebird accelerated, her nose was dipping rather than rising and the sheer volume of water pouring over the rear spar was finding its way into the air intakes and 'putting out

Above: The 'rapid response' team. Left to right: Jack Lavis, Bill Vanryne, Ken Pearson and Tony James.
© A.E. James

Leo observes from a Fairline support launch, while Bluebird still fails to plane.
© Mirrorpix

Still nose-heavy.
© Getty Images

the fire'. After about 30 minutes, Donald reluctantly decided to bring Bluebird in. The frustration was evident on his face for all to see and his comments about Bluebird were less than charitable. A more comprehensive rethink of the situation was required and further modifications to the spray baffles were put in hand.

In the fading afternoon sun, Donald brings Bluebird back to the slipway.
© A.E. James

Donald standing on
Bluebird's nose as she is
pulled onto her cradle
© A.E. James

Above left: Sitting atop
Bluebird as he makes his
way towards her stern .
© W. Vanryne

Above right: 'This rather
stony path'.
© W. Vanryne

Among all these problems, Donald found time to entertain two schoolchildren who had won a competition run by the *Daily Sketch* on 7 November. First prize was the chance to spend the day at Coniston with Donald Campbell. On the face of it, they could not have arrived at a worse time. The continuing problems with getting Bluebird to plane raised the worrying prospect of a major redesign of the intake structure. Donald gave the two children plenty of attention, though, showing them round Bluebird, letting each one sit in the cockpit and taking them out on the lake for a quick spin in the Jetstar.

In the evening, he had arranged for the children to come to the bungalow for dinner, with Tonia doing the honours in the kitchen, assisted by Julia Goossens. When the prizewinners had been returned to their hotel and waiting parents, Donald went back down to the boathouse to resume work on the spray baffle problem.

News of Bluebird's trials on the 18th and 19th had sparked renewed interest in the project and combined with kinder weather brought the crowds to Coniston. Backstops were made to fit between the spray guards and air intake cowlings. Bluebird was launched again but, frustratingly, the problem had not been fixed – she resolutely refused to 'unstick'.

The press corps, which up until then had only comprised the *Daily Sketch*, the *Daily Express* and the Press Association as its permanent members, was now boosted by reporters from the *Daily Mirror* and other newspapers, attracted by the previous week's runs.

Sunday
20 November to
Monday
21 November

Weather:
Bright and dry

Donald poses for
the press.
© Mirrorpix

Why Mr Campbell do you want to break this record when you yourself already are the holder of it?'

'You know, I think 'you' ought to be substituted for the word 'we'. it's the last British-held world speed record. Ten years ago, we had all three major ones and now we've got one. If someone does not do something about it, we shall lose that, and I believe these records are very definitely symbolic of a nations ability technically and of their virility.'

Donald Campbell speaking in November 1966

Bluebird sitting on the slipway in the late autumn sunshine.
© Leo Villa's Film and Picture Archive

'There is no form of record-breaking where you get it smooth.'
© Press Association

Donald was called upon to give lengthy interviews and make himself available for photographs. That he was shown smiling in many of the resulting images was more down to his patience and good nature than anything else.

On the Monday, Bluebird was again launched, but the backstops proved ineffective and she was winched back ashore for further modifications. It was a frustrating business, carried out in the full glare of the media. Work carried on throughout the afternoon and into the evening, fitting 12-inch extensions made of aluminium sheeting to the spray baffles.

The weather had been kind now for almost a week and Bluebird had made numerous outings on the lake, but Donald had still not been able to travel much faster than 30mph. He was increasingly impatient to resolve the problem before the calm conditions gave way to winter weather.

Although Bluebird was launched twice that day, in both the morning and afternoon, the trials with the extended baffles provided no solution, although Bluebird did travel further, heading off down the lake for about a mile in repeated attempts to plane before being towed back to the slipway when the water became too churned up. Leo again observed progress from a boat alongside. Over the weekend, Donald had experimented with water flow from a tap over the back of a spoon, speculating that the convex shape of the spray baffles meant that water would stick to the surface and be drawn towards the intakes. After the afternoon run, he decided to make a more fundamental modification by swapping the spray baffles from one side to the other. Instead of matching the shape of the intakes, they now formed wing-like structures with their concave side face down to the water. This once again meant working late into the evening in cold, draughty but mercifully dry conditions. The forecast promised calm weather in the morning and everyone retired to the hotel hopeful that the problem had finally been fixed.

Tuesday
22 November

Weather:
Bright and cold

Above left:
Donald carries out further spray baffle modifications.
© C. Glynn

Above centre and right:
Bluebird about to be towed to the centre of the lake.
© C. Glynn

. . . Still failing to plane . . .
© Mirrorpix

Left: Back at the jetty.
© G. Hallawell

Below: 'Better tow me in boys'.
© Mirrorpix

Above right: Donald's
face says it all . . .
© C. Glynn

Right: Donald gets back
into Bluebird's cockpit.
© C. Glynn

NORMAN LUCK ON DONALD CAMPBELL

'Bluebird K7 was ready and waiting, a wonderfully powerful product of superb engineering by the Campbell team, as they painstakingly prepared for the ideal conditions for the eagerly awaited high-speed attempt. It was to be a long wait – weeks of watching and hoping for the right climate as winter shrouded the lake and on many occasions the wind speed and visibility made it impossible for Bluebird to leave the boathouse.

Donald despairs at the thought of yet more spray baffle modifications.
© J. Wardhaugh/Ruskin Museum

It became a strict work regime. Up and dressed at 6.30 a.m. to go to the boathouse for the latest weather reports. Hopes were raised as the Campbell team went through a rigid schedule of checks to ensure an attempt was feasible.

The checks included a boat to ensure that fallen tree branches swept into the water by the overnight wind and rain would not be a hazard to Bluebird – it travelled the full length of the lake and returned. The timekeepers took their places on the lake shore, and the atmosphere was tense as the team chatted over crackly radio links to co-ordinate the detailed preparation. I lost count of the number of times this happened and at the last minute was told an attempt had been aborted because of a swell or bad weather made it perilous for Bluebird to be pitted against the elements.

The weeks went by. Donald Campbell was living in a bungalow close to the Sun Hotel, where his team and all the journalists gathered each night to speak to him and get the latest news on how he planned to proceed. Donald's wife, Tonia, was at Coniston throughout November. A night club singer, she had accepted a regular gig in Carlisle and the journalists ran a regular 'taxi' service for her to and from the club.'

Much of the previous night had been spent in the boathouse making further refinements to the spray baffles. Donald woke on the 23rd feeling tired and worn-down by the problems of the last few days, but stepping out onto the balcony of the bungalow (a feature made possible by the steeply sloping site), he noticed that there was not a breath of wind. Louis was once again on standby and presently reported that the lake was like a millpond. Coniston Water had a habit of remaining placid until just after there was enough light to make a run. More often than not, about half an hour after everyone arrived at the slipway a south-westerly breeze would blow up, disturbing the water and making any trials impossible. The team assembled at the boathouse, and Bluebird was made ready for a run. The usual launch procedure was witnessed by the press cameramen, TV crews and a small crowd. Surely this time, with the lake displaying a tranquil reflection of the ridge of Grizedale Forest on the eastern shoreline, K7 would finally get up onto her planing points and show her paces.

Donald took Bluebird slowly towards the middle of the lake, trying to create as little disturbance as possible. Arriving in the desired position, he began to apply more power. The boat lunged forward, shadowed by Leo and Robbie in the Dory. Although less water was being thrown towards the intakes and the engine continued to run, Bluebird would still not rise onto her planing points. After four attempts, Campbell returned to the slipway.

As K7 was winched in, Donald's dejected mood said it all. He was staring failure in the face – conditions had been perfect, but Bluebird had continued to wallow in the water. Again he had barely exceeded 30mph, never mind attempting to set a record of 300mph. It looked to many observers as if Bluebird would have to return south for a fundamental redesign.

'You'd better go and get a proper breakfast,' Donald said, when Bluebird was back ashore. Slowly, a convoy of cars made its way up the muddy track and onto the road linking the lakeside with the village. It was still early. This time, rather than joining the team, Donald stayed behind on the jetty with Robbie, apparently brooding about K7, perhaps thinking what he would like to do with that 'cow of a boat', a description he had used a few days earlier. About 45 minutes later, the phone rang at the Sun.

Mrs Robinson came into the kitchen, where toast and marmalade were being consumed, with a message for Leo: Donald wanted everyone down at the slipway again as soon as possible. Campbell had used the time to instruct Robbie to get hold of a couple of potato sacks and have them filled with sand. These were obtained from the local greengrocer, who also happened to have a pile of sand in his backyard. The sandbags were tied securely to the transom towing eyes either side of the jet-pipe cowling, with another rope running around the tail fin. This rather makeshift modification was just being completed when Leo arrived back at the lakeside. Immediately, Donald gave instructions to prepare for another run.

Unbeknown to most of the team, Donald and Leo had had one of their periodic differences of opinion about the best way of getting Bluebird into the planing position. Donald had wanted to modify the air intakes to stop water getting in, while Leo believed that unless the air intakes were completely redesigned it would also be necessary to shift Bluebird's centre of gravity rearwards by adding ballast to the stern. Until that morning, Donald had

Launching Bluebird with
the sandbag ballast
© J. Wardhaugh

prevailed with the repeated redesigning of the spray baffles. With everyone
out of the way getting their breakfast, Donald had now wasted no time in
fixing up a temporary ballast solution in the form of the sandbags. Rather than
being motivated by an 'I know better than you' attitude, Campbell genuinely
believed that shifting the centre of gravity back would affect K7's stability at
high speed. He thought the spray baffle modifications combined with the extra
power of the Orpheus engine would allow Bluebird to get into the planing
position, and that the nose would be less likely to pitch up at very high speed
with the more forward weight bias of the Orpheus-equipped boat. Hence his
reluctance to try weighting down the stern, but this now looked like the last
chance of making progress.

   With K7 afloat and Leo and Robbie again shadowing her in the Dory,
Donald applied power. This time, K7 behaved like a lady, quickly rising to
her planing points and speeding off down the lake, dousing Leo and Robbie
in a cocktail of spray and kerosene vapour. Donald travelled south for about
a mile before turning round and heading back. When he returned to the jetty,
his broad smile seemed to take five years off his age. 'We're back in business,'
he shouted to the assembled pressmen at the jetty. 'This is the best thing that
has happened since we got up here. I wasn't using the engine at full thrust by
any means, but by golly that boat can go! We were up to 120mph in about
250 yards.' Bluebird was hauled ashore and refuelled, with the sandbags still
in place.

With sandbags attached, K7 ready to go . . .
© Mirrorpix

Robbie and Leo look on as K7 accelerates.
© Mirrorpix

Planing at last . . .
© Mirrorpix

Passing through 100mph.
© Mirrorpix

As the news of Bluebird's success spread, Campbell decided to make further runs. Sightseers drawn to Coniston by the perfect weather saw Bluebird touch about 160mph. On the final run, one of the sandbags fell off, but that didn't worry Campbell. 'I didn't even notice it had gone until we got back to the slipway,' he said.

They now had to find a way of making the ballast permanent. Donald was interviewed by the assembled journalists. 'I've always said that world records do not come easily. We expect problems and we are prepared to work night and day to solve them, but given more weather like this, we could be getting some really fast runs in by the weekend. We can see daylight at last, we're back in business.' He felt he had to stick his neck out and promise fast runs, but he was also at the mercy of conditions.

Campbell had done 160mph in little more than 300 yards and was now well aware of the increase in power of the Orpheus engine over the old Beryl. The nose heaviness was down to the modifications made to Bluebird during the refit, including the different location of the much lighter Orpheus engine in the hull. This had the effect of moving the centre of gravity forward. Correction of Bluebird's centre of gravity would involve a process of trial and error until the correct balance was found. But at least the sandbags had proved the theory. In effect, they gave Bluebird a similar weight distribution, by moving the centre of gravity backwards, to that she had had when equipped with the Beryl engine.

Telephone calls were made to Ken Norris regarding a permanent solution and it was decided to affix lead weights to cross-members at the stern. The next problem was where to obtain 170lb of lead to make the weights.

Morale had soared, and the team planned to celebrate its success by putting-in another night of hard work. Donald made one concession to Leo: 'Unc, make sure you have an early night tonight, I want you in bed by 1.00 a.m.!'

Norman Buckley, one of the official observers, sent a member of his team to the boatyards in Bowness-on-Windermere in search of lead. He returned with a quantity of lead ingots. These were manhandled into the boat shed. Meanwhile, one of the locals told Donald about a nearby factory building that was being demolished, the roof of which also contained a substantial quantity of lead. Donald dispatched Louis and RAC man Bill Jordan to negotiate its purchase. They returned an hour or so later with the boot of the Morris Traveller laden with sheets of roofing lead.

Top left: Bluebird starting to plane.
© Mirrorpix

Top right: A victory of sorts . . . '200 miles an hour by the weekend . . .'
© Mirrorpix

Above: Returning after her successful run.
© Mirrorpix

Left: Winching K7 ashore.
© Mirrorpix

Louis was then sent to the Sun Hotel and returned with three biscuit tins. The caravan got a new supply of biscuits, and Donald took the tin lids. The process of melting down the lead using an oxyacetylene torch now began, with the tin lids serving as moulds to create individual slabs. Once the lead had hardened, holes were drilled into the slabs at strategic points ready for them to be bolted onto Bluebird's frame at the transom.

From the outset, Donald had decided that he would take charge of this task, from planning through to installation of the ballast. They worked late into the night, but the casting proved very time consuming so at about midnight they packed up and headed for their beds.

Everyone was back at the jetty by first light, eager to complete the work of fitting the lead slabs to Bluebird's stern. It was a difficult and fiddly job, with access to the lower part of the hull being extremely tight. While Leo and Maurie finished preparing the last of the slabs, Donald and Louis set about fixing them to Bluebird.

They had decided to try to do this without removing the engine. Onlookers would have been amused by Campbell's previous talk of advanced engineering. Louis and Donald found themselves with their faces pressed hard against the bodywork, manhandling each of the slabs onto two makeshift frames which had been bolted to Bluebird's stern. The job would have been easier with the engine removed, but that would have meant calling in the heavy lifting gear again and having Bluebird out of commission for at least a day.

Donald was delighted that they were finally making real progress towards their goal. While the lead ballast was being fixed, Leo and Maurie spent the rest of the morning fashioning new spray baffles from half-inch flat perspex sheets which had been obtained from the Vickers shipyard in Barrow. These would replace the original, much-altered curved baffles, which were now discarded.

The new design was such that although the baffles had a bigger surface area they would not cause any additional lift at high speed. In the afternoon, with the modifications finally finished, Donald took Bluebird out. The conditions were by no means perfect and Donald didn't use the full length of the lake, but five runs were achieved with a maximum speed of about 150mph. With the weather deteriorating, Bluebird was winched ashore and activity for the day was stopped.

Thursday
24 November

Weather:
Bright and calm

Left: Donald directs launching operations from the cockpit.
© P. Allonby

Top left: Bluebird about to float free of her cradle.
© P. Allonby

Top right and bottom left: Donald standing in the cockpit as K7 is launched.
© E Simpson & S Wilde

Bottom right: Donald takes his usual position by Bluebird's tail as she is winched ashore.
© P. Allonby

Friday
25 November

Weather:
Cold with a
blustery wind

Until now, Donald had been reasonably lucky with the weather and the locals predicted that it could take a turn for the worse any day and more likely than not continue in that vein for the rest of the year. Coniston might well be held in the grip of gales, rain and snow right through to the New Year. It was typical of Donald's luck that when Bluebird was in pieces the weather conditions would be calm, and when Bluebird was ready to run the biting north-west wind would sweep over the Old Man of Coniston and whip up the lake surface into 3-inch waves. The weather did indeed take a substantial turn for the worse now and the team had to content themselves with making sure that Bluebird would be ready to go when the break came.

Saturday
26 November to
Sunday
27 November

Weather:
Showers and
windy

The weekend failed to bring any respite in the typical winter Lake District weather, leading to a period of enforced inactivity. Donald spent Saturday morning fishing off the end of the jetty as his own wry comment on the weather. He caught nothing.

On the other side of the lake, knowing that no runs were possible, the stoical team of Swiss timekeepers from Longines spent their day setting up timing points at each end of the measured kilometre. They were led by a bald-headed gentleman of short stature named Raoul Crélerot, who had been given the nickname 'Old Father Time'. When they had arrived at the start of the month, none of the timekeepers were proficient in English, but constantly being around Donald and his crew meant that the two younger members now spoke the language with reasonable fluency. Leo, with his Swiss heritage, acted as interpreter between Donald and Raoul. Crélerot had spent most of his life timing great sporting events around the world and was looking forward to something entirely new to him. Like Donald, he couldn't wait to get going, but the blustery weather conditions that had turned Coniston Water into something resembling the North Sea meant they would all have to wait a bit longer.

The weather continued wet and windy and there was little that could be done to Bluebird except ensure she was in perfect condition for when the weather finally improved. Leo, Maurice and Donald also worked on the Jetstar, a turbo water jet-powered ski-boat they were developing, with Norris Brothers, through their new company, Bluebird Marine. Part of the reason for making the attempt in the first place was to use the publicity to help launch the Jetstar. The Daily Express Boat Show at Earls Court in London was due to open on 4 January 1967, so the sooner the attempt could be wrapped-up the greater the likelihood of getting the new company off to a successful start with Bluebird on display alongside the Jetstar.

On Tuesday 29 November, they were down at the boathouse before dawn as usual. The lake was calm but conditions were by no means perfect and more rain looked imminent. Donald wanted to experiment with a new streamlined launching procedure. He was concerned that valuable time was being lost through Leo being present at the boathouse while Bluebird was being launched. His plan was that once they had decided to run, the course boats should move off to their positions as quickly as possible. This would allow the water to settle again by the time he and Bluebird were ready to go.

The new procedure was duly tried out. Donald took the line attached to Bluebird's stern and made his way onto the jetty. Meanwhile, Maurice removed the red jet-pipe cover and the two yellow air intake guards. He then got into the Land Rover to operate the winch. Leo was nowhere to be seen – he had already left in one of the Fairlines for the northern end of the measured kilometre. The winch was started and Bluebird slowly eased down the rails of the slipway.

When Bluebird had floated free from her cradle, Donald pulled her down to the end of the jetty and gently manoeuvred her until she pointed down the lake at a 45° angle. He then jumped down onto the ledge on the transom, unhooked the line and tossed it back onto the jetty. Crawling across the engine compartment cover, he stepped down into the cockpit. The new launching procedure worked. Later, a further enhancement was introduced: Clive would take Donald's place on the jetty and Donald would climb aboard Bluebird in the boathouse. Today, however, the weather took a turn for the worse before any meaningful high-speed run could

Monday
28 November to
Tuesday
29 November

Weather:
Showers and windy, but easing

Donald in the prototype Jetstar.
© Press Association

Above: Bluebird rises on
to plane.
© Press Association

Right: Back on the slipway.
© P. Allonby

be made and Campbell had to be satisfied with a couple of 160mph average runs halfway down the lake and back.

His commentary gave away the struggle he was having getting K7 to perform:

'Starting to put the power on now ... Leo ... level with the yellow bouy, passing through 4, attempting through 5 ... and now accelerating to 5 and ... 6 ... water all over the place, nose lifting ... a lot of water flying around ... and she's away. Passing through the boundary layer and now she's ... we're through the 100 now ... and er ... testing stability and steering, about 140 and of course beginning to tramp like hell, tramping very fast indeed at 200 and I don't think I can hold her much longer than that without having to back off. No I can't hold her any longer ... 200 and I'm having to back off ... I'm backing off right now ...'

Back at the slip, he had at least satisfied himself that Leo, Louis and the other course boats could be at their stations before Bluebird was launched.

Donald takes to the water on a Vespa 'water scooter'.
© G. Hallawell

By coincidence, on that Tuesday an enterprising businessman had turned up at Coniston with an amphibious scooter that took the form of a normal road scooter with long floats attached to it. Donald seized the opportunity to give the scooter a trial run off the jetty, so at least the spectators and pressmen would get some photographs. It brought a bit of much-needed amusement to the lake shore. Donald's opinion of the scooter went unrecorded.

Wednesday
30 November

Weather:
Cold, wet and windy

Once again, all hands were down at the boathouse, but there had been no dawn standby because the weather remained unsuitable. Further modifications and adjustments were made to the Jetstar and her Evinrude V4-powered turbo water jet. Bluebird was now essentially ready and merely waiting for a break in the weather. Leo and Maurice finished off the work they had started the previous evening on the flat-pane spray baffles, which were strengthened by the addition of an L-shaped perspex strip to mitigate against lift and prevent water surging up the pane when Bluebird was getting under way.

Just after lunch, Donald made himself scarce. In the middle of the afternoon, there was a phone call for Leo. It was Donald, could Leo pop up to the bungalow as soon as possible? Leo jumped into the car and made the short journey to the centre of the village. Meanwhile, Maurie, Clive and the other team members, along with the waiting pressmen, made their way up to the Sun.

Arriving at the bungalow, Leo was greeted by Donald, Tonia and Leo's wife, Joan. Donald had arranged for her to travel up by train, from their home in Reigate, to surprise Leo for his 67th birthday. The four of them headed to the Sun, where everyone had assembled in the lounge. Leo found all the fuss and the chorus of 'For he's a jolly good fellow' a little embarrassing, but he was delighted that Joan had been able to make the trip up to Coniston. The party enjoyed a special birthday cake, baked and iced by Connie Robinson, and more than a few glasses of champagne were consumed as proceedings continued into the evening.

The record attempt was now almost a month old. The fastest speed achieved to date was only 160mph, but they had overcome the problems of the damaged engine and having to re-trim the boat. Now they just needed a break in the weather to commence the build-up to a record-breaking run.

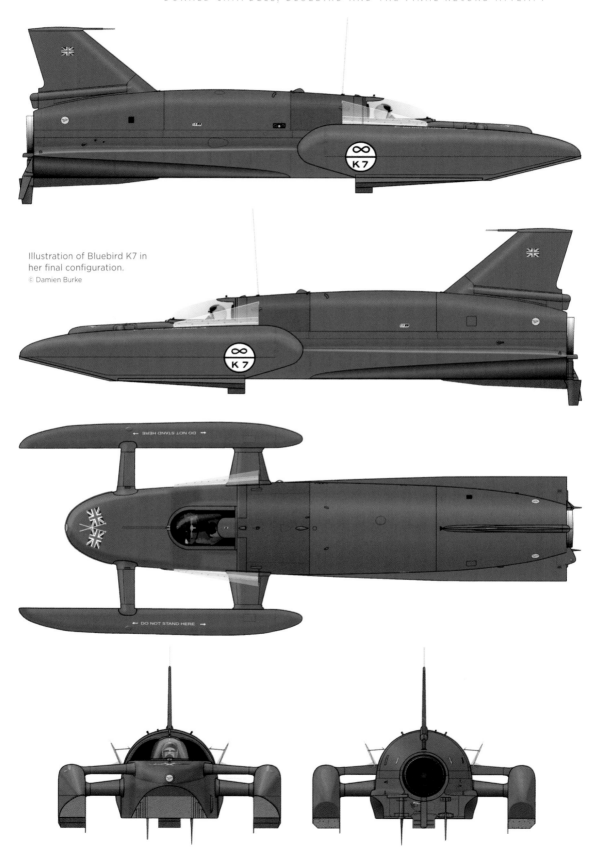

Illustration of Bluebird K7 in
her final configuration.
© Damien Burke

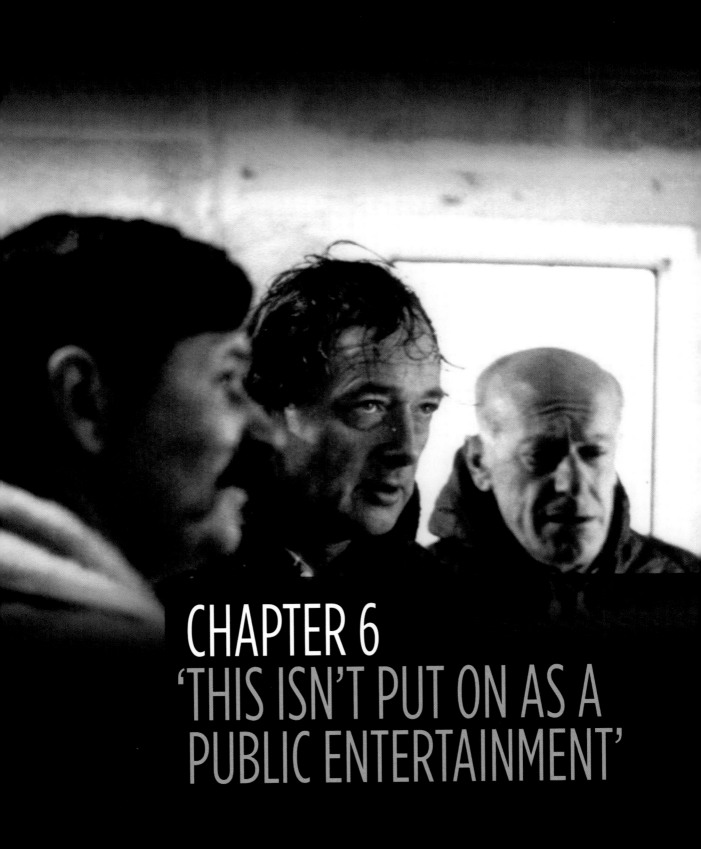

CHAPTER 6
'THIS ISN'T PUT ON AS A PUBLIC ENTERTAINMENT'

Thursday
1 December

Weather:
Wet and windy

Donald and Tonia had decided to head back to London for a few days. The weather forecast was bad until after the weekend and Donald's back trouble had flared up again, necessitating a visit to his osteopath. His back complaint was the legacy of an injury received at school playing rugby, and had been exacerbated by a wartime motorbike accident. It made sitting in the cramped confines of Bluebird's cockpit for any length of time excruciatingly painful.

They left Coniston at midday for the 300-mile drive back to their London pied-à-terre, a flat in Dolphin Square, arriving at about 6.00 p.m.

Friday
2 December to
Saturday
3 December

Weather:
Wet and windy

© E. Whitham

Donald spent the day in London meeting friends, attending to business and seeing his osteopath. The team took the opportunity of Donald's absence to have something of a break, with Leo and Joan taking a drive around the lakes.

On the Saturday, Leo received a phone call from Donald to say he would be returning to Coniston the next day. Word soon got round that Donald would be back on Sunday. Following his departure to London on the 1st, spectators and some less well-informed commentators had openly speculated that Donald would use his back injury as an excuse to cancel the attempt.

'The attempt will be cancelled on doctor's orders,' they said knowingly. The attitude was representative of a significant minority of the public and commentators who believed that Donald was either spinning the attempt out for the sake of extra publicity or had lost his nerve and was too scared to go for the record.

Sunday
4 December

Weather:
Wet and windy

Donald returned from London, arriving back mid-afternoon. Tonia had stayed on, due to a series of cabaret engagements in the south-west of the country during much of the rest of December. The weather at Coniston remained totally unsuitable for running Bluebird, but K7 was ready to go at a moment's notice if conditions improved.

Despite the fact that Donald had returned to Coniston and that the hopeless weather conditions were a matter of public record, many pundits saw Donald and his so-called prevarication and delays as fair game for criticism, even hinting at a streak of cowardice in the process.

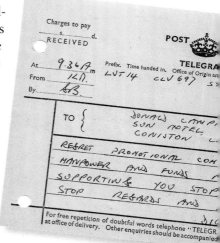

What's it like to drive Bluebird?

Leo Villa, December 1966

'She's not an easy boat to handle, you know. I've only had experience of her up to a hundred mph or so.

'In Australia, we were having the same trouble as Donald is having now – water getting in the air intakes. One evening, the skipper said, "Unc, I've heard all you have to say. I've heard what others have had to say and I've seen the slow-motion films – now I'm going to see for myself. Tomorrow, you'll take her out!"

'Well tomorrow came, I got in, the skipper said, "Well goodbye old man, it's been nice knowing you." With that, he slammed the canopy shut over my head, grinned, and jumped into the launch.

'It's all very well to have seen what happened when he was at the controls, the point was to give him an accurate assessment of what happened when I was there. To do that meant that I had to follow instructions whatever my personal reactions to the result might be!

'I lined her up, with the launch at my flank. The drill was for the launch to keep pace with Bluebird at close quarters in order that a close-up view of the bow and sponsons could be obtained. I gave the throttle a steady push. Bluebird got under way in the slow, ponderous manner common to any vehicle of her weight – to which in the case of a boat, the resistance of the water proved a formidable brake.

'Having got under way, it was now up to the launch to match my speed, as at low speed its acceleration was superior to that of Bluebird. I gave the jet the "gun". My instinct was to study the resulting turbulence, but I soon found that all my attention had to be centred on control. She's tricky to handle as the speed mounts. You've a feeling of tremendous power which is straining at the leash. You're trying to find the point somewhere between the delicate and heavy touch which will bring about a controlled transition from forging through water to skimming over "ice" . . . She was cutting away her bonds . . . she was up . . . pressured at the back . . . 40 . . . 50 . . . 70 then it happened as I expected! A wall of white water completely obscured my vision! My foot held its pressure . . . When would I be able to see? I prayed the old boat was still heading in the pre-ordained direction, I know I was piling on the knots at a terrific pace, then . . . the curtain of spray was flicked aside, and the lake was leaping towards me . . . she was free . . . all restraint gone . . . 90 . . . 100 . . . 120 . . . skimming over the surface like a dart. To hell with boat sheds, tow ropes, spanners, and being filled up, charged up . . . from morning till night. In part, that's how I felt, but I had fulfilled my mission, and I slowly reduced power.

'It's quite an experience . . . He'll do it alright, will Donald . . . He's got guts, that boy.'

Monday
5 December to
Friday
9 December

Weather:
Windy and wet

The weather remained unsuitable all week. Although the rain eased on Monday and Tuesday, a persistent south-easterly wind blew-in, causing a 4-inch popple on the lake's surface. The cumulative rainfall of the previous ten days had made the water level rise some 2 feet, leaving it lapping at the tarpaulin at the end of the boathouse.

The wind continued to batter the boathouse until Friday evening, when it finally dropped. The sky cleared, and as night set in a heavy frost descended on Coniston. It was a good sign; the weather was finally changing. Now the high-speed trials could begin. Given a fair chance, the record attempt would surely not be far off.

The damaged Orpheus left out in the elements.
© E. Whitham

Bluebird ready for action.
© E. Whitham

As dawn broke over Coniston, it was soon apparent that Bluebird would be going out. The heavy overnight frost had flattened the lake into a mirror-like calm. By 8.00 a.m., with the sun rising over the Grizedale fells, preparations were being made at the boathouse. This was to be the first timed run of the campaign. The Swiss Longines timekeepers had been at Coniston since early November and were impatient to get down to business. Raoul Crélerot and his two young assistants had set up their chronometers and telescopes on the eastern shoreline at each end of the measured kilometre.

Campbell told the pressmen gathered at the slipway that he intended to make a steady run to test Bluebird's trim and systems. This run would not give him the opportunity to test the water brake, though, since it had been removed from the boat's transom a few days earlier. The rear stabilising fin had resumed its previous position in the centre of the transom behind the rear planing shoe instead.

Saturday
10 December

Weather:
Clear, frosty and calm

Preparing to get Bluebird afloat.
© News International

Timekeeping

To set a new Water Speed Record, the rules of the Union of International Motorboating must be adhered to. They state that the craft must complete a run each way through a measured kilometre or mile within a one-hour time period (the kilometre was chosen for the Coniston course, with its restricted overall length, to ensure sufficient room for both acceleration and deceleration). The average speed of the two runs must exceed the existing record by 0.75 per cent.

The measured kilometre was surveyed in October 1966 by the Lancaster firm of Proctor, Birkbeck & Batty and was positioned centrally along the lake's length, with Fir Island marking the midpoint of the course on the eastern bank. The northern marker point was some 35 metres south of Cock Point, while the southern marker post was a further 1,000 metres south, diagonally opposite Moor Gill Foot. This allowed a northern acceleration/deceleration zone of around 2.4km (with 0.5km overshoot for deceleration) and a corresponding southern deceleration and acceleration zone of at least 3km. Bluebird's course was down the centre of the lake, which was approximately 400–420 metres wide throughout the measured distance. The measured distance was marked by two large wooden slatted marker buoys covered with red plastic sheeting. These 2 metre by 3 metre buoys were each tied on to the top of two anchored rowing boats towards the western shoreline.

Longines' M. Crélerot setting up his timing equipment.
© P. Allonby

The timekeeping positions were at either end of the course on two 3-metre long wooden stages that were built out into the lake on the eastern shoreline.

Swiss watchmakers Longines of St-Imier sent a team of three timekeepers under the direction of Raoul Crélerot. Timekeeping was by means of Longines Chronocinégines. These took the form of Bolex cine-cameras to take up to 100 photographs a second of the external scene, and rotating discs whose speed was controlled by a quartz oscillator, the natural frequency of which was a precise number of vibrations per second. Each disc was engraved with numbers, the markings of the fastest disc recording down to thousandths of a second. Two Chronocinégines were positioned at each end of the measured distance. After synchronising two pairs of chronometers so that they show the same time, it is simply a matter of deploying them at the start and finish points and comparing time differences after each run. The Chronocinégines would film Bluebird as she entered and left the measured distance on each run, recording the time as Bluebird passed each marker point by triggering the chronometers. An auxiliary telescope was used to position the line of the Chronocinégines at an exact right angle to the moving object (Bluebird) and to trigger the high-speed camera with sufficient time to photograph the start and finish line.

The average speed is calculated from an average of the elapsed time taken to complete each run.

The launching procedure.
Donald in the cockpit,
Maurie in the Land Rover
and Clive with the line on
the jetty.
© News International

Donald settles in to
Bluebird's cockpit as she
is launched.
© News International

In his coat to keep warm, Donald in Bluebird's cockpit.
© News International

Bluebird leaves the jetty and (*inset*) heads towards the course.
© News International

There was no question of any attempt on the record just yet. Both Donald and Bluebird would, as he put it, have to be worked up. The first course boats – consisting of the Dory with Louis at the helm, acting as refuelling boat, and one of the Fairline cruisers, commandeered by Keith Harrison – had headed for their positions at the southern end of the lake.

Leo left next to take up his station at the northern end of the kilometre as course marshal.

The surface of the lake was glassy as Bluebird commenced her first run shortly after 8.20 a.m., following Leo's all-clear.

Campbell started Bluebird's Orpheus engine at the jetty and slowly cruised out towards the centre of the course. He piled on the power and Bluebird quickly rose onto her planing points, trailing her usual comet's tail of spray behind her. Over the radio intercom Donald shouted, 'I'm all over the bloody place.' He covered the measured distance at an average of

Above: Bluebird's comet tail of spray.
© News International

Left: Travelling at about 200 mph on the return run.
© Press Association

202mph on his first run and exited the kilometre with the forward planing shoes well immersed but 'tramping' quite noticeably.

Bluebird sped off to the southern end of the lake to turn round and wait for the wash of her first run to die down. After about ten minutes, Leo was able to give the OK and Bluebird started back on her second run. This was completed at an average of 196mph. Back at the jetty, Bluebird was immediately refuelled, but before Donald was able to make any further runs a wind sprang up from the south-west and rain set in.

Donald stood by to hear radio reports from out on the lake, but they were not favourable. Leo reported: 'There are now two-inch waves, conditions are quite hopeless.' Donald then had Bluebird drawn back into the boathouse and the course boats were called in.

'What do you think, Unc?'
© News International

It had been a reasonable day, and it began to look as if the long weeks of waiting would soon be over. Donald's old smile returned as he answered journalists' questions while the boat was being winched back into the boathouse. During the afternoon, Bluebird's water-brake was refitted. Donald did not want to risk any really high-speed runs without it. The stabilising fin was moved back to the starboard side of the transom. It is not clear why the brake was removed in the first place, although some days earlier Campbell had complained that Bluebird's steering felt unusual, so he perhaps wanted to revert to the 1964 configuration with its central fin for comparison purposes.

Sunday
11 December

Weather:
Dry, bright and calm

Right, below and opposite:
Preparations before dawn.
© C. Rogerson

Everyone was on the slipway before sunrise, making preparations to get Bluebird afloat and running as soon as there was sufficient light. The Longines timekeepers had been informed and were standing by at their stations. Shortly after 8.00 a.m., Donald arrived at the jetty and after spending a few moments observing conditions gave instructions to launch Bluebird. The boat slowly emerged into the daylight, the sun glinting on her sapphire blue paintwork.

Donald climbs aboard
Bluebird.
© Carl Rogerson

Above: Donald issues instructions as K7 slides slowly down the slipway.
© J. Griffith

Above right: Settling down in to the cockpit
© C. Rogerson

Clive Glynn attached the line to K7's stern and made his way along the jetty. Donald donned his yellow lifejacket, leather helmet containing the radio earphones and his silver RAF-issue jet pilot's crash helmet. He radioed the course boats to obtain a report on water conditions. Bluebird floated free of her cradle, and with Clive pulling on the line and Robbie using a boat hook, her nose was pushed round until she was positioned at the end of the jetty, ready to go. Donald settled down into the deep cockpit until only his head was visible to the few assembled spectators. He strapped himself into his four-point safety harness. The cockpit cover was pulled shut over his head and shortly afterwards the now-familiar hiss of compressed air was heard as Campbell pressed the Orpheus's starter. Crowds lined the banks of the lake, having heard and read about the runs of the previous day. As the jet engine roared into life, they looked forward to being rewarded with the sight of another run at high speed. But while Bluebird was taxiing towards the centre of the lake, conditions suddenly deteriorated – the mirror sheen on the surface

CLIVE GLYNN ON DONALD CAMPBELL

'xand then spent the rest of November making lots of unsuccessful trail runs. It became a routine, and everyone in the small team had a role to play. When Bluebird was launched, I would pull her down the jetty on the end of a line, and Maurie would use a boat hook to push her round so she pointed down the lake. After I undid the line, Donald would take his time, speak to Leo on the RT, and eventually start up and cruise to the lake's centre. Eventually, by mid-December, we made a few quick runs, but a lot of the time the lake was never that smooth, and by mid-morning, the wind would often get up and disturb the surface.

Donald was always friendly and sociable. He appreciated your efforts, and took many of the frustrations we experienced in his stride. He usually had time for a joke.'

Left:
A line pulls Bluebird to the end of the jetty.
© C. Rogerson

Below left and right:
Bluebird heads out to the track.
© C. Rogerson

Right:
Bluebird heads out to the track.
© C. Rogerson

Far right and below:
K7 heads back to the slipway, after weather conditions deteriorate.
© J. Griffith & C. Rogerson

Far right:
Donald climbs from the cockpit.
© J. Griffith

Below: The waiting game continues
© C. Rogerson

disappeared and the stillness of the air was disturbed by a strengthening breeze that began to whip up the lake into an inch-high chop.

Daylight had brought back the troublesome south-west wind. Donald cruised out into the centre of the lake, communicated again with the course boats to check conditions in the measured kilometre, and then reluctantly abandoned the run. The surface was definitely no longer suitable for him to reach high speeds. Campbell carefully turned K7 round and returned to the slipway. Leo was already on his way back from his position out on the lake.

As the engine died, the cockpit cover slid open; Donald stood up and climbed out of the cockpit, taking hold of the line passed to him by Clive and attaching it to the two towing eyes at the root of the forward spar. Bluebird was pulled forward until her nose rested between the two padded posts at the front of her cradle. Donald removed his lifejacket and placed it together with his crash helmet on the driver's seat, then pulled the cockpit cover closed. Once the boat was aligned at the bow, he commenced the rather hazardous task of crawling along the engine cover in order to step down onto the fin-like platform at Bluebird's stern to align it with the cradle. Taking the other end of the boat hook held by Robbie, he pushed against it until he had straightened up the stern into the cradle. Bluebird was slowly winched back up the slipway into the boat shed.

Donald jumped down off the stern, left the boathouse and got aboard one of the Fairline cruisers. Starting it up, he made his way round to the bay in front of the Bluebird Café, as if to check conditions, and let the assembled crowd get a look at him. After a few minutes, he returned to the

jetty. Conditions remained tantalising for the rest of the day but never cleared up. Although the team stayed on standby, no further runs were attempted.

During the afternoon, large red marker buoys were towed into position and anchored at either end of the kilometre. They took the form of huge slatted wooden boxes, covered in fire engine red plastic sheeting and fixed on two rowing boats. The stage was being set – Donald wanted to be fully prepared for his next chance.

K7 is drawn back into the boathouse.
© C. Rogerson

> AW: 'If you break this record, what does it prove?'
> DC: 'I think perhaps most important of all, it still proves British leadership in engineering terms and it does I think, also show, the British, when they make their minds up and overcome all obstacles, they can achieve anything.'
> AW: 'So really this is based on British patriotism?'
> DC: 'Well we're all playing for a team, old boy, and we're all playing for the same team.'
> AW: 'Can you describe the feeling you experience in this boat, because you are riding on a knife-edge?'
> DC: 'Well your feelings depend on the exigencies of the moment, if everything is going fine and stability is on the top line, that's one thing but if not . . . well, this boat can get pretty hairy . . .'
>
> **Donald Campbell talking to Alan Weeks of *BBC Sportsview*, December 1966**

Donald jumps into the Fairline to cruise out into the bay to check water conditions.
© C. Rogerson

Leo and Maurie examine
Bluebird's water brake.
© C. Rogerson

From top:
That's it for the day.
© C. Rogerson

GLM 37C, Donald's E-Type Jaguar.
© C. Rogerson

Overlooking Pier cottage from the eastern
side of the lake.
© C. Rogerson

Camera's lined up to capture some action.
© C. Rogerson

Raoul packing up for the day.
© C. Rogerson

Monday dawned bright, but the wind that had sprung up the previous day still blew across the surface of the lake, albeit with decreasing strength. The dawn standby had once again proved unnecessary, but preparations were nonetheless made to ensure Bluebird was ready to go if conditions improved.

By early afternoon, the wind had died down completely and the lake assumed a glassy calm. The course boats made their way to their positions and Bluebird was launched. Donald then suddenly noticed they had left Mr Whoppit, his lucky mascot, back at the bungalow. A hurried phone call was made from the caravan to ask Julia Goossens to rush the little bear down to the slipway. Donald waited 20 minutes for the mascot to arrive but luckily conditions remained favourable.

Monday
12 December

Weather:
Bright and calm

Above top:
Bluebird afloat and ready for action.
© P. Allonby

Above centre:
Donald draws the canopy shut.
© P. Allonby

Left and above bottom:
Weather conditions about as good as they get.
© P. Allonby

Mr Whoppit

Woppit made his debut in March 1953, in the very first issue of *Robin*, a weekly comic aimed at very young boys and girls. It was published by Hulton Press, who had already enjoyed huge success with *Eagle*, their boys' adventure comic. 'The Story of Woppit' began when the little teddy bear fell out of his owner's pram and was left behind on a country road. Things looked bleak for the abandoned toy but, as he sat there, lost and alone, along came a little shaggy donkey called Mokey. The pair became instant friends and decided to travel together, exploring the countryside. Later on, they were joined by Tiptop, a scarecrow, and the three settled down to live at Mrs Bumble's farmhouse, where they helped with the chores and continued to have fun learning about the plants and animals. Woppit himself was a rather odd-looking teddy; with his pointed ears and prominent snout, he sometimes looked more like Winnie the Pooh's pal Piglet. However, he was always a kindly and amiable little soul who liked to do good deeds, such as sending a Valentine card to cheer up a lonely old lady.

In 1956, soft toy manufacturer Merrythought produced a teddy bear named Woppit. The bears were 9 inches tall, and made of brown plush with blue felt inner ears and matching shoes and a red felt jacket. Woppit only appeared in the Merrythought catalogue for that one year before being dropped.

One of the bears had an extremely interesting life history – as Donald Campbell's mascot.

Donald was given the reject bear in the summer of 1958 by Peter Barker, who was his commercial manager and friend and had been in charge of merchandising at Hulton Press. Donald always referred to the teddy as Mr Whoppit and had a soft spot for the little bear because of his reject status.

Mr Whoppit travelled with Donald in the cockpit of Bluebird on all of his subsequent record-breaking attempts at Coniston, Bonneville, Lake Eyre and Lake Dumbleyung. He had a little Bluebird badge sewn on his jacket to mark his role as the official Bluebird team mascot. In 1963, Tonia made him a set of Bluebird overalls to match the ones worn by Donald.

'The Record Breakers'.
© Press Association

The first run commenced at 2.43 p.m. and was made at a speed of 250.78mph. Just 7 minutes later, without waiting to refuel, Bluebird made her return run at a slightly more leisurely 237.72mph. While doing so, K7 ran into water disturbed during the first run. This set off 'tramping', with Bluebird rolling from one planing surface to another in very rapid succession. The sound of the sponsons alternately striking the water could be heard by the spectators on the lake shore as the boat went past.

Campbell gave his usual indistinct commentary as he made the second run:

> *'... tramping like buggery ... you were quite right about the water ... nine six, about 200 coming up ... she's tramping like hell, I don't know whether you can see her at the moment ... about er, half way down ... nine five, about 240 ... 250 now ... full throttle ... 250 ... she's settling down a bit ...'*

The second run was to be the last of the day; with daylight fading, Bluebird was winched ashore. Donald had not been able to reach maximum engine revs on either run and he was concerned that his speed had been substantially below his existing record.

Left from top:
'Full Power'.
© Press Association

'Tramping' over disturbed water.
© Press Association

Bluebird noses back in towards the jetty.
© P. Allonby

Left: The man in the mask.
© P. Allonby

Far left: A relaxed Donald chatting to David Benson after the run.
© G. Hallawell

The engine cover was removed and another check made on the Orpheus, but there was no indication of anything amiss. Later in the evening, the team returned to the Sun satisfied that things were beginning to look up. The weather forecast remained good. If they could only get to the bottom of the lacklustre engine performance, a few days of calm would allow Donald and Bluebird to reach their potential and attack the record.

Tuesday
13 December

Weather:
Clear and calm

Donald Campbell was known to be an intensely superstitious man, so the date aroused much speculation as to whether he would run or not, regardless of the weather. In fact the day had dawned with clear skies after a heavy overnight frost, so conditions were perfect. The assembled reporters nonetheless assumed that Donald would find himself needed elsewhere that day and Bluebird would remain safely tucked up in the boathouse.

Donald did indeed fail to appear during the morning, which was spent by the team combing the lake's surface for driftwood. Around midday, Campbell arrived at the boathouse and immediately asked Leo his opinion on conditions. A report on water conditions at the southern end of the lake was sought and came back favourable, so instructions were given to get the course boats to their stations.

Getting ready to time a record?
© P. Allonby

After the usual launch procedure, Bluebird was ready for the first run just after 2.00 p.m. The sun was shining brightly at the southern end of the lake, but was already very low in the sky at this time of year. Donald commenced his first run at 2.15 but only achieved an average speed of 197mph. 'It was like driving into arc lights,' is how he later described conditions during the first run. Within 4 minutes, again without waiting to refuel, he commenced the second run at a much faster pace, recording an average speed of 261mph.

A beautiful winter's day. One of the course Fairlines heads out for the southern end of the kilo.
© Leo Villa's Film & Picture Archive

The outward run.
© P. Allonby

Top:
Returning, as the wash of
the first run heads back to
the course.
© Rex Features

Below left: 260mph plus . . .
© Press Association

Below right:
The plume of spray from
the water brake.
© J. Wardhaugh

Conditions just about
perfect.
© Leo Villa's Film & Picture
Archive

Bluebird was inching closer to the record and witnesses felt sure there would be another couple of runs to take advantage of the perfect conditions.

However, they reckoned without Donald's almost habitual misfortune. Arriving back at the boathouse, he requested that Bluebird be brought ashore immediately. Onlookers assumed this was for refuelling, but Donald looked tense and distracted. It soon became clear why: Bluebird had hit a seagull on the return run. The bird had struck the port rear spar, close to the main hull and just inches away from the cockpit canopy and air-intakes. The unfortunate creature would have known little about it, but Donald's superstitious nature saw killing a seabird on the 13th of the month as a bad omen. He later admitted that he had been terrified about running on the 13th: 'I knew something was bound to happen, because it was the 13th.' Describing the collision with the seagull, he said: 'I saw it begin to rise from the water but I was travelling way too quickly to take any avoiding action, for a moment I thought it was going to hit the canopy, then it would have been curtains for me. A few inches the other way and it would have gone down the air-intake and wrecked the engine but something was bound to happen on the 13th.' To another reporter, he said: 'I'm all right but that poor bloody little bird isn't, you can bet your life on that.' Bluebird would be out of action for the rest of the day. The impact of the bird had punctured a water seal around the junction of the rear spar fairing and the hull. This would need to be resealed before K7 could take to the water again. Maurie spent the rest of the afternoon on the repair, knocking the dented fairing back into shape and tightening its fastenings.

Donald feared that part of the seagull may have gone down the port air intake. Not wanting to risk his only good engine, he ordered an inspection.

Donald examines the seagull damage.
© Press Association

The long laborious job of removing the engine cowling and the top casing of the axial compressor commenced. Donald put a call through to Bristol Siddeley, who advised that their engine specialists, Jack Lavis and Ken Pearson, would travel up from Bristol that evening. Leo's initial inspection revealed no damage, but with the engine again having failed to achieve maximum revs on either run, they decided to do nothing further until Lavis and Pearson arrived to carry out a proper check.

The weather remained calm, with nightfall bringing a heavy frost. Things were looking promising for the next day's conditions.

BILL VANRYNE ON DONALD CAMPBELL

'Once my work at Coniston was done, and I had provided Leo and Maurie with specific instructions in operating the air charging system for the engine starter, I headed back to London with Ken Norris, both of us taking it in turns to drive Donald's E-Type Jag. I followed the attempt closely on the news. I knew that Donald was not having a smooth time of it over those next few weeks.'

Weather:
Calm and bright

Maurie and Jack Lavis work
on K7's Orpheus.
© E. Whitham

Work on the engine began in the boathouse as dawn broke, with Jack Lavis and Ken Pearson having arrived in Coniston late the previous evening. They were now working alongside Leo and Maurie, checking that the errant seagull had not been drawn into the air-intake and caused damage to Bluebird's engine. Fortunately, everything was found to be clear.

It was decided to shackle K7 to the slipway once more and conduct a series of static tests to try to identify the cause of the engine's inability to reach maximum revs. Like a racing piston engine, a turbojet engine develops most of its power in the last 10 per cent of its rev range, but with the power jump being even more pronounced. Failure to achieve more than 90 per cent of full revs thus meant that Campbell might have been missing as much as

Clive removes the securing brackets from Bluebird's stern after the latest static test.
© E. Whitham

23 per cent or almost 1,000lb of the engine's stated maximum of 4,500lb of thrust. K7 probably had less power at this stage than it did when equipped with the Beryl!

Adjustments were made to the engine and it was run-up on the slipway. Although a marginal improvement was achieved, full revs remained elusive and fuel boost pressure remained low. The two Bristol Siddeley engineers suspected a faulty fuel pump, but with no spare to hand it was decided to make a further trial run anyway and take advantage of the favourable conditions on the lake.

The course boats were prepared and the timekeepers informed. Leo and Robbie set off to take up position at the northern end of the kilometre, while Louis and Bill Jordan took the Dory with a supply of fuel to the bay south of

Donald prepares for another run.
© E. Whitham

Above and top centre:
Calm all around as
Bluebird slips slowly into
the water.
© E. Whitham

Top right and above right:
Beautiful Bluebird K7.
© E. Whitham

Peel Island. They would be ready to refuel Bluebird should Donald decide to use that option.

Maurie, Clive and the Bristol Siddeley engineers finished preparing K7 and disconnected the chains and ropes that had secured Bluebird to the slipway and her cradle. Once the course boats were in position and the timekeepers ready, Donald contacted them over the radio link for a report on conditions. At the boathouse, at the northern end of the lake, conditions were perfect, but Leo reported: 'Conditions are a rather mixed bag, a disturbance near the shore and a swell running down the centre of the lake from the north. Not as good as it has been.' Campbell asked: 'Is it as good as yesterday?' to which Leo responded, 'There's not much in it, Skipper.' 'Then it's worth a try,' Donald replied. Bluebird was afloat a little after 11.25 a.m. and the usual process of Clive and Maurie positioning her off the end of the jetty at a 45° angle was carried out.

At the slipway, only a handful of people witnessed the launch, while over at the beach a few photographers positioned themselves to capture Bluebird's departure. Just after 11.30, Bluebird was under way. Conditions were as good as they had been at any time during the week and Donald would not be heading into the low sun this time.

The measured kilometre was entered at 11.33 a.m. and completed in 8.37 seconds, at an average speed of 267.25mph – Bluebird's fastest run to date. Over the intercom, Donald gave his usual running commentary, 'jumping like hell' being the main point of note. Bluebird roared off to the southern end of the lake past Peel Island and within a matter of minutes, without bothering to refuel, had turned and was on her way back. She entered the measured kilometre at 11.37 and took 8.54 seconds to cover the distance at an average speed of 261.85mph.

Beautiful Bluebird.
© E. Whitham

'Here we go.'
© P. Allonby

When Donald arrived back at the slipway and climbed out of Bluebird's cockpit, he wore a look of bewilderment and dejection. It had clearly been a record attempt (which are rarely announced as such in advance – usually they are referred to as a trial run to see how conditions are).

'And she's away.'
© E. Whitham

Donald was certainly not holding back in terms of using all of Bluebird's power, but although the speed seemed high the average of the two runs – 264.55mph – was 14mph short of the speed he would need to break his current record. Back on the slipway, as the pressmen returned from their lakeside vantage points, Donald faced some searching questions. The rumour had gone round that he had had his foot flat to the floor on both runs and could not get Bluebird to go any faster. 'Did you have your foot hard down that time, Don?' he was asked. Quick as a flash, Campbell countered with his own question:

Returning to base. Still no new record.
© E. Whitham

Bluebird drifts to a rest.
© E. Whitham

'Where exactly has the power gone?'
© E. Whitham

'Do you give away your trade secrets? No? . . . Well neither do I.'

He went on to give his explanation of what he suspected to be the reason for Bluebird's poor showing. 'It looks like we have not heard the last of our friend the seagull,' intimating that a part of it could have been sucked into the engine intake and be affecting performance.

The truth was a little less dramatic. Donald and Leo had long suspected that the fuel system was at fault, with K7 simply not getting sufficient fuel into her engine to achieve maximum performance. Both were keen not to say anything to the press that might show the Bristol Siddeley engine in a bad light, though, especially given the amount of support they were receiving from the company.

Lavis and Pearson were still on site and now called their Bristol headquarters to request that a replacement fuel pump be sent up to Coniston. The item was dispatched later that afternoon. In preparation for arrival of the replacement component, the team set about the task of lifting K7's engine out of the hull in order to access the fuel pump at the base of the engine, underneath the axial compressor. This was a laborious business, but Donald did not want to lose any opportunity and was mindful of the fact that the weather conditions had been perfect for the last week.

Back at the slipway . . . © E. Whitham

'I must look how I feel.'
© E. Whitham

Above and above right: Bluebird is hauled back into the boathouse.
© E. Whitham

'The gentlemen of the press'. BBC *Look North* presenter Gerald Harrison records a piece to camera while, from second left, Arthur Knowles, Harry Griffin, Norman Luck and Keith Harrison (behind film camera lens) discuss the day's events.
© P. Allonby

Thursday
15 December

Weather:
Rain, with a south-west breeze

The new fuel pump is fitted by Jack Lavis.
© Leo Villa's Film & Picture Archive

The Bristol Siddeley engineers completed work on Bluebird's fuel system and installed the new pump as soon as it arrived. The engine was refitted to the hull and all system ancillaries plumbed in. Bluebird was now ready and the team hoped she would at last perform to her potential. It was typical of Donald's luck, though, that once the mechanical problem had been fixed the calm, frosty weather they had enjoyed for the previous five days came to an end. Heavy rain and gale-force winds arrived, meaning there was nothing to do but wait. The press again began to get restive. They had had their appetite whetted by the runs earlier in the week and were looking forward to getting the whole thing over with by the weekend, so they could return home the week before Christmas.

DC: 'This isn't done for public appeal . . . it isn't done as a public entertainment. If I was putting on a theatrical play and nobody wanted to roll up and watch it, I should be very worried. This isn't put on as a public entertainment.'

JP: 'Why is it put on?'

DC: 'It's put on to try and reach a certain goal, which is to see a British boat eventually first past the magic 300 mark.'

JP: 'Do you think when you do this that you will receive a certain amount of interest?'

DC: 'I wouldn't know and neither frankly do I care very much, but we don't intend to stop or spare any effort to get it. What others like to think about it is their business . . .'

JP: 'But everyone wants to know why you are doing it.'

DC: 'Well that's . . . good luck to them, let them continue to ask, er . . . we believe there is a goal worth achieving, full stop.'

continued . . .

. . . continued

JP: 'But there is a risk involved for you because something could go wrong on a run.'

DC: 'But I thought you said just now there wasn't any interest?'

JP: 'From my point of view I am saying, but there is an interest in the risk at least when it actually happens – the attempt.'

DC: 'Well this is the good old days of the Roman arena and the chaps coming down to the coliseum to watch the gladiator . . . and let's make no mistake about it John, er . . . if you're not prepared to get your nose punched, don't go down into the arena – we got ours punched yesterday afternoon.'

JP: 'When you're in the cockpit alone, you know, there is nobody else, you're enclosed in this little tiny space, how do you feel?'

DC: 'Well your emotions can vary according to the behaviour of the craft. If you're going straight and everything is behaving well and stability is on the top line, that's one thing . . . if on the other hand, you run into stability troubles and you get that boat going haywire at 200 knots plus, that's another.'

JP: 'What's the feeling like? Do you have time to assess it at all or don't you think about it at the time, this is what interests me.'

DC: 'May I ask you if you have ever been frightened?'

JP: 'Yes.'

DC: 'Full stop.'

JP: 'And that's all it is?'

DC: 'By the same token of course, if you're not frightened you're probably going to kill yourself very rapidly, and if you're too frightened, the result is the same anyway. This degree of tension is necessary because the adrenaline is pumping around the system and this is speeding up your reactions.'

JP: 'A lot of people imply there is a sort of death wish you've got, this is why you're doing it.'

DC: 'Well a lot of people sit on their behinds . . . in the comfort of an armchair and watch television, but what do they know?'

JP: 'So it's not pointless?'

DC: 'Not in my book.'

JP: 'Do you ever sit back and think about why you're doing it, your own motives, what it is that's happening?'

DC: 'No . . . there isn't time . . . you know . . . probably you'll say I haven't grown up, and if that's so, well I am quite prepared to accept it and I am in no hurry . . . too much time to grow up and grow old.'

JP: 'You quite accept the sort of schoolboy accusation they put against you?'

DC: 'Accept it? . . . I think it's a sad day when a man loses the enthusiasm of a schoolboy.'

Donald Campbell speaking to John Pett for *The Price of a Record*, 15 December 1966

CHAPTER 7
'IF YOU'RE NOT PREPARED TO GET YOUR NOSE PUNCHED...'

Friday
16 December to
Monday
19 December

Weather:
Heavy rain,
followed by snow
and strong winds

And still the wind blows.
© News International

> " I am always scared stiff when I make a record attempt.'
>
> **Donald Campbell talking to Brian Boss of the** *Daily Sketch*, **December 1966**

Over the next few days, weather conditions deteriorated even further. The mountains surrounding the lake became snow-capped and the streams feeding it turned into torrents. These swollen streams brought a further hazard to the attempt – masses of driftwood was swept into the lake. Keith Harrison and Robbie spent a lot of time cruising up and down the lake, removing tree branches and the like from Bluebird's course. A particularly large lump of wood required four men to lift it ashore after it was towed in by one of the course boats. Temperatures dropped steadily and the snowline began to creep inexorably down the fell sides. Winter was closing in on Coniston.

Bluebird was now ready, and all Donald needed was a two-hour break in the weather to get things organised and complete two runs. The new record would then be his.

The team busied themselves working on the Jetstar or spent infrequent days-off driving around admiring the wintry Lake District scenery, but their thoughts were always on the hoped-for change in the weather. The water level of the lake had risen again by more than 3 feet, threatening to cut-off the boathouse. The yard between Bluebird's accommodation and the garage became a quagmire and a temporary walkway of wooden planks was put in place to provide safe passage from one to the other.

Above: Donald, Maurie and Louis attend to Bluebird.
© News International

Above right: Clive contemplates Bluebird.
© News International

Right: Leo and Donald work on Jetstar in the workshop.
© News International

The weather forecast of the previous day had offered some hope, with the expectation that the front which had brought the storm to Coniston over the previous five days would finally move away and be followed by a period of calm. The new day duly dawned crisp and still; Louis made his way down to the boathouse as usual and found the lake looking like a millpond. Returning quickly to the Sun, he alerted the team. Shortly after 8.00 a.m., everyone was assembled. Conditions were certainly good enough to have a try. The green tarpaulin at the lake end of the boat shed was lifted in preparation for getting Bluebird afloat. Dismay! Bluebird was trapped on the slipway – the tubular scaffolding poles forming the roof cross-members had buckled and given way.

The sheer weight of melting snow on the roof had pushed the poles down below the level of Bluebird's tail fin. Fortunately, the boat itself was not damaged, but the boathouse would have to be rebuilt.

Louis, Robbie and Clive clambered-up and removed the bent scaffolding poles. They were replaced with new ones and the entire roof beefed-up to guard against a recurrence. The job was completed by the afternoon, but by then the lake was too rough to contemplate a run. As if mocking the team, conditions had remained calm all morning.

The brief respite in the rain and gales was over and they had been unable to seize the opportunity. Later that evening, members of the press confronted Donald to ask him about his intentions. Christmas was only five days away and they wanted to get home. Christmas Day fell on a Sunday and there would be no papers until 28 December, so they were reluctant to remain in Coniston

Tuesday
20 December

Weather:
Cold and calm

Below left and right:
The collapsed boathouse.
© Leo Villa's Film and Picture
Archive and P. Allonby

over the festive period. Donald was non-committal, but he knew that unless he could make the attempt over the next day or two he would have to suspend the project until after Christmas.

Wednesday
21 December

Weather:
Wet and windy

Once again, the dawn standby produced disappointment. The poor conditions ruled out any chance of a run and the prospect of a suspension came closer. The Longines timekeepers now took the matter out of Donald's hands. They announced that they intended to leave for London in order to fly back to Geneva. There was also talk of them pulling out altogether – they had been at Coniston since early November, at their own expense, and like everybody else were getting increasingly impatient with the weather, quite apart from wanting to spend Christmas with their families. Donald pleaded with them to stay, called Longines headquarters in Switzerland and their representative offices in London, but all to no avail. He was forced to agree to a suspension until after the Christmas holidays, announcing that after sundown on Thursday (i.e. the 22nd), the attempt would be suspended until the morning of Wednesday 28 December.

> " We are used to the long waits in this game but this one is heart-breaking – gales, snow and squalls, week after week, and that blasted lake just lies there and laughs at me.'
>
> 'I know what everybody is saying . . . they always say it . . . I'll have a second cockpit put on the next Bluebird and we'll see how many of the bastards want to come out for a ride.'
>
> Donald Campbell in the *Daily Telegraph*, December 1966

Thursday
22 December

Weather:
Wet and windy

Donald decided to stay at Coniston for the Christmas break. Tonia was appearing in cabaret in Somerset over the holidays, so a quiet Christmas with her at home would not be possible. His daughter Gina was working at the Park Hotel in Arosa, Switzerland, so when Connie Robinson asked if Donald would like to spend Christmas at the Sun he jumped at the chance.

At lunchtime, Donald bought everyone who was leaving a drink at the bar and bade them farewell. Leo was uneasy about Donald staying at Coniston, suspecting that he would have Bluebird out on the lake if conditions were good enough. He suggested to Donald that he, Maurice, Louis and Clive should stay behind, but Donald wouldn't hear of it. He told Leo not to be so silly and to go and enjoy Christmas with Joan at their son's home in Derby. Louis, Julia, Maurie, Clive and Coco the dog headed off back to Surrey in the big Citroën.

Friday
23 December

Weather:
Wet and windy

With the team gone and the TV and pressmen having returned to their respective bases in Newcastle, Manchester and London, Coniston prepared for a tranquil Christmas. Donald busied himself with his own Christmas preparations. In the afternoon, he and Robbie made their way over to Windermere and Kendal to do a spot of Christmas shopping. He enlisted Robbie's help in buying a reel-to-reel tape recorder, before spending a quiet evening back at Coniston with his friends from the village.

metalwork measured about a foot across and pushed the streamlined fairing back onto the main structure of the spar. The damage was not structural, but the dent was unsightly and it brought home to everyone that the undertaking was potentially very dangerous. Had it been 3 feet to the right, the duck would have hit the cockpit canopy, with disastrous results. The makeshift team was busy getting Bluebird ashore when Leo arrived back from Derby, having set off at first light that morning. He was far from amused and made a strong case to Donald that it was futile to take such risks without the timekeepers present. Donald countered that he wanted to get in all the practice he could while conditions allowed.

Maurie had returned from the south earlier in the day with Clive, Louis and Julia. He brought with him some new components to add to Bluebird's fuel system. During the week prior to the Christmas break, the Bristol Siddeley engineers had worked with Norris Brothers to devise a modification to Bluebird's fuel system that involved installation of a fuel boost pump and header tank in the fuel line. This would get more fuel into the engine and allow it to run for short bursts at up to 110 per cent of its stated maximum revs, effectively developing 10 per cent more power.

Left: Bluebird's damaged spars.
© P. Allonby

Above: The cramped confines of Bluebird's cockpit.
© P. Allonby

The weather had closed in again, and even though the attempt was now back on there was no chance of getting Bluebird afloat. Ken Norris had travelled up from Sussex and assisted Donald, Leo and Maurie to ensure that K7 was ready for any break in the weather. The fuel boost pump and 1-gallon header tank were incorporated into the fuel line to ensure that the engine could operate at 110 per cent of its stated maximum during short-duration runs. The front spar that had been dented in the collision with the duck the previous day was examined by Norris, but as it was only the fairing and not the load-bearing structure beneath, it was decided to leave it alone. The press and TV crews now returned to Coniston. They had heard of the Christmas runs and high speeds achieved, causing them to prepare stories along the lines of 'a break in the weather would give Campbell the opportunity that he needed'.

Longines sent back two junior timekeepers. Raoul Crélerot had not returned and Norman Buckley was put in charge of timekeeping using the Longines equipment.

Bluebird had now twice struck a bird at high speed, so something would obviously have to be done to eliminate this hazard. Shotguns were suggested as a way of scaring-off the birds and local villagers provided a pair, but when tried they had little effect. Birds returned to the lake's surface within a couple of minutes.

Louis and Clive were therefore dispatched to the Standard Fireworks factory in Huddersfield, West Yorkshire. They returned with the car laden with a number of large rockets, the plan being to launch a couple before each run to frighten the birds away. Donald drove a stake into the ground and then proceeded to test one of the rockets to see if the theory would work in practice. Birds duly scattered in all directions when the rocket exploded in mid-air, not returning for some considerable time. It was decided that the rockets would be launched from the support boats either side of the measured kilometre.

The press now started a round of speculation about the cost of the record attempt, which was being funded out of Donald's own pocket. There were rumours of a large cash bonus being paid to Donald if the record was broken before the end of the year, but the author has found no evidence to substantiate the story and has been unable to identity the two companies involved, which were said to be American. While Campbell did not actively refute the rumour, he would not elaborate further when pressmen questioned him about it.

"The act of dying worries me, I like this life far too much, but one becomes afraid of failure too. On my own behalf and on behalf of the team. I am not sure which comes first. In the boat the feeling is . . . well, the old curtain goes up, the bell rings, the old adrenaline is pumping at a rate of knots and you know, we all have this fright process, and a lot of things can affect it. There are days when you are at a low ebb and others when you are at a high ebb, a lot of things can affect your feeling in the boat. Three prime causes of fear are fatigue, cold and noise, you get very frightened and you need to be. It's like a curve if you could plot it. If you are not frightened at all, you are a dead duck. If you are too frightened you slip down the other side of the curve, you need to be at just about the right pitch.

This waiting and this weather drives one through the roof. You know damned well that sooner or later you could take a thoroughly unjustifiable risk, so the question is: How far do you consider an unjustifiable risk to be justified? Here comes a measure of experience, there are times when you are likely to overstep the mark and then luck comes into play, it's a big factor. Father used to say, don't go before your time, boy.

My father was a terrific example, courageous, colourful, dour, unbending, uncompromising, but that's not the motivation as such. There are things in life you want to do, it's damn difficult to get inside yourself and find out why. Spirit counts very much. It is infectious. All you know is that there is a fire burning inside. . . Father and I were very different characters. I am the sort of idiot who, once he gets tucked into a job, just puts on the blinkers and sees nothing else.

It just so happens that I've been thrown into this, the old sea of fate; there's a saying – Better fish in the ocean than ever came out of it. And boy, you'd better hope your bait's good. . .

This game can be hell. One often wonders how Hillary might have felt. They have climbed the highest mountain there is, and that's it. In my life, the top at the moment is 300 miles an hour. Life is a succession of these mountains. All of us are struggling up and, oh God, isn't it a swine? You get there and you look around and it's great. And you just have time to breathe before you start getting everything in perspective. Then you realise it wasn't a mountain after all. It was a molehill. You look over there and you can see another mountain, the real mountain, and you are going for it, boy, and what hurts, what REALLY hurts, is when you come to the last one and you go down the other side.'

Donald in a
reflective mood in the
boathouse.
© News International

Donald Campbell talking to Geoffrey Mather, Deputy Editor of the Manchester edition of the *Daily Express*, December 1966.

Geoffrey Mather – 'Was physical challenge ever so beautifully described?'

Thursday
29 December

Weather:
Wet and windy

Conditions remained hopeless and there was now little to do but wait; Bluebird and her pilot were both ready. Donald held a press conference down at the slipway, where he repeated the message that had almost become routine: 'We are at a stage of complete readiness for further high-speed trials and we have been for over a week.'

'What's holding you back?' the press would ask.

'The weather,' he replied, without adding much more.

Talk of breaking the record on New Year's Eve went around, almost as if Donald could order up suitable conditions for a specific time. The weather remained unsuitable all day, but the fact that conditions could change very quickly made the waiting extremely irksome. There was no escape from Coniston, no opportunity to get away, because a window of one hour was all that was needed. Inevitably, boredom set in.

Friday
30 December

Weather:
Wet and windy

The holiday period brought the crowds to Coniston, anxious to catch a glimpse of Campbell and Bluebird, but it was not to be. The course was swept for driftwood washed into the lake by the recent heavy rains. A sweep of this kind was scheduled at least every other day or more often if required.

It was decided to anchor the course boats in their positions at the northern and southern end of the measured kilometre to ensure they did not disturb the lake surface ahead of any run. The course teams would drive along the road on the eastern shoreline of the lake and then ferry themselves out to the cruisers by way of inflatable dinghies.

The weather forecast for the next few days did not look promising. The next day, New Year's Eve, was the second anniversary of Donald's successful Lake Dumbleyung record of 276mph, the speed he was now trying to beat.

Saturday
31 December

Weather:
Windy

There was a full team standby that morning, with everyone assembled at the boat shed before dawn. Unfortunately, as the sun rose in the sky, the wind that had persisted since the 27th continued to blow over the lake. At around lunchtime, the press, TV people and photographers congregated in the bar of the Sun. Donald bought everyone a drink and seemed to be in good form despite the frustration of the waiting. He knew that Bluebird was now ready at last and the runs over Christmas had finally confirmed he had the power needed; all that was holding him back was the weather. It was sure to break at some time and then he would be able to seize his chance. The record attempt was clearly imminent and the mood of those at Coniston reflected the fact. In the hallway of the Sun Hotel, a noticeboard had been in use throughout the attempt for team announcements. Often early risers were treated to the witty contributions of stragglers from the night before. One notice read: 'Standby at dawn, Bluebird team, driver: Clive Glynn, reserve: Donald Campbell.' A faded photograph depicting a group of shipyard workers standing next to a large vessel was also stuck to the board for a number of weeks. Ken Norris skilfully applied a pair of sponsons to the ship and added the caption: 'Bluebird and team'. The captain standing on the bridge was given a blue bobble hat. On New Year's Eve, a new notice appeared:

> 'The Team, the staff and hangers-on are invited to a fancy dress party to be held in the lounge at ten o'clock on New Year's Eve. Hostess: Lady Aitkin, Host: Old Misery Himself.
>
> **Note**: staff will be on duty at 7 a.m. New Year's Day.'

Donald dressed as a French chef/waiter with black pencil moustache and a striped apron, while Louis struggled into a miniskirt. David Benson made a convincing Batman, and Dr Darbishire transformed himself into a black-cloaked witch doctor complete with headdress. Donald moved from group to group, quipping and teasing. He chastised those who had not made the effort to come in fancy dress, including Leo and Maurie, but although the party was a riot by any normal reckoning, Leo wrote years later that it was not up to Donald's usual standards. The tension of the waiting still weighed on the atmosphere. At midnight, 'Auld Lang Syne' was sung and a toast drunk. Donald brought a tear to Connie Robinson's eyes as he thanked her on behalf of everyone present for being such a wonderful mum to them all.

He also toasted the assembled journalists, photographers and TV people, saying: 'You are all here to see me turn Bluebird on her back.'

NORMAN LUCK ON DONALD CAMPBELL

'As the weather worsened, the army of reporters and photographers made regular trips to Lakeland Fashions – a knitwear shop in Lake Windermere where one of the hacks had a contact to buy cut-price woollies to ward off the chill of dawn sorties to the boathouse.

Christmas came and went. New Year arrived. Journalists had grabbed whatever time off they could to return home to their families for the festive period and soon returned to continue their assignment.

New Year's Eve in the Sun Hotel was a fancy dress party. David Benson, the late Daily Express motoring correspondent and close friend of Donald Campbell, my photographer colleague, John Wardhaugh, and I all attended. There was a poignant moment as Campbell was asked a question about his bid. He said if he fired Bluebird up to full potential to achieve the 300mph plus aim to get the record and the conditions weren't right he would just loop the loop. I stood beside him as he simulated the loop with his hand and informed us that such an occurrence could be fatal. As it was just days later on the morning of 4 January.'

Sunday
1 January 1967

Weather:
Windy, dry

There was no dawn standby on New Year's morning. It had been a hectic night, and as the team, press and TV people assembled for breakfast their collective state could best be described as fragile. Nobody was in any hurry to get down to the lakeside. The unsuitable weather did not deter the crowds, though. For no apparent reason, they came to Coniston in their thousands, with hundreds of cars clogging the narrow road on the eastern side of the lake looking for a vantage point. The beach by the Bluebird Café was packed with onlookers, all eager to get a glimpse of Donald, Bluebird or anyone associated with the attempt. The police had their work cut out dealing with the crowds. Sensing that the spectators would at least like to see something, Donald took out the Jetstar and drove round into the bay close to the shore. As dusk fell, the crowds began to disperse and an early night was enjoyed by all. The celebrations of New Year's Eve had taken their toll on tired bodies.

Waiting for a break in the weather.
© Press Association

The two Bristol Siddeley engineers, Lavis and Pearson, were back at Coniston. Since the modifications to Bluebird's fuel system with the installation of an auxiliary header tank and boost pump, the Orpheus had not been given a static test. Donald was anxious for them to confirm that the improved engine performance he had experienced on Christmas Day was not just a flash in the pan. The engine cover was once again removed – involving the undoing of over 120 'Dzus' fasteners. The engineers got to work checking the fuel system and making minor adjustments. The crowds had not gone away; Monday was a public holiday and the dry, cold weather brought them to Coniston again in droves. After the engineers had completed their work, preparations were made for the static test. Bluebird was again shackled to the slipway rails with heavy chains. The inner tarpaulin that hung over the yard end of the boat shed was rolled up onto the roof, all loose equipment moved out and the Land Rover reversed back to the very end of the slipway. Donald expressed concern about the number of onlookers and issued instructions as to where it would be safe for them to stand. Campbell then climbed into the cockpit and slowly began to apply more and more throttle. The engine roared to full revolutions and the jet-stream hurled spray right across to the other side of the lake.

Engine speed went past the stated maximum, indicating that fuel starvation was indeed a thing of the past. Amid general elation, the engine cowling was refitted and Bluebird fuelled up, ready to go. Later in the afternoon, the biting wind that had persisted for the last five days suddenly dropped and the lake became very calm. Preparations were made for a run. Leo and Robbie, together with Keith Harrison and Press Association photographer Eric Shaw, set off to drive to the beaches adjacent to where the course boats were positioned at the northern and southern end of the measured distance. They would row themselves across to the tethered Fairlines. The timekeepers were already in position, but Norman Buckley and Andrew Brown as official observers had to be present at the timekeepers' stations.

Having witnessed the sharp improvement in the weather, the crowds abandoned the beach by the café and made their way to the eastern shoreline road. Bluebird was soon afloat and ready to go once confirmation came through that the official observers were in position. The minutes ticked by, half an hour passed and the light was beginning to fade but still there was no word. What was the hold-up? A perfect opportunity was being missed! Finally, when daylight had faded, the course boat crews and official observers drove back into the yard. The traffic on the road along the eastern shoreline was so heavy that they had been unable to reach their positions. There was nothing that could be done. Once darkness fell, the crowds would leave of their own accord and the road would be passable again. The local police promised to introduce a patrol along the road to make sure there would be no recurrence of the blockage. The extended New Year's holiday was expected to bring large crowds to Coniston, perhaps for the rest of the week, raising the prospect of further disruption on a road normally used by just a few cars a day in winter.

Monday
2 January

Weather:
Windy and dry

> 'The heartbreak of this project is you are not only fighting the unknown with the technicalities involved, but you are being continually frustrated by this appalling weather. I never remember such an intensely foul spell as we have experienced in these last two months.'
>
> Donald Campbell, *The Price of a Record*, January 1967

Tuesday
3 January

Weather:
Windy with
showers

The crowds turned up again in the morning, but they were to be disappointed. The wind blew and occasional showers rendered conditions unsuitable. Donald was not seen much that day and did not put in an appearance at the boat shed until the afternoon. Tentative arrangements were being made to move Bluebird and the Jetstar to London for the Boat Show after the record had been broken. The show was due to open the next day, and displaying K7 alongside the Jetstar after setting a new record of over 300mph would give Donald's Bluebird Marine venture a significant boost.

> 'We're at complete readiness for further high speed trials and we've been at a state of complete readiness now since before Christmas.'
>
> *'What's holding you up?'*
>
> 'The weather. It's been holding us up now for 8 long weeks. We've had some development troubles which we expected, but they have been minor in comparison to the weather.'
>
> *'Mr Campbell, when you do make your attempt, the best of luck. Thank you.'*
>
> 'Thanks so much and all the very best to you.'
>
> Donald Campbell, speaking to ITV on 3 January 1967

Towards the end of the afternoon, the wind dropped and the lake began to flatten and reflect the surrounding hills. It was half an hour too late, however, because the light was also fading. Donald ventured out to the end of the jetty with his binoculars to scan the lake surface, but there was insufficient visibility to see his sighting point, at Brown Howe at the southern end of the lake, with any clarity.

It was yet another frustrating episode to add to the growing catalogue he had experienced over the past nine weeks. The general consensus was that this would be the week the attempt would be made. The weather forecast indicated that colder, frosty conditions would be arriving at Coniston once the wind subsided, so Campbell would get his chance.

Newspaper photographers and TV crews discussed where they would position themselves for the attempt – down at the slipway to see Donald set off and catch his triumphant return, or out on the lake to record Bluebird as she streaked through the measured distance on her two runs. The *Daily Express* had two photographers at Coniston, John Wardhaugh and Peter Jackson. They decided to divide responsibilities by tossing a coin. The loser would be positioned on the lake shore, the winner at the jetty. John Wardhaugh won the toss.

Early that evening, Donald spoke to Tonia, who had now finished her singing engagements and was preparing to travel to Coniston. He was not happy about her driving up overnight and arranged to call her when he awoke the next morning so she could start her journey early. A little later on, Donald dropped into the bar at the Sun. He looked tired and his mood was subdued, but he made arrangements with a few of the press boys to have a game of cards at the bungalow later.

At about 8.30 p.m., while waiting for the arrival of Keith Harrison and another of the pressmen, he was playing Russian patience in the company of David Benson. In one of the games, Campbell turned up the ace of spades followed by the queen of spades. He remarked immediately to Benson that the queen was the death card. He was noticeably upset and told Benson that Mary, Queen of Scots had turned the same cards the night she was beheaded. Benson tried to reassure his friend, telling him not to worry about his superstitions. Stephen Darbishire's son, also called Stephen, paid a call on Donald to introduce him to his girlfriend, Kerry. Donald immediately told them of the cards and his premonition, leaving Kerry speechless and causing Stephen to tell his friend not to be ridiculous. The incident clearly bothered Campbell. Presently the others arrived at the bungalow and a game of pontoon got under way. Julia Goossens brought some fresh cards, but they had green backs and Donald, who detested the colour because he believed it to be unlucky, refused to play with them.

Donald's mood lightened as the evening progressed; he was playing well and remarked: 'That's the first time I have ever won at cards.' He ended the

Donald plays Russian patience at the bungalow.
© Mirrorpix

evening up about £2 (modern equivalent: £28). His early unlucky cards were still obviously playing on his mind, though. David Benson later claimed that he had said: 'I have the most awful premonition that I am getting the chop this time, I have had the feeling for days.' Benson told him not to be silly and that it was just the hanging around that was getting him down. Benson also claimed that Donald had said: 'Well, it's somebody in my family that is going to get the chop, I pray to God it's not me.' Campbell's daughter, Gina, vehemently rejects the idea that her father would even consider that form of words: 'My father was always far too worried about everyone else, he would never be so selfish as to wish bad fate upon anyone in the family.' Certainly it was not in keeping with the selfless nature of Donald's character to think like that or use such words.

Card games would usually break up the same way. Donald would say: 'Let's make this the last hand, we might have a bit of business to attend to in the morning. The forecast isn't too bad, is it Keith? I think you had better stir yourself and Louis and get down there early.'

As the three pressmen left the bungalow there was a chill in the air. 'It looks like tomorrow could be the day,' Donald said as he looked up at the clearing night sky, 'I only hope it's not my last.'

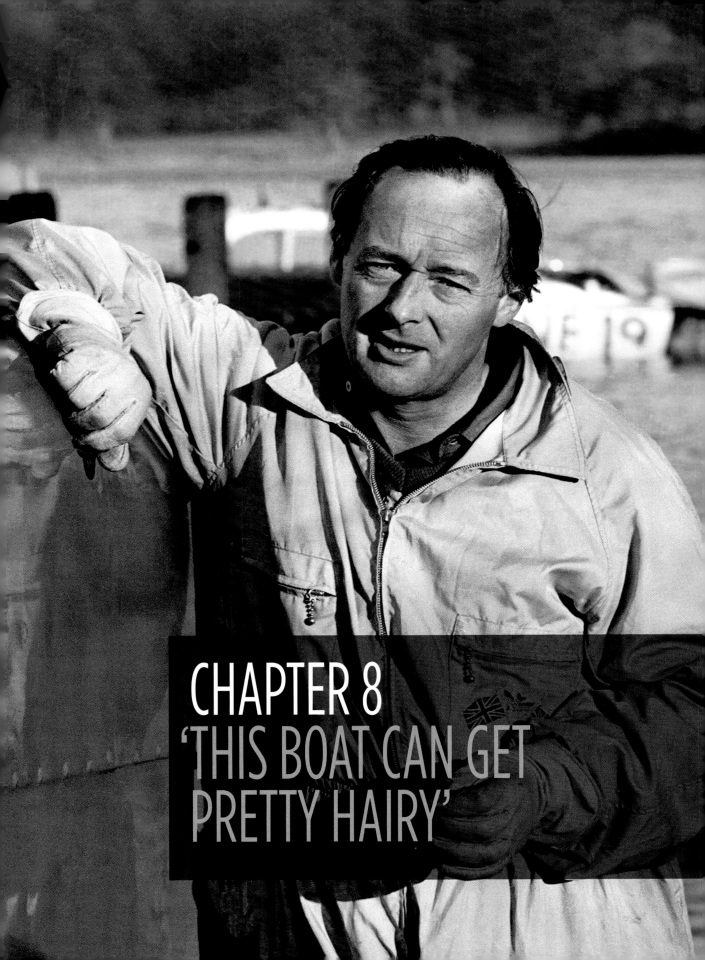

CHAPTER 8
'THIS BOAT CAN GET PRETTY HAIRY'

Weather:
Cold, dry and calm

Donald was awake long before dawn, having slept uneasily owing to the anticipation of the coming day. He phoned Tonia very early to tell her to put off her journey to Coniston. If this was to be the big morning, the attempt would be over by the time she arrived and preparations would be under way to pack Bluebird off to London for the Boat Show. He did not want her to make a wasted journey. For Keith Harrison the day began, as so many had, at 6.30 a.m. He was down at the lakeside to assess whether conditions were suitable for calling out the rest of the team. He had received a favourable weather forecast from RAF Bawtry the previous evening and a provisional standby had been ordered at the boathouse for 7.00. The lake was calm in the still, dark conditions and there was no discernible breeze. Harrison made his way back to the Sun to rouse the team. His next stop was the bungalow, where Donald was having his usual early breakfast – a bowl of cereal and a cup of coffee, laced with brandy to keep out the cold. 'What's the weather like, Keithy?' Donald asked. Harrison replied that he had seen it better, but that he had also seen it worse, and suggested that they might get a run in that day. They walked out onto the balcony and looked away from the lake towards the snow-capped mountains behind the village. Campbell remarked that their chances were 50/50 at best. 'I don't like the way the wind is coming from the north-east.' Harrison said there had been no breeze at all down at the lake shore.

Donald decided that his odds might be better after all: 'All right, Keithy, you'd better get them out then.' His mood was cheerful; after nine long weeks, the waiting was finally coming to an end. He went back to his breakfast and Harrison carried on to the boathouse.

He was the first one there. He started the generator and a string of naked light bulbs that illuminated the boathouse flickered on. Other team members began to arrive – Leo and Maurie in the Vauxhall, Louis and Clive in the Citroën. Paul Evans arrived and started up the radio truck so he could get his equipment ready. Next came Robbie and Dr Darbishire. Robbie would be piloting Leo's course boat and Darbishire would be acting as one of the official observers. The rubber dinghies used to get out to the anchored course boats at each end of the measured kilometre were loaded onto the Land Rover. Pressmen, including the old hands who had been at Coniston from the start and the new boys who had only arrived a couple of days before, had also begun to assemble at the boathouse. The camera crews were checking their equipment and making sure that film magazines were loaded, ready to record the day's events as they unfolded. Donald arrived shortly after 7.30, parking his E-Type in its usual position beside Pier Cottage. 'Another bloody false alarm,' he remarked, 'but let's just have a look and see how quickly we'll be back for a proper breakfast.'

TONY JAMES ON DONALD CAMPBELL

'Through November and December of 1966 and the start of January 1967, if the weather promised to be fair Donald would be up at 6 o'clock and be down at the lake soon after, to see conditions for himself. I felt he was suffering, because he never knew which day he would risk his life, but he had to be prepared to do so each day.'

Gary May, a reporter for the *London Evening News*, grabbed a quick comment from Donald: 'It looks like no breakfast and no lunch, we should be able to go at 3 o'clock this afternoon.' Donald walked to the end of the jetty with his binoculars to study conditions in the half-light before the sun finally rose behind the Grizedale fells. Earlier, on the back of Keith Harrison's report, Donald had rung Andrew Brown at his home. Brown was to be one of the official observers for the attempt. 'I think the water is smooth,' Donald told Brown. Brown used to refer to the water as having an 'oily calm' whenever conditions were favourable, now Donald poking gentle fun at Andrew's detailed description: 'I'm sorry we haven't got an oily calm, Andy, but it has distinct possibilities.' Scanning the lake, Donald saw Keith's 'smooth' for himself.

He went looking for Leo. In his book *The Record Breakers*, Leo described their encounter as follows:

> 'I found Donald in the boathouse leaning against Bluebird, staring out over the lake, his thoughts miles away. "Morning Skipper, the lake doesn't look at all bad today." "Oh, hello Unc, don't waste time, you'd better get everybody out to their stations and tell Maurie to launch the boat," he replied.'

This struck Leo as a rather curt dismissal, quite unlike Donald, who had usually had time for a chat and a joke before previous record attempts. He obviously had a lot on his mind and wanted to get on with the job in hand.

The crews for the course boats – Leo, Robbie and Geoff Hallawell for the boat at the northern end of the measured kilometre, Keith Harrison and PA photographer colleague Eric Shaw for the boat at the southern end – left Pier Cottage to drive round to the other side of the lake. Leo, Robbie and Geoff took the Vauxhall, Keith and Eric the Land Rover. Ted Hamel had already ferried the two young timekeepers to their posts in the Morris Traveller, where they joined Norman Buckley, Andrew Brown and Dr Darbishire, who was acting as radio man at the northern timekeeper's station.

At the slipway, preparations for Bluebird's launch were in hand – Clive and Maurie were detailed to get the boat afloat. Paul Evans, the Signals corporal, had been given permission by Donald to set up his radio link alongside the course. He was preparing the remote control facilities in his army Land Rover

Leo being rowed out to the Fairline by Robbie.
© G. Hallawell

and would shortly set off for the northern timekeeper's position. He would be in touch with four locations out on the lake and with Donald in K7's cockpit.

Leo, Robbie and Geoff in the Fairline at the northern end of the kilometre were call sign Alpha. Keith Harrison and Eric Shaw in the other Fairline at the southern end of the kilometre were call sign Kilo. In the refuelling boat in the bay south of Peel Island were Louis Goossens and Bill Jordan, call sign Charlie. The timekeepers' call sign was Tango, Paul was Base, and Donald in K7 was Skipper.

Above: Donald in the cockpit as K7 is launched.
© Norman Hurst

Above right: Getting ready to leave the jetty for the last time.
© Norman Hurst

Donald stepped into Bluebird's cockpit just after 8.10, still some 25 minutes before sunrise proper. Clive removed the red jet-pipe cover from the jet and set it down on the floor of the boathouse. Donald passed the two yellow air-intake covers to Maurie, who then took control of the winch in the Land Rover. It was the familiar launch procedure that had been refined and perfected over the past few weeks.

Donald asked *Express* reporter David Benson to fetch a demister cloth out of the Jag. Bluebird's cold perspex cockpit canopy had begun to mist over. Donald now went through his standard superstitious ritual. Mr Whoppit, dressed in his miniature blue overalls, was placed in position down by Donald's seat. Next, Donald had a 'word' with Tiki, a small wooden model of the Polynesian god of happiness. As he slid down into his seat, he reached into his pocket and pulled out his pipe and tobacco pouch. He handed them to Benson, saying: 'Hang on to these, will you . . . they are sticking in my arse.'

With a smile and his usual wink, Donald donned his leather helmet and began to do up his four-point safety harness (two shoulder straps and a lap belt). The boat was lowered down the slipway and Clive pulled Bluebird round to the edge of the jetty once she had floated free of her cradle.

> 'When you go down into the arena, you know, you go down with your eyes open, and when you go down into the arena, you know that sometimes, you're likely to get your nose punched. You do it with your eyes open, you take the risks.'
>
> 'Of course you're under tension, of course you're frightened – everybody concerned is. If they weren't, you'd be very frightened of them, but you keep these fears to yourself.'
>
> 'Make no mistake about it, we are going into the unknown. We don't know what is going to happen, but we do know if we go too fast, she will take off.'
>
> **Donald Campbell, BBC interviews, autumn 1965 and 1966**

Donald reaches for his silver pilot's helmet.
© Norman Hurst

Maurie then used a boat hook to push K7's nose into position so it pointed down the lake. At 8.30, Leo called Keith Harrison at the southern end of the kilometre to enquire about water conditions. The answer came back that there was a slight swell, but otherwise the water was moderately good.

Paul Evans, in his effort to get round to the northern timekeeper's position on the lake shore, had got stuck in traffic. Even at this early hour, the road around the eastern shoreline was jammed solid with spectators' badly parked cars. Paul radioed Donald to brief him; Donald instructed him to make his way back to base, saying that he would wait. Some 10 minutes later, Paul was back at the jetty. At 8.40, Donald asked for a conditions update from Leo and Keith and received positive responses.

Donald then issued the instruction to fire one rocket from each of the course boats to clear the lake's surface of birds. They fizzed into the air and exploded with a series of staccato bangs. Next, Donald radioed the timekeepers to ask if they were all set. After receiving their confirmation, he announced that he was preparing for the first run. Maurie got the thumbs up from Donald and told Clive to release the line from the stern. Immediately, the air starter system hissed and the engine burst into life within seconds. Clive only just had time to get the line free. He noticed that Donald was not hanging around this morning.

Below: Bluebird heads out to the course.
© Getty Images and Norman Hurst

Radio telephone
transcript:

Donald Campbell
Call Sign: Skipper

Leo Villa
Call Sign: Alpha

Keith Harrison
Call Sign: Kilo

Timekeepers:
**Stephen
Darbishire**
Call Sign: Tango

Paul Evans
Call Sign: Base

Louis Goossens
Call Sign: Charlie

GMT 08.43

Leo, Leo, how's your water? OVER

There appear to be no birds in the way at the moment, and there is a slight down swell on the water, but it could be caused by our own boat. OVER

Kilo, Kilo, Kilo, Kilo, how's the water? OVER

Kilo to Bluebird. The water surface is smooth, but there's a slight ground swell, erm, otherwise conditions are reasonably good, visibility is quite good. OVER

Roger Kilo. We are going to try a slow run. Charlie do you read? OVER

Yes Skipper, read you loud and clear.

OK . . . all stations . . . rockets fire one . . . NOW!
From Bluebird, Tango, do you read?
Tango, Tango, Tango, do you read? OVER
Base, do you have contact with Tango? OVER

Wait there Skipper, I'll try calling him. Base for Tango, Base for Tango, do you read? OVER

Tango to Base, loud and clear. OVER

Roger. Please listen out on your sets, Skipper has been calling you. OVER

Tango, you're just ready to build up about runs, how's your . . . are you set? . . . ready? . . . OVER

Base for Tango, Skipper wishes to know if you are all set. OVER

– Silence –

Base for Tango, Base for Tango, Skipper wishes to know if you are all ready. OVER

Tango to Base, Tango to Base, yes, we are all ready – we are all ready. Will you pass that message on to Skipper – Tango to Base, OVER

Base for Skipper, Tango all ready.
OVER

Roger Paul, assume you'll relay . . .
Charlie, Alpha, Charlie and er . . .
now Kilo, have your rockets fired?
OVER

Alpha calling Skipper, one rocket
fired Skipper, one rocket fired, not
particularly brilliant, we had it too
low but it went off. OVER AND
OUT

Kilo, Charlie, confirm please. I said
fire one, fire one, not two. OVER
Kilo . . . confirm.

Base for Kilo, do you read Skipper? OVER

Go!

GMT 08.45

Kilo, we are under way [21-second
pause]

OK Leo, do you read me? OVER
[Start of first run]

Coming in loud and clear, Skipper
. . . Coming in loud and clear
(Point A)

Two bloody swans have just taken
off going down the lake.
I'm under way, all systems normal;
brake swept up, er . . . air pressure
warning light on . . . coming onto
track now and er . . . I'll open
up just as soon as I am heading
down the lake, er doesn't look too
smooth from here, doesn't matter,
here we go . . .
Here we go . . . [pause 3 seconds] . . .

Campbell commenced the first run of his last record attempt at just after 8.45. Bluebird moved slowly out towards the middle of the lake, where she paused for a brief second as Donald lined her up. With a deafening blast of power, Donald now applied full throttle and Bluebird began to surge forward. Clouds of spray issued from the jet-pipe, water poured over the rear spar and after a few hundred yards, at 70mph, Bluebird unstuck from the surface and rocketed off towards the southern end of the lake, producing her characteristic comet's tail of spray.

She entered the measured kilometre at 8.46. Leo Villa witnessed her passing the first marker buoy at about 285mph in perfect steady planing trim, her nose slightly down, still accelerating.

7.525 seconds later, Keith Harrison saw her leave the measured kilometre at a speed of over 310mph. Campbell lifted his foot from the throttle about ³⁄₁₀ of a second before passing the southern kilometre marker. He had made his usual commentary throughout the run.

'Nose beginning to lift'.
© Author's Collection

'OK, we're up and away . . .'
© Author's Collection

Bluebird accelerates towards the measured kilometre.
© Mirrorpix

Below: Passing north timing on the first run at 285mph.
© G. Hallawell

. . . Passing through four . . . five coming up . . . a lot of water, nose beginning to lift, water all over the front of the engine again . . . and the nose is up . . . low pressure fuel warning light . . . going left . . . OK we're up and away . . . and passing through er . . . tramping very hard at 150 . . . very hard indeed . . . FULL POWER . . . Passing through 2 . . . 25 out of the way . . . *tramping like hell Leo* . . . I don't think I can get over the top, but I'll try, FULL HOUSE . . . and I can't see where I am . . . FULL HOUSE – FULL HOUSE – FULL HOUSE . . . POWER OFF NOW! . . . I'M THROUGH! . . .

The emotion in Campbell's voice as he shouted 'I'M THROUGH!' combined relief, elation, surprise and fear and is a least two octaves higher in pitch than the rest of the commentary. The '25 out of the way' comment was a reference to using Leo's course boat as a marker point 25° from the straight ahead, aligning the tip of the port sponson with it.

As Bluebird left the measured kilometre, Keith Harrison and Eric Shaw both noticed that she was very light around the bows, riding on her front stabilising fins. Her planing trim was no worse than she had exhibited when equipped with the Beryl engine, but it was markedly different to that observed by Leo at the northern end of the kilometre, when she was under full acceleration.

The usual procedure following the first run of any record attempt – and this was now most definitely a record attempt – was that when Bluebird reached the bay at the southern end of the lake beyond Peel Island, Leo Villa would give the skipper his view on how the boat had looked as it passed the northern end of the measured kilometre. Leo would then prompt for a similar response from Keith Harrison at the southern end of the kilometre. Campbell would relay his impression of the run and Leo, as course marshal, would make a

Bluebird leaves the measured kilometre at the end of the first run.
© Press Association

decision as to when the second run should commence, bearing in mind the water conditions. They would also decide if they were going to refuel.

Campbell's commentary continued and was delivered at a more measured pace as he headed to the southern end of the lake.

> *. . . power . . . (garbled) er* er passing through 25 vector off Peel Island
> . . . passing through 2 . . . I'm lighting like mad . . . brake gone down
> . . . er . . . engine lighting up now . . . relighting . . . passing Peel Island . . .
> relight made normal . . . and now . . . down at Brown Howe . . . passing
> through 100 . . . er . . . nose hasn't dropped yet . . . nose down . . .

Just as he left the measured kilometre, the engine flamed-out for some inexplicable reason. He again made a vector reference of 25°, this time to Peel Island, again off the port sponson tip. The water brake was applied as he came up to and passed Peel Island at around 200mph. He referred to relighting the engine, and then said 'relight made normal', but given the indistinct, excited voice coming from the cockpit, no-one listening in on the radio loop *at the time* picked up on the comment. If it had been picked up, it would have alarmed Leo. The flame-out would not have been caused by water entering the intakes – Bluebird was still in the planing position – but by an interruption in the fuel supply, caused by a fuel system or electrical problem. If that was repeated under maximum jet thrust, it could have catastrophic consequences.

. . . 'I'm THROUGH!' . . .

Leo, do you read me? OVER

Hello read you . . . er Skipper, come in [16-second-long static]

Base do you read me? OVER

Reading you Skipper, come in.

Base will you get a message from Tango, please? OVER

Base, roger, in actual fact that was Alpha that answered you, Skipper. OVER

Don't worry about Alpha, I want a message from Tango. OVER

Roger, Skipper . . . Tango, Tango, do you read? OVER

Tango to Base, Tango to Base . . . Stand by. OVER [static]

Tango to Base, OVER, Tango to Base, OVER . . . Message for Skipper . . . +47 +47 +47 do you copy that, repeat. OVER

ROGER – ROGER – ROGER . . . Base for Skipper, Base for Skipper, from Tango, +47 +47 OVER

It was now 8.47 and Campbell had the speed from his first run. Taking 250mph as a baseline, '+ 47' meant 47mph over that figure; he had in fact averaged 297.6mph. Bluebird had peaked at around 315mph just as Campbell lifted off, before she left the measured kilometre.

Under the rules laid down by the UIM, an hour was allowed in which to make both runs. This was enough time for the wash to disperse and the lake to regain its glassy appearance, assuming there was no adverse change in the weather. At speed, Bluebird's planing created comparatively little wash and it took quite some time for the slow-moving wash to be reflected back into the centre of the lake. This gave the option of making the return run very soon after the first one. Donald knew how long he would have to do this, and indeed had practised fast return runs after between 4 and 7 minutes in mid-December, albeit at lower speeds.

Leo and Robbie (Alpha).
© G. Hallawell

Paul Evans (Base).
© P. Allonby

The Timekeepers (Tango).
© Mirror Pix

Bluebird was now turning in a wide arc at the southernmost tip of the lake, adjacent to Brown Howe and about 1 kilometre south of Peel Island. Having heard his speed, Donald announced that he was starting his return run. In a significant deviation from previous practice, for the first time during a record attempt Donald had not checked water conditions with Leo and received the OK. This was against the procedure that had previously been agreed and against the whole way the team had always operated. Alarmed by this, Leo could only look on, unable to contact Donald because the latter's radio mic was still in transmit mode. Leo would have been even more worried if he had known at the time that Donald had referred to the engine flaming-out as he decelerated.

. . . 'I'm starting the return run now' . . .
© Author's Collection

GMT 08.48

[Campbell manoeuvring Bluebird
ready for return run in the bay south of Brown Howe]
Roger, Paul . . . I'm starting the return run now . . . (3 minutes 18.5 seconds after start of first run)
[20.5-second-long 'non-speaking' pause including 8-second period of static. Campbell may have been speaking, but the signal is not being picked up by base, Bluebird's location south of High Peel Near is masking any transmission]

Campbell commenced what was to be his final run at 8.48 – less than 2 minutes after exiting the kilometre on his first north–south run. The condition of the water 2 kilometres south of the actual measured kilometre was much rougher than Donald could have anticipated. He had used the water-brake to shed about 130mph of Bluebird's speed at the narrowest part of the lake past Peel Island. The wash this created was now rippling back into the centre of the course, giving the water surface a corrugated profile.

There was a significant pause between Donald's last communication with Base and the start of his commentary. When he resumed talking, his comments were all the more chilling. His description of the water conditions left none of his listeners in any doubt that he was suffering one hell of a rough ride.

His foot was hard down, but Bluebird was tramping badly. By the time he passed Peel Island, still almost 2 kilometres from the start of the measured distance, K7 was already travelling at over 150mph, bouncing over the rough water from one planing shoe to the other. Donald maintained full power and the tramping continued. Bluebird was accelerating rapidly towards the measured distance, but was off course, travelling much closer to the eastern shoreline and heading diagonally across the lake at about 5° in the direction of the western shore.

Campbell was now in the middle of the deceleration zone of the previous run and the swell resulting from deploying the water brake was badly destabilising Bluebird.

Just 10 seconds after passing Peel Island, Bluebird was travelling at about 270mph, still accelerating and pitching violently across the rough water. About 700 metres from the

CLIVE GLYNN ON DONALD CAMPBELL

'On 4 January, it seemed a usual sort of day. The lake was pretty still, but initially we were not sure if there would be any runs or not. Donald came down pretty early, and seemed his normal self with the usual 'good mornings' and then he had a chat with Leo. Once he decided to have a go, things began to move pretty quickly. Bluebird was launched, and I pulled her round the jetty on the line as usual. This time, I only just managed to get the line off her stern before Donald started Bluebird's engine and he was away – in a flaming hurry! The lake surface was not perfectly still but conditions were pretty good. We watched as Bluebird made her first run, and heard the speed from the radio truck. By now there was a faint north-east breeze starting, and the surface was not completely smooth. Quickly he turned round, but never got back to the boathouse . . .'

K7 about 700m from the start of the measured km on the return run travelling at about 270mph.
© Author's Collection

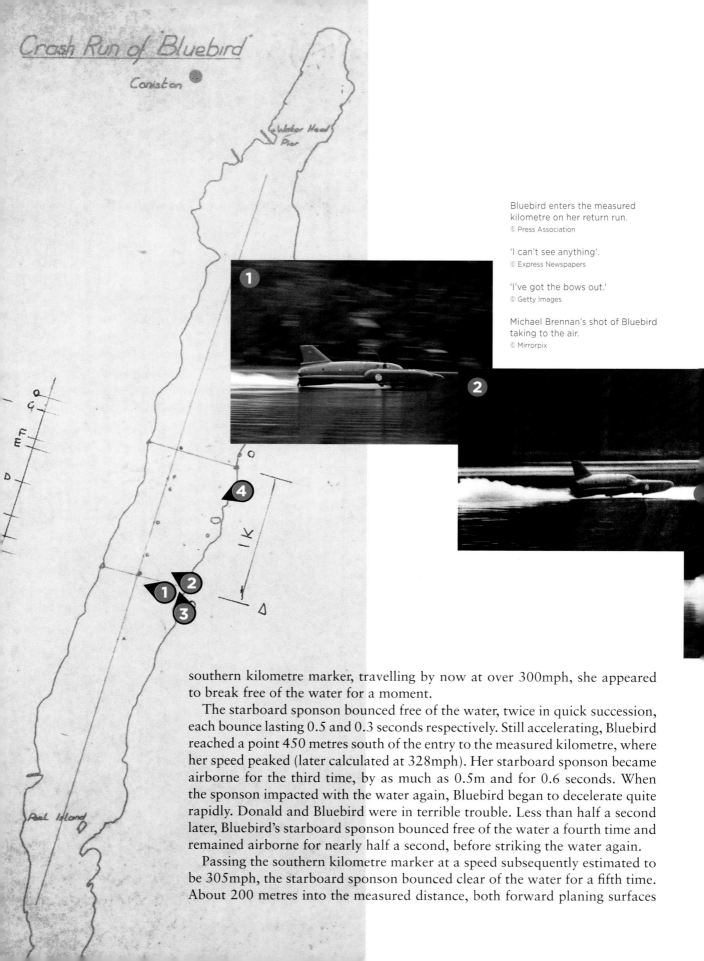

Crash Run of 'Bluebird'

Coniston

Water Head Pier

Peel Island

southern kilometre marker, travelling by now at over 300mph, she appeared to break free of the water for a moment.

The starboard sponson bounced free of the water, twice in quick succession, each bounce lasting 0.5 and 0.3 seconds respectively. Still accelerating, Bluebird reached a point 450 metres south of the entry to the measured kilometre, where her speed peaked (later calculated at 328mph). Her starboard sponson became airborne for the third time, by as much as 0.5m and for 0.6 seconds. When the sponson impacted with the water again, Bluebird began to decelerate quite rapidly. Donald and Bluebird were in terrible trouble. Less than half a second later, Bluebird's starboard sponson bounced free of the water a fourth time and remained airborne for nearly half a second, before striking the water again.

Passing the southern kilometre marker at a speed subsequently estimated to be 305mph, the starboard sponson bounced clear of the water for a fifth time. About 200 metres into the measured distance, both forward planing surfaces broke free of the water for the last time. Bluebird exceeded her safe pitching angle of 5.5° and slowly took to the air.

Some 220 metres further down the course, at about 290mph, she stood on her tail. There was no jet thrust to disturb the water beneath the jet-pipe. Bluebird's engine had ceased to produce any meaningful thrust, either because Campbell had lifted the throttle, or the ange of attack during the rotation, meant K7's intakes were starved of airflow. She climbed about 10 metres above the water and performed a near 360° flip before plunging back into the lake at an angle of around 45°. The boat began to break up on impact and a massive cloud of spray briefly hid the worst of her gyrations from view. The impact broke Bluebird in half just behind the cockpit, the sponsons were torn from their spars. The rear section of the hull barrel-rolled along the lake for approximately 80 metres before coming to rest momentarily facing the direction she had just come from. As the spray settled, Bluebird slipped from sight and sank into the depths of Coniston Water.

Full nose up . . . Pitching a bit down here . . . coming through our own wash . . . er getting straightened up now on track . . . rather closer to Peel Island . . . and we're tramping like mad . . . and . . . er . . . FULL POWER . . . er . . . tramping like hell OVER . . . I can't see much and the water's very bad indeed indeed . . . I'm galloping over (I can't get over) the top . . . and she's actually giving a hell of a bloody row in here . . . I can't see anything . . . I've got the bows out . . . I'm going . . . U-hh!

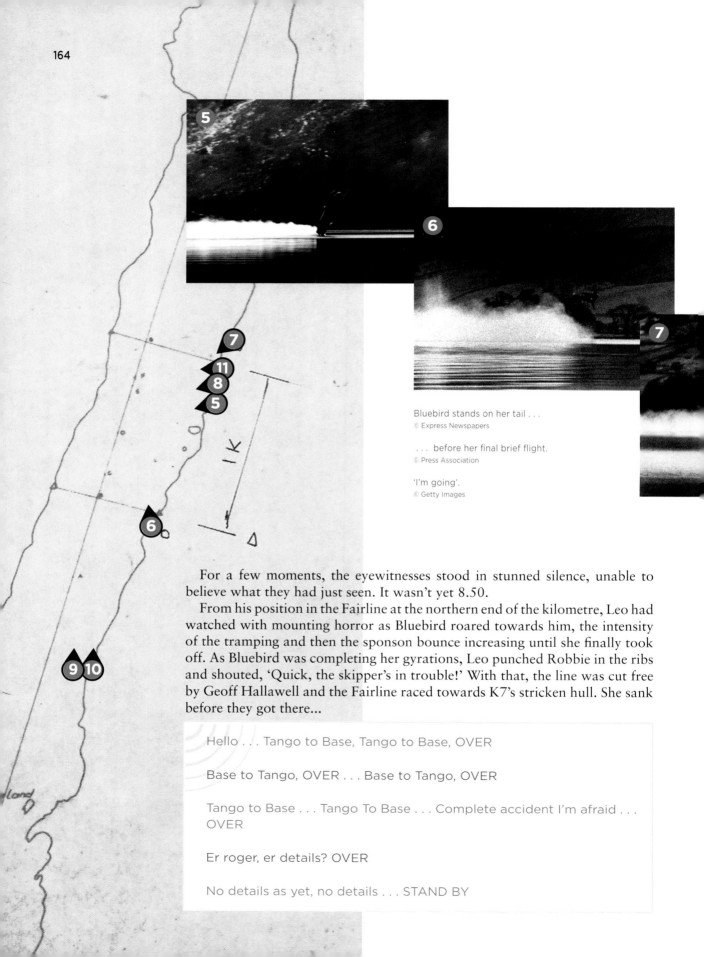

Bluebird stands on her tail . . .
© Express Newspapers

. . . before her final brief flight.
© Press Association

'I'm going'.
© Getty Images

For a few moments, the eyewitnesses stood in stunned silence, unable to believe what they had just seen. It wasn't yet 8.50.

From his position in the Fairline at the northern end of the kilometre, Leo had watched with mounting horror as Bluebird roared towards him, the intensity of the tramping and then the sponson bounce increasing until she finally took off. As Bluebird was completing her gyrations, Leo punched Robbie in the ribs and shouted, 'Quick, the skipper's in trouble!' With that, the line was cut free by Geoff Hallawell and the Fairline raced towards K7's stricken hull. She sank before they got there...

Hello . . . Tango to Base, Tango to Base, OVER

Base to Tango, OVER . . . Base to Tango, OVER

Tango to Base . . . Tango To Base . . . Complete accident I'm afraid . . . OVER

Er roger, er details? OVER

No details as yet, no details . . . STAND BY

Within seconds of Bluebird sinking, Donald's lifejacket and what looked like his silver crash helmet bobbed up onto the lake's surface. After managing to get close, Geoff grabbed at the silver object. It wasn't Donald's crash helmet, it was a sponson now devoid of its blue fairings. As he reached out to grip the heavy object, he overbalanced and toppled into the icy water. He was quickly hauled back into the boat and went forward into the cabin to try to dry off. The sponson was lashed to the boat and the search continued. Robbie got on the radio to contact Base to ask them to organise some divers. The call was logged at 8.58.

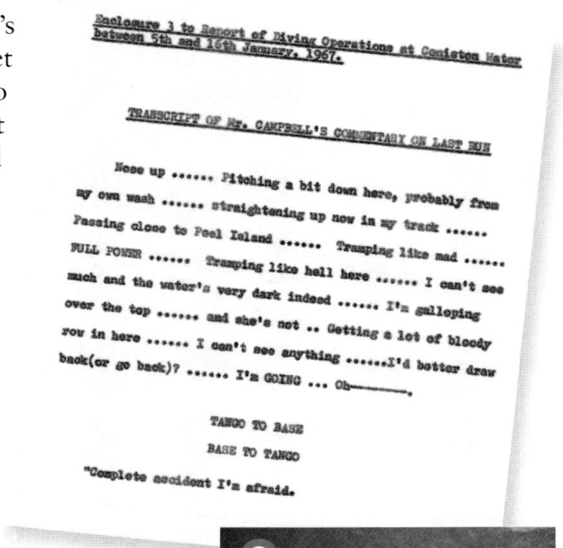

Enclosure 3 to Report of Diving Operations at Coniston Water between 5th and 16th January, 1967.

TRANSCRIPT OF Mr. CAMPBELL'S COMMENTARY ON LAST RUN

Nose up ...... Pitching a bit down here, probably from my own wash ...... straightening up now in my track ...... Passing close to Peel Island ...... Tramping like mad ...... FULL POWER ...... Tramping like hell here ...... I can't see much and the water's very dark indeed ...... I'm galloping over the top ...... and she's not .. Getting a lot of bloody row in here ...... I can't see anything ......I'd better draw back(or go back)? ...... I'm GOING ... Oh————.

TANGO TO BASE

BASE TO TANGO

"Complete accident I'm afraid.

Bluebird dives back into the water.
Note vapour coming from the jet-pipe.
© Mirror Pix and Authors collection

Impact.
© Author's Collection

The severed main hull of K7 moments before sinking.
© Express Newspapers

Leo's Fairline searches in vain.
© Author's Collection

By 9.20, divers had been located and were on their way from Barrow. Piece by piece, debris floated to the surface – Donald's silver jet-pilot's helmet, breathing mask and mic, his red socks, his fur-lined suede boots, a driving glove, and his leather helmet containing the RT headset. Finally, Donald's mascot, Mr Whoppit, appeared on the surface, still wearing his miniature blue overalls.

On the shoreline, the onlookers stared across the lake at the two cruisers circling the crash site. There had been anguished cries when Bluebird took off, but now they watched in silence. Back at the slipway, where the scale of the accident had not been fully appreciated, David Benson of the *Daily Express* tried to reassure others about Donald's fate, pointing out that he had 30 minutes of air on board Bluebird when she sunk. Some thought his survival plausible, those who had been on the lake shore already knew the truth: Donald could not have survived an accident of such ferocity. By now, shortly after 9.30, the worst fears began to be reported. The telephone in the caravan became a hotline for journalists filing their copy with their editors. The news soon hit the airwaves.

Andrew Brown and Norman Buckley entered the yard and made for the caravan. They were going to phone Tonia to break the terrible news. Even this private phone call was filmed by a TV news crew, the story being simply too big for them to ignore. (The broadcaster in question, Rediffusion, was

Below: Bluebird's wrecked port sponson.
© Norman Hurst

Below Centre: Leo's grim task – bringing parts of the wrecked K7 ashore.
© Mirrorpix

Below Right:
A heartbroken Leo is lead away from the Lake by Andrew Brown (L) and Keith Harrison (R)
© Mirrorpix

understandably criticised for this intrusion and offered a full and unreserved apology shortly afterwards.)

Daughter Gina heard of her father's accident in a telephone call from her mother (Donald's first wife). She was working in Switzerland at the Park Hotel in Arosa. When she was unexpectedly told there was a call for her from England, she knew instantly what it meant. 'It's strange, but it never crossed my mind that it might be good news,' she said later.

The Fairlines and the BBC camera boat cruised around the accident site until Dr Darbishire and Maurie went out in the Jetstar to meet Leo's boat mid-morning. Leo transferred to the Jetstar and was brought ashore. Keith Harrison's boat

NORMAN LUCK ON DONALD CAMPBELL

'Everyone had turned up. Bluebird was peeping out of the boathouse, Campbell was clearly frustrated that the attempt had taken so long to co-ordinate. My usual station was at the northern kilo marker down the lake and I barely had time to get in position when I saw Bluebird being launched. It seemed that Campbell was determined to get on with it. Many of the usual meticulous safety checks seemed to be scrapped as he piloted Bluebird to the starting point at the head of the lake.

Then suddenly over the radio came the signal that Bluebird was up and running – a beautiful sight on full plane as it powered past us on the epic voyage. After the first run, it was total confusion. The radios crackled and excited voices confirmed the speed and that this could be the moment when history was made. The signal came that Campbell had turned and was starting his return run.

Bluebird came into view, nose up at full speed with only the tail-plane skimming the choppy surface of the lake and suddenly it happened. It was as if Campbell had predicted days before, as the nose bucked into the loop and jack-knifed into the murky water.

I was in total shock. I scanned the water for the bobbing figure of Campbell coming to the surface. There was total silence. The only objects bobbing on the surface were the air filled bags used for buoyancy in the fractured hull of Bluebird. Minutes went by and it became clear that Campbell had failed in his dream to be the first man over 300mph on water.

Later that night I found myself driving across the Pennines with the ITN film to the RAF Bomber Command HQ in Huntingdon where experts were asked to analyse each frame to help determine the cause of the crash.'

Far left: Andrew Brown and Norman Buckley examine Bluebird's wrecked sponsons.
© *Mirrorpix*

Left: Clive Glynn carrying one of Bluebird 's sponson fairings.
© P. Allonby

Bluebird's port sponson and its upper fairing.
© P. Allonby

The wrecked sponsons. Donald's E-Type is in the background.
© Mirrorpix

PAUL ALLONBY ON DONALD CAMPBELL

'On the day of the fateful run, I thought the weather was doubtful, so I phoned ahead and spoke to Clive Glynn who told me that there was not going to be a run at first light as there was a slight breeze and that lake conditions were not suitable.

I decided to go along a little later and when I did it was all over, Bluebird had crashed, and everyone was walking around in a daze and I had missed photographing Donald leave the jetty. I was told later by the northern editor of the LEP, Harry Griffin, that 12 countries were waiting on the line for my pictures!

A few years ago I travelled to Spain with a journalist to interview Brian Wilson – I was by this time a TV cameraman. Brian was the cameraman for Border TV who actually shot the colour footage of the two final runs. He told us that he too had phoned Clive that morning and was told the same story but had felt uneasy about it, so had travelled to Coniston anyway. When he arrived on the east side of the lake, he came across the ITN cameraman who was cooking breakfast and who invited Brian to join him. It was while they were in the middle of their bacon and eggs that they heard the distinctive engine of Bluebird being fired up. Dropping everything, they set up their equipment just in time to record the event. Had Brian continued down the lake to his usual position he would not have got the footage which became part of the documentary The Price of a Record.

I often think how different it would be today, the solitary phone in the caravan by the slipway, totally inadequate, replaced by individual mobile phones. Photographers would send their pictures within seconds of the event direct to the news desks around the world, likewise TV picture via scanners and satellites, Bluebird would probably have numerous cameras on board and there would be certainly better communications with the cockpit.

But for all this, the 1967 attempt was unique, no media circus, just a regular bunch of "snappers and hacks" who were privileged to be able to record the last few weeks in the life of a very brave man.'

had collected the other sponson. Geoff Hallawell now moved across to Keith's boat. The sponson he had salvaged was fastened to the third course boat along with the sponson recovered by Harrison, to be towed ashore. Harrison had also found a sponson rear fairing, which he hauled aboard his boat.

Leo had given up all hope for Donald. Arriving back at the boathouse, he was mobbed by pressmen. He looked pale and crumpled – a broken man, for whom the activities on the lake were no longer of any interest.

At the slipway, the pieces of wrecked boat brought ashore were left on the rails or the jetty – the sponsons, sponson fairing and then the cockpit seat, which brought home the awful realisation that nobody would see Donald again.

At lunchtime, back at the Sun the story was unfolding on the television news. Both the ITV and BBC footage of the fatal run was played and those who had been at the jetty were able the see the full horror of the crash for the first time.

The divers from Barrow realised that they did not have the specialist equipment to dive down the 140+ feet to the bed of the lake where Bluebird had sunk. The Royal Navy were contacted. They agreed to send a team of divers, who were expected to arrive in the village later that evening.

Far left: Leo, Maurie, Clive and Louis examine the salvaged sponsons on the slipway, in front of the empty boathouse.
© PA

Upper Left: Donald's E-Type where he had parked it that morning.
© Mirrorpix

Lower Left: Donald's coat lies on the passenger seat.
© Mirrorpix

The recovery of Donald's body was now the priority. Subdued groups gathered, reminiscing about the man who had brought them to Coniston in the first place. Pressmen had been drawn by his dogged, never-give-up patriotic attitude, his ability to have everyone in stitches of laughter and to be the centre of attention. His close colleagues remembered his friendship, his vulnerability, but above all his immense bravery; they also knew they would miss him terribly. They returned to the slipway and remained at the boat shed until light faded, but there was nothing except emptiness.

Leo was shattered, tired and bereft, yet he carried on with dignity, doing his duty as he saw it. He made the 60-mile trek to the TV studios in Carlisle to appear live on *24 Hours* late that evening. He faced the cameras out of loyalty to Donald, his friend, not arriving back at Coniston until 2.00 a.m. the next day.

TONY JAMES ON DONALD CAMPBELL

'When the news of the accident came through to my office early on the morning of 4 January, I felt a deep sense of loss. There were those who said at the time that being proud of being British was an outmoded concept. There are still those who say it today. Donald was a patriot and prepared to put his life on the line.

I said earlier that Donald was a legendary figure, so he was, but there was warmth, humour and a real concern for those helping him achieve his goal. Subsequent attempts to break records on land have been high-tech, high-cost endeavours, which the Brits have excelled in. Long may that continue. My only regret is that Donald is not here to see and applaud them.

Much has been written by others concerning the technical aspect of the attempt and all sorts of theories put forward to explain the tragic accident that befell Donald and Bluebird. At the end of the day, it was one very brave man against the elements.'

CHAPTER 9
'HE BELIEVED IN THE POTENTIAL OF BRITAIN...'

Donald Campbell's life had ended spectacularly, as he always thought it might, and with as much publicity as if a head of state had died. Evening papers, both local and in London, Manchester and other large cities, all carried the same front-page news story about the Coniston crash.

In the aftermath of the accident, there were only two things that mattered to the Bluebird team – finding Donald's body, and identifying the cause of the tragedy. Ken and Lewis Norris had travelled up from Sussex the previous day. They now got to work, together with John Stollery from Imperial College, to try to understand why the accident had occurred. Ken Norris believed that Donald would have been killed outright as K7 plunged back into Coniston Water after her brief flight. He also suspected that the 'g' forces Donald was subjected to as Bluebird completed her back-flip would have caused him to lose consciousness prior to impact. They interviewed eyewitnesses, including Leo, Anthony Robinson, Norman Buckley, Andrew Brown, Dr Darbishire and Keith Harrison, to build up a picture of what conditions were like on the final run. The general opinion was that the measured distance itself was still quite calm, although they had no knowledge of what water conditions were like further down the lake. Keith Harrison remarked that Bluebird's starboard sponson was at least a foot clear of the water as it passed him going into the measured kilometre

CLIVE GLYNN ON DONALD CAMPBELL

'Later, Louis and I had the horrible task of hauling ashore the pieces of wreckage the support boats brought back. That was when it really hit home. It was my first experience of this sort of thing, and I just felt numb. I also noticed the silence. We seemed to do things automatically for the next few days, and then it was all over and I returned south in the Land Rover I had brought to Coniston 9 weeks earlier.'

on that last run. He had not seen Bluebird do that before. Leo remarked that Bluebird had been tramping quite noticeably before she took off. But what no one had been a direct witness to, and what would hold the key to what happened, were the events that unsettled Bluebird before she entered the measured distance.

The ten-man Royal Navy diving team from HMS *Safeguard* in Rosyth, Scotland, led by Lt Cdr John Futcher, had arrived late the previous evening. They set up base at the slipway early that morning in preparation for their first attempt to locate Donald and Bluebird.

Daily Sketch.
© Author's Collection

Daily Mirror.
© Author's Collection

The divers commenced their search at 12.30. Futcher believed that Donald's body would be either at the point of impact, in the main wreckage of the boat, or at a point between the two locations.

The first three dives that afternoon found small pieces of wreckage, indicating the team was on the right track. On the fourth dive, the main hull of K7 was found in 142 feet of water, some 130 feet east of her track, resting in her correct attitude but facing south east.

A more detailed search was impossible as the divers had only a hand-held torch. With such limited illumination, the jagged metal of Bluebird's broken hull posed an unacceptable risk. Lady Campbell, Donald's mother, and his sister Jean observed diving operations from the boathouse and later in the afternoon from the lake shore.

Earlier that day, a lone RAF Vulcan piloted by Sqn Ldr Don Dale had diverted from its specified course and flown down the lake at 2,000 feet, dipping its wings three times. As Dale recounted later, his salute was dedicated to 'a very brave man who had just lost his life.'

All the newspapers that morning had placed the accident squarely on the front page, with headlines ranging from '300mph to disaster' (*Daily Mirror*), 'Bluebird's leap of death' (*Daily Express*) and 'Beyond the limit' (*Daily Sketch*) to a more factual tone – 'Campbell killed, 200 yards from triumph' (*Daily Mail*). They made much of the final words Donald had spoken over the intercom, although many editors saw fit to embellish the commentary with phrases like 'the water's not good and I'm on my back'. The game of patience that Donald had played the previous evening, and his premonition of his own death, also featured prominently. In addition, there was speculation as to how fast Bluebird was travelling when she left the water, with some suggesting that Bluebird was doing 300mph and others putting the figure as high as 320mph.

Tonia had travelled to the Lakes the previous day with her manager, Mel Collins, after the *Daily Mirror* arranged a private flight at short notice. She stayed with Norman Buckley and his wife at their home on the shores of Lake Windermere. She was preparing to travel over to Coniston that morning when she suffered a recurrence of a previous heart problem. She was visited by a doctor and advised not to make the journey that day.

In the late afternoon, snow flurries began to fall over the lake. With the light fading, diving operations were suspended for the rest of the day.

BILL VANRYNE ON DONALD CAMPBELL

'After the Christmas and New Year holidays, I was back in the laboratory at Rotax, when news of the accident came through, on that morning of 4 January. My colleagues and I were, of course, deeply shocked and saddened. We regarded Donald as a patriot, a great believer in Britain and in British achievement. Today, Donald is an icon, revered by many, and not just of my age, but younger generations who still admire his drive and courage and what he was trying to achieve.

Looking back over the years, I have been fortunate to attend many annual meetings of the K7 Club where I made friends with those who were involved with Donald's record-breaking Bluebird ventures. The days I spent at Coniston working alongside Donald were very special. I shall never forget them.'

Friday
6 January

Weather:
Biting cold wind and snow flurries

The first two dives that morning were carried out to ascertain if Donald's body was in or near the remains of Bluebird's main hull. Underwater lighting equipment was now being utilised to make the divers' task less hazardous, but conditions on the silt-covered lake bed meant that visibility was still limited, especially when the lake bottom was disturbed. No sign of

Above Right: The divers continue their heroic search.
© Mirrorpix

Above Right: Do you remember when Donald...? *L - R:* Joan Villa, Lady Dorothy Campbell, Leo, Jean Wales, Charles Wales and Maurie reminisce over lunch at the Sun Hotel.
© Rex Features

Donald's body was found. The dive team discovered that Bluebird had broken in two behind the cockpit, which was now no longer attached to the main hull.

After locating Bluebird's hull, Futcher decided to devote the rest of the day's diving operations to working back along the trail of the wreckage. Three more dives were carried out, producing small fragments of Bluebird, but a fourth dive hit an area clear of wreckage. Moving the search 60 feet to the west relocated the line the boat had taken. This was the last dive of the day, and there were still no clues as to the whereabouts of Donald's body.

Having recovered from her illness, Tonia now made the journey to Coniston to observe the search operation. The snow had continued to fall and she stood for several long minutes by the northern timing station, looking across the lake to where the divers were working. She thanked Lt Cdr Futcher and his team when the fading light brought them back to shore. 'I am very grateful for what you are doing,' she told them. Later that evening, after a visit to the bungalow, she was driven back to London.

On the Saturday morning, the front page of the *Daily Express* featured two photographs of the wreck of Bluebird lying on the lake bed. The paper had hired a 37-year-old professional diver named Peter Joel to photograph the boat using a special underwater camera. He captured an image of Bluebird's main rear spar on the port side and her tail fin complete with Union Jack. The report also commented that K7 was largely intact aft of the cockpit.

Saturday
7 January to
Monday
16 January

Further dives were made and minor pieces of wreckage recovered. In the early afternoon, while diving at a point 280 feet south west of the main hull, the broken steering wheel was found, still attached to the steering column and steering box. Futcher identified this as the probable point of impact. Accordingly, the rest of the day was spent searching the same area, but Donald's body was not found. Bluebird's instrument panel and parts of the light aluminium internal cockpit structure were recovered and brought ashore.

The next day, the broken steering wheel, complete with attached assemblies, was also brought back to land.

Although the search was extended 200 feet further south, there were no more signs of wreckage or of Donald's body. Ken Norris had done some calculations based on the point of impact and the sinking position. He told Futcher that these could not be more than 400 feet apart, given the maximum estimated speed when the crash happened and the time and thus distance taken to decelerate to 0mph and sink. This information confirmed Futcher's search area.

On Monday 9th, Futcher took the search north to cover an area where two splashes appeared on still photographs taken by *Sun* photographer Michael Brennan. This search yielded two pieces of wreckage.

On Tuesday and Wednesday, the search continued along the central line of travel between the impact point and the area where Bluebird had sunk, but extending this line to the east and west. On Tuesday evening, a memorial service was held at St Andrew's Church in the village. Leo, his wife, Maurie and other team members, Norman Buckley, Andrew Brown and Dr Darbishire, pressmen, Lt Cdr the Hon. Greville Howard (representing the Campbell family), police officers, the local fire brigade and villagers all came to pay their last respects and tribute to Donald Campbell.

The lesson was read by Norman Buckley, and the Revd John Hancock, Vicar of St Andrews, gave the address:

'Donald Campbell was a man of determination who had surmounted delays and difficulties which must have been tiresome. He was courageous but knew what he was undertaking and took no irresponsible decisions. He was a great patriot and believed in the potential of Britain – that there was nothing the country could not achieve, if she put her mind to it. It was in demonstrating this belief that he lost his life.'

The congregation sang Donald's favourite hymn, 'God be in my head, and in my understanding'.

On Wednesday evening, with nothing of further significance having been found, Futcher was about to abandon the search. Before he could announce his decision, however, he was asked to view film taken by a Tyne Tees cameraman from a vantage point north of the measured kilometre, looking south. This gave a more complete picture of the accident than the BBC or ITN footage, which essentially showed a side view as Bluebird took off.

Crash search area.
© Author's Collection

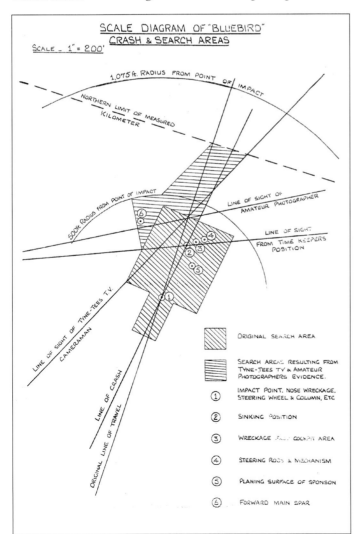

On Thursday 12 January, John Futcher travelled to the Border TV studios at Carlisle with Leo, where they viewed the film frame by frame. It showed an object emerging from the spray after the initial impact which they estimated was the approximate size and shape of a human body. Futcher decided to continue the search until the object was found. Leo was less optimistic that it was Donald. The splash point where the object hit the water was not visible in the film, but Ken Norris calculated the possible trajectory and this information was communicated to Futcher in a telephone call, Norris having already returned south to continue with crash analysis at Haywards Heath. A new search area was identified and the next day systematic diving continued, but without success. In the early afternoon of the following Saturday, an amateur photographer came forward with footage of the crash that showed the splash point for the object. The search was narrowed down and on Sunday 15th the object was located. It turned out to be the forward spar that connected the sponsons to the hull in front of the cockpit.

Futcher now had no option but to abandon the search, so the disappointed divers returned to their base at HMS *Safeguard* on the evening of Monday 16 January. The search had covered the entire crash area, including the cause of every splash shown on the available film material from ITN, the BBC and Tyne Tees. (It is not clear whether the colour Border film for the Four Companies documentary, filmed south of the measured kilometre, was made available. The actual documentary, *The Price of a Record*, was not shown until June that year.)

John Futcher paid tribute to his team, praising their efforts to locate Donald's body under extremely difficult circumstances. For the first seven days of the search, the weather had been bitterly cold and on several mornings the surface of the lake at the northern end was frozen to a thickness of a quarter of an inch. The depth of water in the search area varied between 130 and 142 feet. All light from the surface was absorbed by the time 70 feet was reached, and the bed of the lake consisted of thick mud with a 1-foot layer of fine silt on top. Any movement near the bottom caused a disturbance of this fine silt, making it billow up around the diver and totally obscuring everything.

Shortly after the Navy search was called off, the boathouse was dismantled and Leo and Maurie headed back to Surrey.

The lone cradle left on the slipway.
© Leo Villa's Film and Picture Archive

On 18 January, the *Daily Express* published an analysis of Bluebird's two final runs, assisted by RAF photographic experts. On the first north–south run, when Bluebird averaged 297.6mph, the RAF suggested that the peak speed achieved was 320mph, but by the end of the measured kilometre Campbell had decelerated to around 280mph. The water-brake had been applied south of the measured distance to help slow K7 down.

On the return run, K7 reached a peak of 328mph just before entering the measured kilometre, decelerating to around 300mph as she passed the first marker boat. When she took off, Bluebird was travelling at less than 290mph, well below the average of the first run.

Ken Norris was intimately involved with every aspect of the RAF crash investigation on which the *Express* article was based. He stated that at 300mph the take-off angle was calculated to be 6°. A 2-foot lift on the starboard sponson, which had been noted as K7 travelled into and then through the measured kilometre, would give the equivalent of 4° at the centre of the boat. The question was, what had caused the boat to rise the extra 6 inches that made it take off? The *Express* speculated that Bluebird had hit a piece of submerged driftwood, citing evidence of two large indentations in the starboard stabilising fin. It went on to say that, rendered unstable by the impact, the boat then ran into its own wash, which was sufficient to lift it above the critical safety angle. No mention was made of the flame-out of the engine on the first of the two runs, or that the engine could have possibly flamed-out on the return run as it was throttled back. The report concluded that Campbell had sensed he was out of control and had lifted his foot from the accelerator, since there was no thrust disturbance from the jet-pipe when Bluebird was standing on her tail above the water. The engine had actually flamed-out on the return run as it was either throttled back or starved of air as Bluebird bounced free of the water before her brief flight. (Photographic evidence appeared to indicate that the Orpheus, which had been set up for continuous ignition, tried to relight itself as it completed its loop. A stream of unburnt kerosene could be seen issuing from the jet-pipe.)

The accident had been caused by a combination of circumstances which Donald and Bluebird were capable of overcoming in isolation, but not together. The result was the destruction of the fastest boat the world had ever seen.

On 22 January, John Futcher wrote a personal letter to Leo Villa at his home in Surrey. In it, he said:

Items recovered from the lake and left at Coniston police station.
© Author's Collection

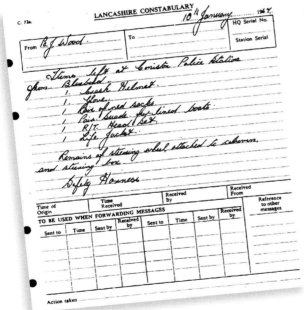

'I was terribly disappointed to have to leave Coniston without having found Mr Campbell's body, but after thoroughly searching the crash area and investigating under and finding the cause of every known splash, the only thing I could have done, even looking at it in retrospect, was to have started a systematic search of the whole lake.

'I sincerely hope, Leo, that the shock and personal grief you suffered as a result of the disaster is gradually being dimmed, and now that you are back in your own home, you'll be able to pick up the threads of your life and continue with the project in which Mr Campbell had placed so much hope. You can in no way whatsoever blame yourself for the accident, indeed if Donald had listened to you, he would have been alive today. I know you know this, and I am sure every other thinking person knows it also. However, this gives little relief when the loss is so personal.'

It would transpire, thirty-four years later, that the diving team had missed finding Donald Campbell's body by a relatively small distance. A more complete analysis of the course of the accident also became possible when new evidence came to light after Bluebird was recovered from the lake bed in March 2001 by Bill Smith and his Bluebird Project Team.

Coniston returned to its winter slumber, the boathouse site was cleared of any debris and the media spotlight shifted to other stories. The village was left to grieve in peace. As a stark reminder of Donald and Bluebird, the wheeled launching cradle was left on the slipway, before eventually being towed to its head and remaining there for the next thirteen years. The specially equipped Land Rover was found a new home at local Land Rover agent Hadwins in Torver Village, just down the road. Plans were made to erect a memorial to

Donald on the village green in Coniston, made of local slate in the form of an offset cross with a bench seat.

An all-party House of Commons motion sponsored by six Members of Parliament asked for public recognition in his memory. On 28 January 1967, it was announced in the *London Gazette* that Donald had been awarded the Queen's Commendation for Brave Conduct for his courage and determination in attacking the Water Speed Record. There were many who felt that this award was insufficient, that Donald deserved greater recognition, but as his actions did not involve saving a life he could not be awarded the George Cross or the Albert Medal, the two highest honours available as posthumous awards for brave civilians. A knighthood, which many felt he deserved following his success in 1964, could not be awarded posthumously.

On 23 February 1967, a memorial service for Donald Campbell CBE was held at St Martin-in-the-Fields in central London. Tonia, Gina, Lady Campbell and Donald's sister, Jean, were among the 500 relatives and friends who attended the event. The Duke of Edinburgh and the Prime Minister were represented, members of the Bluebird team from previous attempts in the UK, USA and Australia were there, as well as everyone who had supported Donald during his last attempt in Coniston. Tonia sat with Leo and the team, Gina with her aunt and grandmother. Donald's solicitor, Victor Mishcon, delivered the address:

The Royal Parish Church of
ST. MARTIN-IN-THE-FIELDS

A SERVICE OF
THANKSGIVING AND PRAYER
for
DONALD CAMPBELL,
C.B.E.
Queen's Commendation for Brave Conduct
23rd March, 1921
4th January, 1967

THURSDAY, 23rd FEBRUARY, 1967
at 12 noon

Service of Thanksgiving.
© C. Glynn

'Speed is not the only thing that manages to break through barriers. Amongst nations and amongst various sections of the community within a nation, amongst all creeds and colours, outstanding courage and outstanding character break through barriers too, of boundaries, languages, cultures and classes. Donald Malcolm Campbell did not break the sound barrier on land or sea but he broke those more important barriers during his all too brief life, so that we who are gathered here today are but a few of those who loved and honoured him, and who now mourn him in their many thousands in these islands, in the United States of America, in Australia and throughout the length and breadth of the world where the spirit of adventure and bravery still thrill the blood of man. "And thou shalt love the Lord thy God with all thine heart, and with all thy soul, and with all thy might." These are sacred words in the house of God, often heard as they are in the place where I usually worship. If ever a man gave himself with all his heart and soul and might it was Donald Campbell. So did he love his God, so did he love his Queen and country, so did he love his ever-loyal team with its Leo Villa and the lady whom they called

Fred [Tonia]. So did he love the cause of human progress for which in his own field he was prepared to devote and indeed sacrifice his life. So did he love and cherish the memory of his father. So did he love people. Humbly but proudly, as a friend amongst other friends of his do I pay my tribute to him today in the presence of distinguished personages including representatives of His Royal Highness the Duke of Edinburgh and the Prime Minister and before members of his family including his wife, his daughter, his mother and his sister. Britain and the world have such need of the indomitable spirit, the sheer determination, the unconquerable determination he had. Our poet Tennyson might have written of Donald Campbell as he wrote of another:

> "Such was he: his work is done.
> But while the races of mankind endure,
> Let his great example stand
> Colossal, seen of every land,
> And keep the soldier firm, the statesman pure;
> Till in all lands and thro' all human story
> The path of duty be the way to glory.'"

A research fellowship to endow a seat into the study of aerodynamics was established at Imperial College, London, to perpetuate Donald's memory. The fellowship ran until 1973. Some years later, the wind tunnel where so much research had been carried out on both K7 and CN7 was renamed the Donald Campbell Low Speed Wind Tunnel in his memory.

On 21 March, the Home Secretary announced that there would be no inquest into the death of Donald Campbell. There were sufficient witnesses to testify that he had been killed in his Bluebird hydroplane on Coniston Water.

On 3 April, a £25,000 insurance cheque (today's equivalent: £360,000) was sent to the estate of Donald Campbell, minus a debit for the amount of £500 to cover the annual insurance premium on the Bluebird K7 hydroplane, which was unpaid at the time of the accident. Lloyd's of London and the insurance syndicate that had covered Bluebird agreed to pay out, notwithstanding the fact that the premium was late. On 20 June 1967, it was announced that Donald's estate had been finally valued at £38,066 gross (today's equivalent: £548,150) but only £10,677 net (today's equivalent: £153,750).

On 10 June 1967, Leo Villa was awarded the OBE for services to record-breaking. On 20 July, at a ceremony at the RAC Club on Pall Mall in central London, Donald was posthumously awarded his fourth Segrave Trophy. Tonia accepted the award and used her speech to rebuke those who had believed Donald was scared at Coniston and who had paid little attention to his efforts before his death, but afterwards praised him as a hero.

'Many people today see Donald as a big hero, but to say it today is one thing, to have said it yesterday, when he was there to hear it, was a much more important thing. The Segrave Trophy was given to Donald three times while he was alive and I know how happy he was. This honour goes to the Bluebird team and their skipper. Thank you in his name.'

There were Segrave gold medals for Leo Villa, Ken Norris, Lewis Norris, Maurice Parfitt, Tony James and John Stollery. Framed copies of the citation went to Louis Goossens, Ken Reaks, Jack Lavis and Ken Pearson.

Twenty-one days earlier, on 30 June, American Lee Taylor had finally broken Donald's 1964 WSR with a new two-way average of 285.213mph in his jet boat, Hustler, at Lake Guntersville, Alabama. The American threat that Donald had spoken of one year earlier had not been a figment of his imagination. Although he no longer held the official World Speed Record, Campbell's peak speed of 328mph, achieved on that final run, lived on in the record books for another ten years as the highest speed ever achieved on water. It was finally eclipsed in October 1978 by Australian Ken Warby, when he averaged 317.596mph to set the current Water Speed Record with a pass through the kilometre on his second run at over 329mph.

On the second weekend in November 1968, the K7 Club gathered in Coniston for their annual meeting at the Sun Hotel. On the Sunday 10 November 1968, the slate memorial to Donald Campbell was unveiled by Lady Campbell on the village green at Coniston. Villagers had raised £300, with contributions also coming from the K7 Club. Some 200 villagers and members of the K7 Club, as well as family members, attended the unveiling.

'Who says Campbell's not popular?'

Courage is not the act of going quickly; it is the act of knowing what could happen and then carrying on anyway. Campbell never forgot the Utah crash or the crash that destroyed Bluebird K4 in 1951 or, for that matter, the nightmare drive at Lake Eyre when he finally took the LSR. He was not without imagination. Campbell talked about death because he lived with it, *not* because he wanted to die. He knew there was no safety net when he walked out onto the tightrope. Everything depended on him, and him alone, he *had* to perform. That brought with it pressure – it meant that he would eventually have to take what he once described as 'a thoroughly unjustified risk'.

On that cold Wednesday morning, in the eyes of the uninformed he did just that, and he paid the ultimate price. But at the same time the legend of Donald Campbell was born.

Top left: The memorial before the unveiling ceremony.
© A.E. James

Top right: Anthony Robinson, Lady Campbell, Betty Buckley and Norman Buckley at the unveiling of the memorial.
© W. Vanryne

Above left: Leo Villa, Andrew Brown, Joan Villa and Norman Buckley.
© A.E. James

Above right: The memorial plaque revealed.
© A.E. James

Like the death of John F. Kennedy, everybody knew where they were and what were doing when they heard of Donald Campbell and Bluebird's demise. He was the Ayrton Senna of his day, pushing the boundaries of what was possible. The manner of his passing immortalised him. That day is now almost 45 years ago, yet the memory of Britain's last and greatest speed king lives on.

Donald Campbell never really left the public consciousness. Rather, he remained latent in the memory of a generation who never forgot his achievements or the grainy black and white film that recorded the accident. They remembered that he was intensely patriotic, that he was incredibly determined – and that he was in possession of quite exceptional courage.

His close family, friends and colleagues and the people of Coniston protected his memory and commemorated each anniversary of his passing, but in terms of the wider world he drifted from sight as one generation gave way to the next.

And then a strange thing happened.

The light of his memory, which flickered precariously for the first twenty years after his death, grew a little brighter. First the BBC cast Sir Anthony Hopkins to play him with considerable aplomb in a prime-time TV drama.

The light grew brighter.

Coniston Water. The calm after the storm.
© Leo Villa's Film and Picture Archive

Then the Internet came along and linked like-minded enthusiasts who never knew of their shared interest.

The light grew brighter.

In late 2000, Bill Smith, an amateur diver from Newcastle, contacted Gina Campbell to tell her of his plan to locate Bluebird. She wished him well, and didn't think much more about it. Months passed and then Bill contacted Gina again to report his success. Gina visited Coniston to meet the dive team. She told Bill that he would have to recover K7 from the lake bed and, much more importantly, find her father before the information got into the public domain. The Rawden Smith Trust, owners of the lake bed, gave permission and the main wreckage of Bluebird was recovered from Coniston Water on 8 March 2001. In the following months, in a quite remarkable operation, other parts of Bluebird, including the shattered front end, were recovered.

Finally, after a heroic search, Donald's body was located on 28 May 2001 just to the east of one of the areas that Lt Cdr Futcher and the Royal Navy divers had searched 34 years earlier. The well-preserved remains were placed in a blue casket and lifted to the surface. Draped in a Union flag, they were brought ashore in Gina's presence. She greatly valued the fact that her father's body had been recovered with absolute respect and dignity, and could now be given a proper funeral. Gina wanted it to be a celebration of Donald Campbell's life – 'I want people to say "Wow!"'

The funeral took place in typical 'Campbell at Coniston' weather of torrential rain on 12 September 2001. St Andrew's Church was packed to capacity and hundreds of well-wishers also gathered outside, eager to pay their respects. Donald was then laid to rest in Coniston's cemetery.

The light was now shining.

Plans were made to restore Bluebird to her former glory. More than 80 per cent of the original fabric of the boat was recovered. Bill Smith and a team of dedicated engineers, metalworkers and enthusiasts have come together to restore Bluebird to full working order. Sometime in 2013, she will go on display in a purpose-built wing at the Ruskin Museum in Coniston and be demonstrated in her element, on Coniston Water.

Who says Campbell's not popular now? After an absence of 34 years, Donald Campbell and Bluebird made front-page headlines once again. Bill will at some stage write his own account of the 'Bluebird Project' – this is not the place to comment further, save to say that he has shown huge respect for the memory of Donald Campbell. I salute his tenacity, determination and his engineering prowess. Thanks to him and a small but hugely dedicated band of supporters, a British engineering icon will be preserved so that future generations can be touched and inspired by the story of Donald Campbell and Bluebird.

The renewed interest in Donald's achievements brought enthusiasts out of the shadows, and new friends and acquaintances were made. New information came into the public domain and discussions started about what had actually happened on that fateful day in January 1967. One such enthusiast was Dr Keith Mitchell, a retired physicist from Newcastle, with whom I entered into correspondence in early 2009. We shared theories and information, learning much from each other over the following two years.

When I decided to write this book in May 2010, I thought I should only go ahead if I could add something to the story, whether new facts or new images. I also decided that I would require both Gina's and Tonia's blessing, for the book I had in mind would concentrate on the last 18 months of Donald Campbell's life and I wanted to respect their opinions, given the subject I was about to document. Both were very generous in their support.

Armed with access to over 300 largely unpublished images, some from press agencies but many from unseen private collections, and the promise of help from many people who were close to the attempt in 1966/67, I decided to press ahead. I realised at the same time that one person was eminently well qualified to write the final chapter – the analysis of the accident – and provide the detail I required: Dr Keith Mitchell.

I am grateful that Keith agreed to undertake the task. I asked Tony James, who played a key role in Ken Norris' post-crash investigation, if he would mind if I gave Keith his contact details so they could discuss his initial research. That was in June 2010. I suspect they were in contact with each other pretty much every other day for the next eight months, developing their analysis! I feel enormously privileged to have had the help of these two fine gentlemen with this project. The final chapter would not have been possible without them.

It is their chapter that now follows. I hope you will agree that it is a fitting tribute to a great man, and a total vindication of the way Donald Campbell conducted himself on that day as he went about the final record attempt.

DONALD CAMPBELL CBE
A TRIBUTE BY ANTHONY 'ROBBIE' ROBINSON, FRIEND AND TEAM MEMBER

We are here today in unique circumstances, it being more than 34 years since Donald Campbell lost his life on Lake Coniston. That the circumstances are unique is quite appropriate, as he was indeed a unique man.

He was born on 23 March 1921. The son of Malcolm Campbell, later Sir Malcolm, a legendary figure in motor racing circles in the 1920s and 1930s, and so it was not surprising that he should follow in his father's footsteps.

Donald's record achievements, 7 World Water Speed records, and 1 World Land Speed record, between 1955 and 1967, stand as testament to his success, but they do not tell the complete story of the man behind the public face. They do not tell of the problems and setbacks he had to overcome, and of the determination and courage required achieving them.

Determination was perhaps his greatest attribute, and the one he was to need most over the ensuing years. Having made the decision to continue his father's record-breaking exploits, it was not long before it was tested for the first of many times. He immediately found that Sir Malcolm had already sold some of the boats, engines and equipment, before his death. Perhaps being aware of the dangers of record breaking, he had deliberately tried to put them beyond Donald's reach. If so, he had badly miscalculated his son's determination. He had soon re-purchased them all, and with the faithful Leo Villa, his father's mechanic, at his side, set out to improve his father's records.

continued . . .

The disappointments, set backs and near misses of the next six years would have defeated almost anyone else, but not Donald Campbell. 'The Skipper', as he was affectionately known, was not to be deterred, and in spite of all the problems, by July 1955 he had his first World Water Speed record, 202.32mph.

In continuing his father's record-breaking attempts, he was accepting the patriotic mantle which Sir Malcolm had worn. But this was not the narrow-minded patriotism of the bigot. It was born of the serious conviction that their countrymen had the technical and practical skills to play their part in the advancement of science. And that these achievements were something to be shared, with pride, for the benefit of all mankind.

Similarly, on a personal level, for a man who achieved so much publicly, he was very modest about his success. If I might borrow Leo Villa's words here, 'with Donald it was always a case of "we" never "I."' He was a team man, never happier than when he was one of the boys, in his overalls, with his hands probably covered in oil, day or night. And after a long day he felt quite at home sitting around the kitchen table at the hotel, with his coffee and sandwiches, planning the next day's work. Remaining on the subject of modesty, he would always be the first person to recognise and admire the success and skills of others, be it paying tribute to a successful competitor, or admiring the equestrian skills of his daughter Gina (yes I think he had finally accepted he was not going to make a mechanic of her). And the singing of his wife, Tonia, enthralled him.

His generosity and kindness towards others equally matched his generosity in praise of others. I think you could talk to anyone who knew Donald, and they would be able to recall some kindness or deed he had done for them or someone they knew. I remember being over at Ullswater in the summer of 1955, when a young man lost his life in an accident on the water. The team had been there for many months, and was under considerable pressure, the Bluebird was all ready to run, when the news that a young man had fallen out of a boat and was missing, came through. Donald immediately abandoned the run, and every man, boat and piece of lifesaving equipment was put at the disposal of the rescue services. Donald arranged for a private room at the nearby hotel to be made available for the missing boy's distraught family, and he himself spent time comforting and supporting them while the search continued. Another occasion concerned the vicar here at St Andrew's Church. During a record attempt in 1956 or '57 he had paid his respects to the vicar as was his custom, in order to avoid running Bluebird during church services. As a result of their talk it transpired that the vicar was short of suitable transport to reach some of the more remote and inaccessible corners of his parish. Donald, as ever quick to size up the problem, soon produced one of those shiny motor scooters that were all the fashion at the time, for our vicar to try out. Perhaps it's still hiding somewhere at the back of the garage at the New Vicarage.

If determination was the attribute that gave Donald the drive to see through to the end what he had begun, then his courage was what made it possible each day. Courage is a word we sometimes use too easily, real courage is

continued . . .

. . . continued

a rare commodity. I am aware from personal experience that some of us in his team had become a little blasé about the dangers of record-breaking, particularly with the Bluebird boat. After all, the record attempts had come and gone successfully, seven in all between 1955 and 1964. This was just another attempt that would have a successful outcome. It is only now with the passage of time that we can fully appreciate just how much courage it must have required each time he climbed into the cockpit of the Bluebird boat or car – knowing as he approached record speeds, that in spite of all the research and calculations, it was he who was putting it to the ultimate test, going where no man had ventured before. To do this time after time, year after year, required a level of courage that would be almost beyond the comprehension of most of us. But Donald seemed to do it with consummate ease.

That Coniston should have been chosen as Donald's final resting place is a great honour for us here in the village, but it is also appropriate I believe, for it was a place he came to like and a place where he knew he was welcome. The lake very rarely made things easy for him, and yet that seemed to give him great respect for it. Maybe it was because it did test him so severely at times, that he felt such a closeness to it.

In recent months, since the recovery of Bluebird, many people have talked to me about how they felt, some thought it correct to recover her; others thought it would have been better to leave things as they were. But all, without exception, remembered the friendly, modest man who was her pilot. Some recalled talking to him in one of our pubs, over a pint of beer, others remember the friendly wave as he passed them on the way down to the boathouse, as they were going to school in the morning. Some recalled talking to him on visits he made to the schools here in Coniston, which he always tried to make, as he was a great believer in youth. He recognised that they were the country's future, and needed to be encouraged.

And so, today, as we finally lay to rest 'The Skipper' beside the lake, and in the shadow of our mountains, and close to some of his friends, I believe that he will have found that other Bluebird, the Bluebird of Maeterlinck's play, that Bluebird of eternal happiness that inspired two generations of racing legends.

No man deserves it more.

Anthony Robinson, 12 September 2001

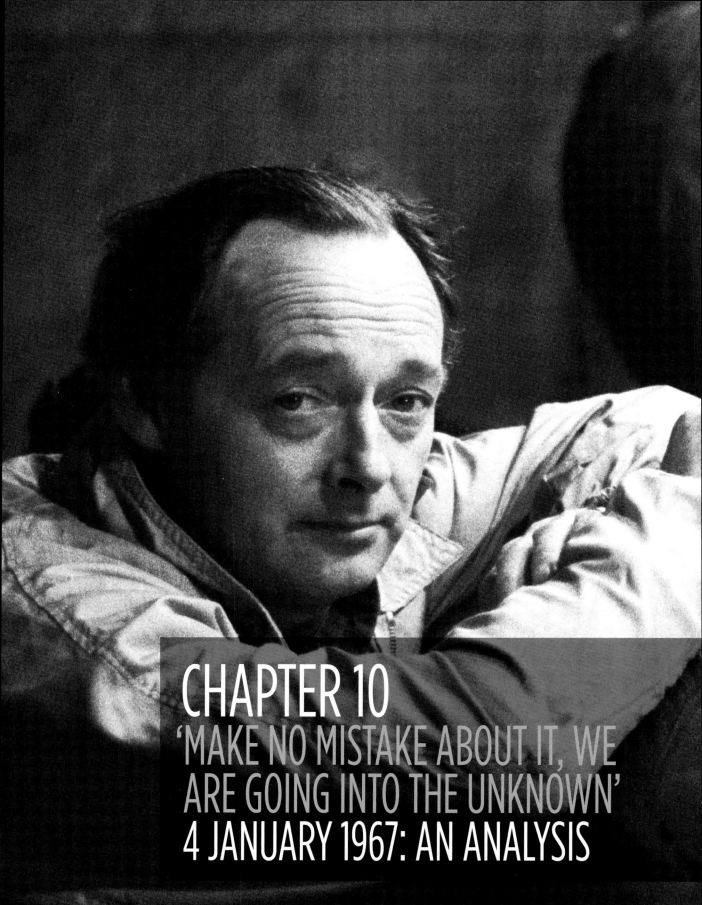

CHAPTER 10
'MAKE NO MISTAKE ABOUT IT, WE ARE GOING INTO THE UNKNOWN'
4 JANUARY 1967: AN ANALYSIS

'Nothing would be done at all, if a man waited till he could do it so well, that no one could find fault with it.'

Cardinal Newman (1801–90)

At the outset of this chapter, it would perhaps be useful to outline my interest in the Bluebird story. I am one of that generation of youngsters in the 1950s and '60s who were profoundly affected by the events and characters surrounding record-breaking. Donald Malcolm Campbell was pre-eminent among our heroes. He was typical of that quintessential 'press-on regardless' spirit which had made the British Empire great and seen us through an unprecedented conflict just a few years earlier. Campbell, with his touch of dash and unshakeable faith in Britain being at the forefront, whether in record-breaking or the design and engineering needed to facilitate it, was an irresistible cocktail to many. That included one youngster predisposed to science and engineering and all things record-breaking, on land, water or in the air . . .

An A-level Maths class at Durham Technical College on the morning of 4 January 1967 was not an edifying place to be. Certainly not one conducive to a lecture on differential calculus, that is. Our teacher was no less the worse for wear than his somewhat unresponsive pupils – excessive libation and its consequences are not only a modern phenomenon! The lecture had just commenced when a late arrival burst into the room bellowing 'Donald Campbell's been killed on Coniston!' He avoided censure because our teacher was as shocked as we were. A sort of deathly pall fell over the room, the intensity of which I can still feel to this day. It also affected the rest of the country and beyond. 'A Day That Shook the World' does not overstate the nation's shock and grief at that time, reinforced in spectacular fashion by the nature of Campbell's demise. He couldn't surely be dead . . . he was indestructible!

So, fast-forward some 37 years and a redoubtable Geordie and his associates, having discovered the remains of Campbell's iconic craft, Bluebird, in the dark dungeon of Coniston's depths, achieved what was thought hardly possible and brought it back to the surface. The nation, and in particular those of my generation whose interest in record-breaking had somewhat waned in the meantime, were once more captivated. But Bill Smith, with characteristic single-mindedness and fortitude, pledged to go further and committed not only to a full restoration but to the 'breathing of life' into Bluebird's once lost and decaying bones.

My interest was reinvigorated. I pored over every publication, book, biography and engineering report of Bluebird's genesis, design and development, plus the career of its illustrious operator. I also studied the many accounts and post-analyses of his final and fated attempt. The latter, I must admit, were a real curate's egg. Some of the reasoning was sound and my knowledge of physics and aerodynamics sat nicely with it. However, much of it was less convincing. As I probed more, I was disquieted by the fact that there were unanswered questions, factual mistakes and often a lack of understanding of hydrodynamics, aerodynamics and turbojet technology. Although misleading, most of these flaws were doubtless unintentional. Nor should they be regarded as surprising in the history of pivotal events. I suspect that if you asked those who attended the Sermon on the Mount what was said and what it meant some 40 years later, you'd elicit a thousand different answers.

When Neil asked me to write this chapter, I was grateful to him for the opportunity to put down the results of my research and the conclusions drawn from it. He has also been hugely supportive. With his possibly unrivalled knowledge of 'affairs Campbell' and very considerable photographic archive, he has filled in my large gaps on the subject. In similar vein, I must express fulsome gratitude to Tony James, the engineer and project manager at Norris Brothers who worked on K7 from summer 1966 up to her final demise and, indeed, beyond it on post-crash analysis in 1967. He has allowed us access to many original papers and reports not available in the public domain. In addition, he sourced many important documents from the Norris Brothers Archive at the Science Museum's Wroughton site in Wiltshire. Perhaps more importantly, he has also devoted much time to re-evaluating and checking the many calculations in this account. Without his contribution, the accuracy, authority and significance of this work would be greatly diminished. I must also thank Prof John Stollery of Cranfield University, David Clarke, BAE Warton (retd.), and Dr Robert Englar, Georgia Tech Research Institute, for their time spent in helpful comment and discussion.

In no way do I have the temerity to claim that this is the final word on the matter, or that it is beyond contradiction. But it is, I hope, another step towards a better understanding of what happened on a very cold and dark January morning, in an all-too-recent but bygone era, to a very British warrior.

Hydroplane basics

For those who do not have an in-depth knowledge of the physics pertaining to hydroplanes, it may prove helpful to take a look at some of the basic concepts underpinning their design. To that end, a simple approach and one which eschews jargon as far as possible has been adopted. However, it must be acknowledged that in its entirety this is a highly complex subject which occupies entire books, never mind a single chapter.

The hydroplane is an exceedingly difficult craft to design such that it performs effectively and safely. Its operation has at least three phases which, unfortunately, are not distinct but blur into one another. Firstly, when at rest it is a pure boat and floats by hydrostatic lift due to water displacement. This is what we know as buoyancy. As it begins to move, there is a transition phase where hydrodynamic lift is generated on the hull. Finally, when speed is great enough, hydrodynamic planing lift comes into play, which combines with aerodynamic lift beneath the craft to support its weight. The latter phase is potentially very dangerous indeed, particularly at speeds above 200mph where proportionately less lift is generated hydrodynamically and more aerodynamically. Depending on the craft's configuration, any disturbing influence, such as swell, can cause it to become airborne and flip backwards, or plunge it into the water's surface – with obviously catastrophic consequences.

Despite the inherent complexities, it is possible to obtain a basic grasp of the main issues which will prepare and inform our subsequent discussions. In doing so, I would crave the indulgence of those under 50 who are used to working in metric units, kilograms, metres and the like. We shall stick with 'old money' in the form of pounds (lb), feet, etc., to conform with the historical context of the subject (those of an analytical bent may find the conversion exercise useful . . .).

i) Moments and centre of gravity (CG)

A designer of a machine which is intended to move, be it a motor car, ship, aeroplane or whatever, will first seek to establish where and how big are the principal forces acting on it. Secondly, the distance these forces act from the centre of gravity (CG) of the craft needs to be known. This is defined as the centre of an object's weight distribution, through which the force of gravity acts. Put another way, if we suspended the craft from a cable at that point, it would hang straight and level. The product of the size of a disturbing force (f) and its distance from the CG (d) is called a moment (magnitude f x d). The distance (d) is called the moment arm. The designer will then calculate all the individual moments and sum them to find their net effect. The outcome will indicate which way the craft will travel – forwards, sideways, up, down, etc. – and by how much. When all these moments balance out, Sir Isaac tells us that the craft will 'continue in its state of rest or uniform motion'.

A good analogy is the ability we humans have to stand on two legs. We are not conscious of it, but our brains, nerve connections and the muscles which they activate are doing some sublimely clever computation and control to keep us upright. We can perform a simple experiment on ourselves to illustrate the concepts of moments and balance. Standing rigid, put one arm out straight in front of you. Easy; balance is maintained unconsciously. Extend it further and a point is reached where, if exceeded, you topple over. Balance can be re-established by extending a leg in the opposite direction. Note, however, that the leg is only extended a small amount compared to the arm. This is because the leg and foot are much heavier than the arm. This illustrates two balancing moments, whereby the gravitational force on the heavier leg times the (shorter) distance from the body's CG equals the gravitational force on the lighter arm times the (longer) distance from the CG. As we shall see, moments are crucial in Bluebird's design and its behaviour when moving.

ii) Lift and drag

When objects move in fluids such as air and water (yes, air is regarded as a fluid!), they produce both lift and drag. These effects are proportional to the density of the fluid and the square of the speed, e.g. doubling the speed will quadruple lift and drag. In air, the lift and drag are referred to as aerodynamic; in water, they are referred to as hydrodynamic. Due to water having a density more than 800 times that of air, it will generate very much more lift than air under similar conditions and, of course, proportionately more drag.

Aerodynamic lift is an unwanted – but unavoidable – effect in the design of high-speed racing cars, Land Speed Record-breaking cars and, of course, hydroplanes. The designer must thus take into account the associated moments. The lift is the result of air pressure being higher underneath the craft than above it, so there is a net force upwards. Hydroplanes also suffer from enhanced lift because of the proximity of the craft to the water's surface, the so-called 'ground effect'. To calculate lift, a mathematical concept known as the aerodynamic centre of pressure (CP_A) is invoked. In aircraft, it is defined as the centre of a wing's lift distribution and – for the purpose of calculation – the point through which the total lift (L_A) is assumed to act. It can also be applied to a hydroplane, and the position of the CP_A in relation to the CG is an important factor in determining the stability of the craft.

Aerodynamic drag in hydroplanes is made up of essentially three constituents:

Form drag
which depends on the shape of the craft, e.g. how streamlined (or not) it is
Skin drag
which, as the name suggests, relates to the area and texture of the skin,
e.g. smooth or rough
Interference drag
which is created at the juncture of two aerodynamic components, e.g. the wing and fuselage of an aircraft or, in a hydroplane, the hull, booms and sponsons

The effects of form and skin drag can be visualised if a flat, thin plate is positioned at right angles to the direction of airflow, i.e. face-on. Form drag constitutes virtually all of the resistance, whereas skin drag is insignificant. If the plate is rotated 90°, i.e. turned end-on to the airflow, the reverse is observed; skin drag dominates, form drag is negligible.

Hydrodynamic planing lift is generated when any object 'skims' or 'skips' along a water surface. Schoolboys need no introduction to this phenomenon. They know intuitively that when a flat pebble is launched at just the right angle and rotational speed onto the surface of a pond, it is observed to 'skip' across the water. There is an apocryphal story that Nelson employed the phenomenon to devastating effect with his cannon shot at the Battle of Trafalgar. What is more certain, is that Barnes Wallis applied the principle highly effectively with his novel dambuster 'bouncing bombs'.

Such lift is fundamental to the operation of a hydroplane. It needs to be known so that the upwards forces and their moments in relation to the CG can be calculated. As for aerodynamic lift, a hydrodynamic centre of pressure (CP_H) can be defined. This is the position where the sum of all upward hydrodynamic planing forces (L_H) is calculated to act. Hydrodynamic drag inevitably accompanies lift. It, too, is made up of form drag and skin drag, but in this case they relate only to those surfaces in contact with the water (see below). Also, there are additional elements referred to as wave-forming and spray-forming drag (so-called 'hump' drag, see below), these being particularly high during transition from the displacement phase to the planing phase. When the craft is planing, form drag alone is used to calculate the various moments (the others, because of their complexity, are highly difficult to determine).[1, 2] It also needs to be appreciated that other 'secondary' appendages immersed in the water, e.g. rudders, stabilising fins, etc., need to have their lift or drag forces assessed and included in the overall moment calculation.

iii) Planing surfaces

The surfaces in contact with the water in a hydroplane are variously referred to as 'planes', 'shoes' or 'wedges' and their design is of crucial importance in such craft. They need to produce maximum lift L_H to support the weight of the hydroplane, but to do so with a minimum of drag to allow the craft to achieve the highest speed possible with the thrust available. The surface area of the planes in contact with the water, the so-called 'wetted area', and their immersion depth depend on the angle the wedges present to the water's surface and on speed. As speed increases, both the wetted area and immersion depth reduce as the upwards force required to support the weight of the boat is generated by 'sweeping' across a greater surface area of water in any given second. At very high speed, the wetted area is relatively small, around 10–20 square inches, and the immersion depth is around 0.1". The planes can have a flat profile – as in Bluebird K7 – or a shallow 'V' shape, like on Spirit of Australia. Technically, the latter is termed 'dead-rise' and the angle between the 'V' arms and horizontal datum is usually between 20° and 30°. As Bluebird's planes were flat, they had a dead-rise angle of 0°. Because of the very high and frankly bludgeoning forces, the planes need to be very strong. They also need to be very rigid so that they maintain consistent planing performance in the face of severe buffeting. Additionally, their design should be such that they minimise pitching oscillations (porpoising) if the craft encounters disturbed water.

iv) Thrust versus drag

Whenever an object, craft or vehicle is propelled through a fluid, energy has to be expended and the rate of using such energy is power. The power derived from the craft's engine is converted to forward thrust. Unfortunately, overcoming drag absorbs disproportionately more power as speed is increased. As a general rule, the power or thrust required is proportional to the cube of the speed, e.g. to double the speed, thrust has to be increased by 2^3, i.e. 2 x 2 x 2 = 8 times. A good example is a car. At 50mph it will require typically 10bhp to maintain that speed, to double it to 100mph will require 80bhp, and quadrupling it to 200mph requires 640bhp!

Likewise, the power of a hydroplane's engine and the thrust derived from it have a significant effect on the maximum speed that the craft can achieve. The speed at which thrust equals total aerodynamic plus hydrodynamic drag is the maximum speed the hydroplane can attain. It was quickly realised after the Second World War that the most powerful internal combustion engines of 3,000bhp in conjunction with prop-riding efficiencies of 45% could not achieve, theoretically, speeds much in excess of 200mph. The thrust generated by this form of propulsion also decreases dramatically at speeds above 150mph. Set against this, the craft experiences a rapid increase in total drag. The two effects converge and balance at around 210mph.[1, 2]

Enter the turbojet. Not only did this power plant produce more thrust, it could do so with no loss of efficiency throughout the speed range of a hydroplane and beyond. At the time of Bluebird's genesis in the early 1950s, turbojet engines of suitable configuration and thrust were becoming increasingly available.

v) Buoyancy

Buoyancy results from the upwards hydrostatic force due to displacement. The centre of buoyancy (CB) is defined as the point at which this upwards force can be assumed to act. If this point and the CG coincide, then the craft will sit level. If they do not, it will list side-to-side or fore–aft depending on the relative position of the CG to the CB. Obviously, this issue is very important in relation to Bluebird, particularly as the low sit of the boat in the water rendered it vulnerable to sinking if water entered the jet-pipe (indeed, this happened at Lake Mead on Bluebird's first trip to the USA in 1955[3,4]). Also, it has an impact on the ability of the craft to transition from the displacement phase to the planing phase. Getting this right, however, is not an exact science, as the designers of Bluebird were to discover, resorting to 'cut and try' methods on the first Ullswater trials in 1955 and the final version of the craft at Coniston in 1966.[4-6]

vi) Stability

Static stability
This is the property of a craft whereby if it is disturbed from its trimmed attitude or direction of movement it will return to that trimmed position or direction when the disturbance ceases. With regard to the hydroplane in particular, if its trimmed attitude is disturbed, e.g. by a wavelet or transient swell, it should return to its original path when that disturbance passes. Such craft can be described as having **positive** stability characteristics. If the craft does not return to its trimmed attitude following a disturbance and assumes a different path, e.g. upwards or sideways, it is said to demonstrate **negative** stability, i.e. it is unstable.

As for the particular situation of longitudinal stability, i.e. in pitch, it is firstly important to understand the concept of 'vertical balance'. This states that for equilibrium conditions in a hydroplane, the sum of the total aerodynamic lift L_A and total hydrodynamic lift L_H must at all times be equal to the weight 'W' of the craft, i.e. $L_A + L_H = W$. A schematic diagram of the vertical forces in a hydroplane such as Bluebird as it planes across the water is shown in Fig. 1.

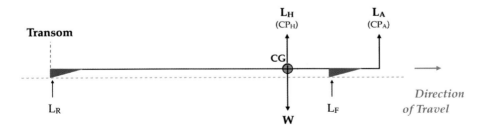

Fig. 1: Schematic diagram of the principal vertical forces acting on a hydroplane.
© Dr K. Mitchell

Where $L_A + L_H = W$

           & $L_R + 2L_F = L_H$

Note that the point where aerodynamic lift L_A acts, i.e. CP_A, is forward of the CG, and the point where hydrodynamic lift L_H acts, i.e. CP_H, is coincident with the CG. The planes are shown as blue triangles and the lift at a front plane is L_F and at the rear L_R. As this type of hydroplane has two forward planes, total hydrodynamic lift $L_H = L_R + 2L_F$.

For static stability in pitch, if the craft is disturbed from its equilibrium, i.e. level trim, it should return to that condition when the disturbance passes. Such disturbances will pitch the craft up or down in relation to the rear plane at the transom, which can be regarded as a 'pivot' about which vertical rotation takes place – see figures 2(a) and (b) respectively.

Fig. 2: Diagram of effects of a pitch-up disturbance (a) and a pitch-down disturbance (b) on the vertical forces of a hydroplane.
© Dr K. Mitchell

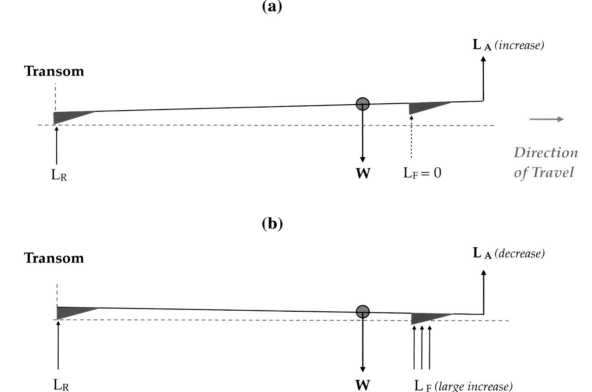

If a pitch-up occurs (Fig. 2(a)), the forward wedges will have left the water at only the smallest pitch angle due to the tiny immersion depth. All hydrodynamic lift at those planes therefore ceases, i.e. $L_F = 0$. This counters to some degree the increase in aerodynamic lift L_A created by the positive incidence of the craft. As long as the net upwards force of L_A and L_R does not exceed 'W', the craft will return under its own weight to a state of level trim on the water. If a pitch-down disturbance occurs – Fig. 2(b) – a very large restoring force will be impressed upwards on the front wedges, returning the craft to the trimmed condition. A reduction in aerodynamic lift L_A will also occur due to the negative incidence of the boat, but a net upwards effect will nonetheless occur due to the overwhelmingly dominant contribution of L_H. (Note that the specific moments resulting from these forces will be considered later in Section 3 viii.)

It will be evident, however, that if the net effect of L_A and L_H exceeds 'W', i.e. $L_A + L_H > W$, the craft will leave the water. This could occur if severe disturbance is encountered by the front planes, for example; the large hydrodynamic restoring force could cause the bows to rear up and if speed was high this would be accompanied by a large increase in aerodynamic lift. This would overwhelm the ability of 'W' to return the craft to level trim and it would flip over. The boat would have exceeded its longitudinal stability limit. It is therefore perhaps most accurate to describe it as having *conditional* static stability.

Generally, hydroplanes are more stable the further forward the CG is located. Additionally, if aerodynamic lift L_A can be reduced – acting as it does in front of the CG – then that too will contribute to stability. However, there is a caveat; if the CG is too far forward the craft will have difficulty rising onto the planes during the low-speed to high-speed transition. Similarly, stability criteria which require the aerodynamic lifting area forward of the CG to be minimised in the high-speed condition will inevitably reduce such lift at low speed, where it assists the rising of the bows when transitioning to the planing phase. Such conflicts serve to underscore the very difficult compromises which have to be made in hydroplane design.

The foregoing discusses stability in the pitching axis, but stability of the yawing axis must also be addressed. All the general considerations regarding stability in pitch can be applied to yaw, but are obviously implemented differently. The craft requires high levels of directional stability such that if its track is altered by surface disturbances or a crosswind it should return to the original track stably and safely with the minimum of control (rudder) input. For obvious reasons, this is often termed 'weathercock' stability. It is possible to improve this stability with vertical 'fins' projecting downwards into the water. This method was initially adopted on Bluebird, but as the evolution of the craft progressed aerodynamic fins of increasing size were attached to K7, culminating in the cropped HS Gnat version of 1966/67. This dramatically improved stability in yaw (see Section viii) b)).

Dynamic stability

This characteristic describes the dynamic response of the craft following an abrupt input or 'shock'. All structures, whether buildings, bridges, aircraft or hydroplanes, demonstrate a natural frequency of oscillation which, if excited by an input such as the above, will cause it to vibrate or resonate. If uncontrolled, this can cause catastrophic damage to the structure. The Millennium Bridge in London is perhaps the most recent high-profile example of this phenomenon. Under certain conditions, it began to wobble as people walked across it. The bridge was closed while shock-absorbing pads (i.e. dampers) were added to the structure.

Damping can best be explained with reference to motor car suspension. If a car hits a bump or pothole in the road and then returns to equilibrium with several oscillations which progressively decay in amplitude, then it is said to be under-damped. The big American saloons of the 1950s and '60s demonstrated this effect somewhat to excess. If the ride set-up is 'hard', then the shock-absorbing qualities of the suspension will be poor and a bumpy ride ensues, i.e. it is over-damped. If the shock absorbing is 'tuned' to respond in about half a cycle – with perhaps a little overshoot – it is said to be critically-damped (this condition is the one most commonly adopted as the 'Sports' setting in modern cars with selectable control of the suspension parameters).

Hydroplanes also need to adopt measures to optimise damping. These effects have to be considered across all axes, i.e. roll, yaw and pitch. A particular concern for a hydroplane is that cyclic disturbances of the water surface can coincide with the craft's natural oscillation in pitch or roll, causing the oscillations to reinforce each other. In situations where the damping is not optimised and the craft is operating at the margins of its stability envelope, a rapid escalation of the amplitude of the oscillations can occur, with extremely dangerous consequences.

Design and development of Bluebird K7

i) Preamble

The 1950s in hydroplane record-breaking dawned with the sharp realisation that the days of the prop-rider were over. As discussed above, burgeoning power requirements and propulsive inefficiencies posed insurmountable problems. The Campbell/Norris team had established this on both theoretical grounds and by practical experience.[1, 2, 4] The advent of jet propulsion for hydroplanes was, as with aircraft (and, interestingly, for exactly the same reasons) not only desirable, but essential.

However, this was a jump that would not be achieved seamlessly or without great sacrifice. The first problem was the sheer increase in speed. Designing a hydroplane which can operate safely at up to 200mph represents a considerable challenge; doing so for one whose peak performance approaches 300mph is a very formidable prospect indeed. The notion of some sort of 'water barrier' at speeds above 200mph – analogous to the 'sound barrier' for aircraft – had often been promoted by Donald Campbell, but possibly for reasons more journalistic than hydrodynamic! If there was any credence to the idea, it was related to the limiting effects of pitching oscillations referred to previously, but it was ultimately shown to have little basis in fact. Nevertheless, dynamic instability of this type is potentially very dangerous and led to the tragic death of John Cobb in his jet-powered boat Crusader on Loch Ness in 1952.

Crusader was designed *inter alia* to minimise aerodynamic lift problems by adopting the configuration of a single planing surface forward and two aft on the usual three-point stability triangle (see below). However, the single forward shoe experiences huge and disproportionate loads and has to be immensely strong. Secondly, the position of the jet engine should, for the purpose of minimising water ingress at the intakes plus potential flooding of the jet-pipe, be some distance above the waterline. The de Havilland Ghost engine used in Crusader was very heavy (2,200lb) and of large diameter, dictating a large maximum hull diameter. The upshot of this was a very high CG. With appropriate streamlining of the hull, outriggers and sponsons, it nonetheless proved possible to achieve the holy grail of static stability, i.e. having the CG forward of the aerodynamic CP_A. Somewhat paradoxically, the opportunity to extend this improvement further was possibly missed by the adoption of a streamlined rear to the craft.[7] Increase of the so-called 'kite area' aftwards (see below) could have shifted the CP_A further back, but as already discussed that might have compromised forward lifting moment in the transition phase from displacement to planing.

Following the crash of Crusader at around 210mph, the Norris brothers performed careful analysis of film recordings of that final run. It has to be acknowledged that this study remains one of the most elegant retrospective scientific investigations ever undertaken in the history of high-speed hydroplanes.[1, 2] It demonstrated that Crusader was dynamically unstable. At such high speeds, swell-initiated pitching oscillations at a frequency of 4–5Hz increased in amplitude with such ferocity that they caused the front plane to collapse and plunged Crusader into the water, fatally injuring Cobb. The Norrises were able to establish that the height of the CG and the large moment arms with respect to the planes (plus other factors relating to the design of the planes, their stiffness, etc.) contributed to the craft's inability to absorb and dampen the critical pitching oscillation.[2] The catastrophe had a profound effect upon Donald Campbell because he revered and respected Cobb and, indeed, all record-breakers. It galvanised him – although further encouragement was hardly needed – to take up the British mantle of record-breaking. Additionally, and importantly, it furnished the Norris brothers with valuable insights into designing a craft which would enable him to do it.

The design aims for the new craft can be summarised as follows:

i)   To attain a speed of 250mph commensurate with an adequate margin of static and dynamic stability in yaw, pitch and roll.[1]

ii)   Very high structural strength and stiffness; the 'g' loadings were to be '. . . some three times that of "Crusader" and five times that of the old Bluebird.'[1]

iii)   Low frontal profile area to minimise aerodynamic drag.[1, 3, 6]

iv)   Every attempt to minimise aerodynamic lifting moments forward of the CG.[1, 2, 6, 8]

v)   Paired forward sponsons mounted on outriggers to reduce loadings at the front planes.[1, 2, 6]

vi)   Planes to have high lift and low drag with good anti-porpoising capability, sponson under-surfaces to permit good transition from the displacement to the planing condition, and good anti-dive characteristics.[1, 2, 6]

vii)   Low CG to minimise potential pitching oscillations at the natural frequency of the craft.[1, 2, 6, 8]

viii)   Turbojet propulsion with low thrust line to minimise thrust on/off moment effects.[1, 2]

ix)   Fuel tank at or near the CG to minimise effects on trim due to fuel state.[1, 2, 6]

To this end, extensive trials of a one-eighth-scale model of the initial 'C' boat configuration were painstakingly undertaken to assess stability in yaw, pitch and roll as well as the transition to planing, effects of swell, propulsive thrust required, etc. This was supplemented by aerodynamic tests of stability in the wind tunnel at the City & Guilds College, London (now Imperial College of Science and Technology) by Mr (later Professor) Tom Fink, who joined the Bluebird team on an *ad hoc* basis throughout the model stage and early full-size trials. These were completed in 1955, but K7 was subject to virtually continuous development throughout its life as problems not predicted by model/laboratory trials manifested themselves (a full account of these issues can be found elsewhere[1–6]). For an easy-to-follow monograph of the development phases, see *The Research & Development of Donald Campbell's Bluebird K7 Hydroplane*, by F.R. Blois.[9]

The approach taken in the ensuing discourse is one whereby the key elements of the initial design are discussed and, where appropriate, summarised for simplicity. Simple calculations will be included in the text, but where they are more involved references will be given to documents that will be available on the book website. The derivations and diagrams relate to the final configuration of Bluebird K7 as this is most relevant to subsequent discussion, but the same general principles apply to the craft throughout its operational life.

ii) Theoretical factors

Using the model data derived from the experiments described above enabled the Norris brothers to make some overall predictions regarding a potential full-size version.[2] The data in Table 1 were generated from water trials of the model 'C' boat.

Table 1

	Model (1/8th scale)	Full size
AUW (lb)	9.0	4,608[1]
Thrust (lb)	5.8	2,970[2]
Thrust/weight ratio (lb/lb)	0.65	0.65
Speed (mph)	79.0	223[3]

Notes:
[1]   Full-size weight = model weight x (scale)^3 = 9.0 x 8^3 = 4,608lb
[2]   Full-size thrust = model thrust x (scale)^3= 5.8 x 8^3 = 2,970lb
[3]   Full-size speed = model speed x $\sqrt{}$ (scale) = 79.0 x $\sqrt{8}$ = 223mph

Furnished with these figures and the wind-tunnel data, they embarked on further comparisons of critical design factors with past and present record-breaking craft, see Table 2. Note that additional data regarding the substantive K7 versions have been added by the author.

The **density** of the craft is important as this has a significant effect on displacement and therefore buoyancy. It can be seen that K7 had significantly higher density than previous craft, and in its final form K7 exceeded that of Crusader by some 94%. Displacement was consequently greater and therefore required considerable attention to be given to the issue of craft buoyancy (note: K7's density of 17.5lb/ft^3 was still, however, nearly four times less than that of water (62.4lb/ft^3)).

Table 2

	Density (Weight/ volume) (lb/ft³)	Aerodynamic loading (Weight /plan area) (lb/ft²)	Frontal area (ft²)	Weight (lb)	Thrust/weight ratio (lb/lb)
Bluebird K4	11.5	24.5	11.5	5,000	0.20 (η = 0.45)
Slo-Mo-Shun	12.2	24.4	29.0	4,900	0.19 (η = 0.45)
Crusader	9.0	32.2	47.2	6,500	0.77 (Thrust/weight ratio) (lb/lb)
Bluebird K7:					
'C' boat configuration	14.4	32.8	26.4	4,800	0.80
Beryl version[1]	17.9	40.7	26.4	5,950	0.65
Orpheusl version[2]	17.5	40.0	28.0	5,813	0.77
Orpheusl version[3]	16.8	38.2	28.0	5,597	0.94

Notes:

1   AUW incl. fuel and pilot (thrust = 3,850lb)[10]

2   AUW incl. fuel and pilot (thrust = 4,500lb)[10, 11]

3   AUW incl. fuel and pilot (condition on 4 January 1967 with 10% boosted thrust = 5,277lb, incl. correction for temp. t = 2°C) plus all structural modifications incl. added lead weights and fuel boost pump for final run.[12]

η = prop-riding efficiency.

Aerodynamic loading is defined as the weight of the craft divided by its plan area (see Fig. 3). The larger the plan area, the more aerodynamic lift will be produced. If the weight of the craft is small, or the plan area is large (or, indeed, both), then the loading will be small and the risk of becoming airborne increases. If the plan area can be minimised and the craft is heavy, then the loading is high and the tendency to become airborne lessens. The loading of K7 was some 63% higher than that of the prop-rider and significantly higher than that of Crusader (24%).

Fig. 3: Bluebird K7 in plan form, illustrating the 'kite area' and stability triangle.
© Damien Burke / Sabrina Pennewiss

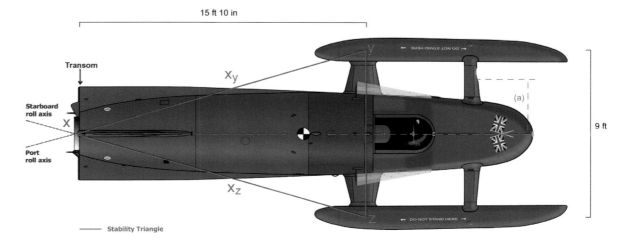

Stability Triangle

Frontal area is an issue in any moving craft; the larger it is, the more aerodynamic drag will be produced, while reducing it lowers drag. The élan displayed by Ken and Lewis Norris as designers was clearly evident here as they managed to keep frontal area to a remarkably low 26.4 sq ft, which was comparable to that of the prop-rider's and almost half that of Crusader. Central to this achievement was the selection of a turbojet with a small cross-section. The Metropolitan Vickers Beryl with its axial compressor had few peers at the time, featuring a relatively small diameter of 36.8". Compare this to Crusader's de Havilland Ghost with centrifugal compressor and a diameter of 53.0" but, of course, considerably more thrust, at 5,000lb.

Thrust/weight ratio is a crucial design consideration as it influences acceleration and the top speed attainable set against the total drag. The overwhelming improvement in thrust due to the adoption of jet power was emphasised by the fact that the prop-riding precursors had around four times less thrust available to them. Indeed, as already discussed, jet thrust was little diminished across the speed range of K7, whereas that in a prop-rider fell off dramatically above 150mph. The Beryl and Orpheus engines fitted to successive versions of K7 had nominal static thrusts of 3,850lb and 4,500lb respectively (note that the latter figure refers specifically to the Orpheus 701 engines 709 and 711).[11]

It was noted earlier that a large increase in thrust is required to increase speed by a relatively small amount in moving craft. We believe that for the final runs of Bluebird the thrust from the Orpheus was boosted some 10% by Bristol Siddeley engineers.[5, 6] That gave 5,277lb of thrust as the absolute maximum (corrected for higher air density at temp. t = 2°C experienced on 4 January 1967). This was some 37% greater than the Beryl's thrust of 3,850lb. The highest peak speed recorded by the Beryl version is generally believed to be close to 300mph. Given the cube law discussed previously – and assuming other factors, e.g. total drag etc. to be similar – then the maximum theoretical speed achievable in the final Orpheus version should have been ≈300 x $\sqrt[3]{1.37}$ = 333mph. This is just a little above the 328mph which most analysts agree was the peak speed on the final run.[3–6]

iii) Configuration

Bluebird K7 was designed as a conventional three-point hydroplane supported on a three-point stability triangle (see Fig. 3). Unlike Crusader, however, the Ventnor convention was adopted as in previous prop-riders such as K4, i.e. two forward and one aft plane (replacing the 'prop'). There are advantages and disadvantages to this method, but in hydrodynamic terms the former far outweigh the latter. Pitching stability is improved with two planes forward, and the extreme front loadings are halved compared to a single front plane. Transition from the displacement to the planing phase is improved by the two sponsons, which increase lift forwards of the CG.[1, 2] Directional control is also improved because an aft rudder can be employed, yielding better low-speed control and reduced loading because it is further from the CG than one mounted forward as on Crusader.[1, 2] Even more importantly, since it is behind the CG it introduces a positive stabilising moment in yaw.

There are, however, also disadvantages. Firstly, the craft is prone to a phenomenon called 'tramping' whereby perturbations in the water's surface can induce an alternate rocking movement about the axes of the stability triangle X_Y and X_Z. The nose of the craft therefore describes a motion with both rolling and yawing components. This results in an overall increase in incidence (pitch-up) of the craft which is proportionate to the severity of the tramping, i.e. the tramping amplitude.

iv) Planing surfaces

As discussed in Section 2 iii), flat-bottomed wedges, i.e. with a zero dead-rise angle, were chosen for Bluebird as it was argued by Tom Fink and Ken Norris that these had better anti-porpoising characteristics.[1, 2] The specific hydrodynamic data to design the wedges were derived from NACA technical data.[13] On the basis of the expected loadings, the angle of attack of the front wedges was chosen to be 3.75° and the rear 2.5°. The length of the wedges was designed to be 57.3" and their width 12". This configuration resulted in a theoretical drag/lift (D/L) ratio of 0.08.[13] The reciprocal of this ratio L/D is therefore 12.5 and is defined as the 'planing efficiency'. This figure means that the planes produced 12.5-times as much lift as drag. However, in discussions between the Norris brothers and Tom Fink it was felt that the planing efficiency would, in practice, be lower than this, so a value of L/D = 6.7 was used in calculations, i.e. D/L = 0.15.[1, 2] It is unclear as to why this figure – which is almost double that predicted theoretically – was chosen; no reasons are presented in the original design documents[14] or in reports derived from them[1, 2].

Following Bluebird's crash, Ken and Lewis Norris and their associates performed extensive analysis of the crash itself and the performance of the craft on the final run.[15] Included in this is a detailed reworking of the calculations of lift and loadings at the planes in the light of more up-to-date NACA technical data published in 1957.[16] At a speed of 312mph and a loading of 1,780lb for each front plane and 1,070lb for the rear, the wetted area for each front plane was 13.2 square inches and 12.6 square inches for the rear. The immersion depth was a tiny 0.072" at the front and even less at the rear, 0.046". From this, it is possible to conclude that the wedge angles were too steep for optimum performance of the craft, particularly when operating at speeds in excess of 300mph.

Re-examining the NACA data[16] suggests that lower wedge angles would have increased immersion depth and wetted area with concomitant improvements in planing efficiency. An element of 'dead rise' would also have improved planing characteristics and tracking.[4] It is of interest here that Spirit of Australia, which captured the world record at 318mph in 1978 more than 10 years after Bluebird's demise, did so with wedges incorporating dead rise; the record still stands. Tom Fink (who had worked on Bluebird K7 in 1955) proposed flat wedges for Spirit of Australia but was overruled by its experienced, hard-nosed constructor and pilot, the redoubtable Ken Warby.[17]

It is important to reflect here that the original Bluebird K7 configuration was designed in 1954 on the basis of planing data available at the time.[13]

It could be argued that the sponson fairing redesign in 1958 offered an ideal opportunity to make modifications to the wedges, but perhaps this was not considered because K7 appeared to be performing very satisfactorily during that period. Also, Bluebird only had an anticipated life of a few more years and, perhaps, two more records. In addition, it would have involved significant engineering effort – and considerable cost – to carry out the work[18] at a time when Campbell was focusing all-out on his Bluebird CN7 LSR effort.

v) Lift, drag and thrust

Gross distribution of lift can be described in simple terms by recourse to the notion of 'kite area'.[6] If we imagine the plan area to be analogous to that of a kite, the largest area will generate the most lift. Compared to craft such as Slo-Mo-Shun where lifting area was concentrated to the fore of the craft, thus producing a propensity to flip backwards at high speed, K7 was designed with a large lifting area towards the transom and every attempt was made to minimise forward lifting area (see Fig. 3). Despite this, the requirement to have two large sponsons and their supporting spars forward of the CG meant that aerodynamic lift thereon could not be eliminated. This was compounded by the fact that the forward under-surfaces of the bow and sponsons were designed to have a steep angle of attack to facilitate transition to the planing condition and improve their anti-dive characteristics.[2] The aerodynamic lift force on K7 plotted against pitch angle 'α' is shown in Fig. 4.

Fig. 4: Aerodynamic lift 'L$_A$' (lb) plotted against pitch angle 'α' (degrees). The upper curve is that derived from the May 1955 wind-tunnel tests following the major revisions, the lower from testing following the 1958 modifications.

© Dr K. Mitchell

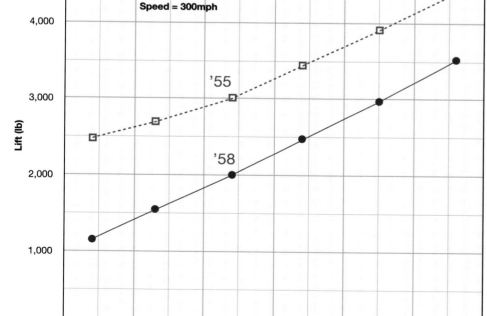

The higher curve is that obtained from wind-tunnel tests[19] performed in May 1955, following the major revisions required to make the craft plane on Ullswater[1-4]. It is interesting to note that nowhere in that wind-tunnel data[19] is there any evidence of the 'kinked' characteristic seen in the original design documents[1,2] or later publications[6]. It is very difficult to justify that feature, aerodynamically.[20] The curves were derived for the highest peak speed observed on the Beryl-engined version of Bluebird. The lift can be seen to increase from some 2,500lb at nominally level trim up to ≈4,500lb at α = 6°. The biggest improvement in respect to reducing such lifting force was made in 1958, when redesigned upper sponson fairings were fitted. These were cleverly designed by Ken Norris so that their upper surface presented a negative incidence to the air stream (see Fig. 7), thus increasing aerodynamic download and reducing lift, see the lower curve. Lift was reduced by nearly 60% at level trim and by ≈35% at α = 6° pitch. The original wind-tunnel data underpinning this curve appear to be lost, a fact confirmed in discussions with Prof John Stollery, Consultant Aerodynamicist to Norris Brothers on K7, 1958–1967. However, a graph derived from John Stollery's original measurements on the revised sponsons in relation to velocity at take-off V_{TO} survives in a Norris Brothers report,[21] and it was possible to derive lift data from it, as presented in Fig. 4[22]. Ken Norris obviously performed a similar exercise, as he refers to it in his design brief of July 1966[23] and to derived data therein in the retrospective analysis of the crash[15] (NB These data are not corrected for mach number [20,53]).

The aerodynamic and hydrodynamic forces experienced by Bluebird and the effect of speed on them can be seen in Fig. 5. These data are compiled from reports of K7's performance in the summer of 1955 following the significant

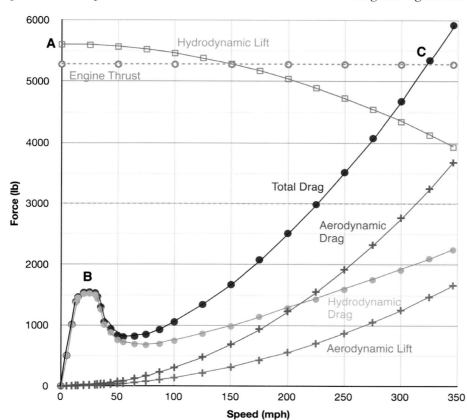

Fig. 5: Aerodynamic and hydrodynamic lift and drag forces plotted against speed for K7 as operated on 4 January 1967.
© Dr K. Mitchell

revisions made, further modifications including those discussed above, and in relation to the craft's final form in 1966/67.[2, 10, 11, 21–25]

Weight and fuel state are those calculated for the condition pertaining at final lift-off.[12, 26] Aerodynamic lift, drag and engine thrust are all corrected for the effect of higher air density at 2°C, which was the temperature on the morning of 4 January 1967. At rest, viz. point 'A' in Fig. 5, there is no aerodynamic component and all lift is hydrostatic, i.e. buoyant. As for drag, initial acceleration from rest creates a highly disproportionate increase in hydrodynamic drag due to wave-making and spray generation, known as 'hump' drag, see point 'B' and images 1 and 2 on page 156. The drag force peaks at some 1,600lb. Overcoming this, and thus transitioning to the planing phase, required a delicate balance of craft trim and power, plus not a little skill from the pilot (conditions which we know were to exasperate Campbell, his support crew and the designers before a solution was found).[4, 6] Once through this phase and rising onto the planes at 50–70mph, such drag falls dramatically before increasing again somewhat more sedately. Aerodynamic drag increases more significantly with speed, eventually overtaking hydrodynamic drag at around 220mph. The total drag curve is the sum of these components. The point at which this crosses the thrust line ('C') is highly significant, because at that point thrust equals total drag (NB Thrust herein is 'static' thrust; no correction for airstream momentum is included[53]). This represents the maximum speed attainable by the boat, which can be seen to be 320–330mph. This is pretty consistent with that estimated in Section 3 ii) using power law calculation.

Returning to lift issues, increasing speed causes aerodynamic lift to increase, but hydrodynamic lift reduces. The net effect of these forces – under equilibrium conditions – equals the weight of the boat. At 300mph, a little over ⅓th is generated aerodynamically, the rest hydrodynamically. However, there is a caveat; these data are for the boat operating at or near level trim. If it begins to pitch up even by a small amount, e.g. α = 2°, aerodynamic lift and drag will be roughly doubled. This will, however, be accompanied by a partially compensating reduction in hydrodynamic lift and drag due to the reduced load on the forward planes. But the reader will not find it difficult to appreciate the gravity of this phenomenon if further increases in pitch occur . . .

vi) Orpheus installation

The BS Orpheus engine was an attractive replacement for the ageing Metropolitan Vickers Beryl as it produced around 20–30% more power at nearly half the weight (913lb as compared to the Beryl's 1,780lb). According to Ken Norris's original design brief of 13 July 1966, it could be fitted without too many serious problems and, most importantly, would allow K7 to attain the maximum design speed of 325mph.[23] There then appears to have been an intense dialogue with BS's Ken Pearson regarding the ancillary equipment needed for the Orpheus and operational requirements of the engine in its new environment.[27] The issues related mainly to air circulation around the jet-pipe to facilitate cooling and to the intakes, spray shields, etc. The former aspect was addressed satisfactorily, but the latter less so. BS made recommendations which required more rounded edges to the intakes, i.e. 'bull nose' entry, modification of the spray deflectors because they masked the intakes, and a blending-in of the step alongside the cockpit – presumably to improve airflow into the duct.

Ken Norris expressed doubt as to the need for the above modifications, but agreed that they should be implemented if time allowed.[27, 28] Given that the deadline for completion of all work was 31 August so that trials at Coniston could commence in mid-September – Campbell was keen to take advantage of the favourable autumn conditions – it is perhaps unsurprising that the work was not done.[18] Neither does it appear that the static running tests of the engine in its new environment as recommended by BS were performed. Both Bill Vanryne and Tony James have confirmed that only starts and idling runs were performed at Haywards Heath; there were no run-ups to high power settings.[18, 29, 30]

These technical issues were not helped by severe financial constraints. Only £1,000 (£15,000 today) was allocated to the conversion, with instructions issued to Norris Brothers staff that all attempts should be made to elicit goods/services from suppliers free of charge, the *quid pro quo* being that they could derive publicity and advertising benefit by association.[23, 31] Installation of jet engines in any enclosure, be it an aeroplane or hydroplane, is not straightforward; it takes time and money. Bluebird's power plant was replaced with one developing potentially 30% more thrust, with a correspondingly higher air ingestion rate, within the same aerodynamic duct. Such a scenario does not bode well for the eventual live running trials of a craft that would attempt to push forward into a new dimension of hydroplane record-breaking.

History would prove that to be the case later that very autumn.[3–6] Rivets from the intake duct were ingested by the engine during a high power static test on 5 November, damaging the compressor blades of Orpheus number 709. A further communication from Ken Pearson to Ken Norris on 9 November detailed the requirements for a new duct, its testing and the constraints on the engine's operation.[32] The ducts were strengthened by the inclusion of a new second inner skin which was both riveted and bonded to the original skin. During these repairs, some rounding-off of the intakes was carried out, but not to BS's full recommendation of a 1.5" radii.[32] Photographs taken following the repairs illustrate that the radius of curvature is perhaps half that. Not rounding off the intake lip leads to 'breakaway' of airflow around the relatively sharp edges of the intake at low speed, which disturbs the flow into the engine's compressor. This has an effect on thrust just when it might be useful for overcoming hump drag, see Fig. 5. (The reader might wish to examine – at a distance, of course – the intake ducts of commercial airliners; they are beautifully rounded to reduce the possibility of breakaway when maximum thrust is demanded at low airspeed, e.g. during take-off.) With regard to the step alongside the cockpit, disturbance of the air stream at high speed resulting from breakaway at the intake ramp creates unwanted turbulence at the intake face. There is no record or recollection of the duct depression tests and blending-in of the intake ramp beside the cockpit specified in that document[32] having been carried out[18]. All photographic and other evidence confirms this impression.[33]

vii) Weight and CG

Given the relative weights of the Beryl and Orpheus engines, it would be reasonable to assume that K7's all-up weight (AUW) was much lighter. However, it was only some 300lb or so less, see Table 3. The weight advantage of the Orpheus was partly wiped out by the amount of ancillary equipment required by the conversion (Appendix I). Trim and CG position were other important factors. In this regard, the Orpheus was mounted further forward than the Beryl,[23] with the ancillary equipment also being mounted as far forward as possible. Ken Norris was understandably keen to garner the benefits of a more forward CG to combat potential aerodynamic problems at the high speeds anticipated.[23] Detailed reassessment of trim and CG position were carried out.[10, 12, 26] The results of these – and recent rechecking of these calculations[12] – are shown in Table 3.

Table 3

	K7 (Beryl)	K7 (Orpheus)		
		Initial (1 Nov. 1966)	Plus 170lb rear lead ballast weight (22 Nov. 1966)	Less 27 gal. fuel (4 Jan. 1967)
AUW (lb)	5,950	5,643	5,813	5,597
Centre of gravity (to transom, in.)	141.00 (11.75')	146.45 (12.20')	142.63 (11.89')	142.12 (11.84')
Weight moment (to transom, lb.ft)	69,913	68,867	69,093	66,268

It can be seen that the conversion did indeed result in a better CG position, improved from 141.00" (11.75') to 146.45" (12.20'). Five and a half inches might seem a trivially small amount when compared to overall length, but it is not trivial in the complex world of aerodynamic-hydrodynamic balance. However, the *bête noire* of the hydroplane designer again reared its ugly head during November 1966 when Bluebird steadfastly refused to plane, presumably because the CG was now too far forward.[3, 4, 6, 10] The sandbag experiment on 22 November and the permanent installation of 170lb of lead ingots with Ken Norris's authority[34] some 16" forward of the transom solved the problem. The trade-off, however, was a regression of the CG to 142.63" (11.89'). Finally, the specific condition of reduced fuel state at lift-off on the last run reduced this slightly – but not significantly – to 142.12" (11.84'). The reason this has little effect is because the centre of the fuel tank is located at 156.0" (13.00'), so the CG change due to fuel burn is innocuous (see Section 3.1, design aim ix). Concluding therefore, compared to the Beryl version's CG at 141.00", K7 in the condition prior to lift-off showed an improvement of only around 1" to compensate for the much higher speeds. (NB Evaluation of the wreck indicates that, actually, 185lb of ballast was added in front of the former at 20" from the transom[54]; this gives an equivalent CG translation to that indicated above, which suggests that Ken Norris recalculated accordingly, though this is unrecorded. Also, he puts the tank distance at 159.0". The effect of these factors on the CG position calculated above is some 0.15" or 0.11%, ie insignificant[55]). The installation of various auxiliary items on the port side of the hull (some 80lb at ~18" off-axis) and its effect on lateral trim has been assessed. The resultant moments indicate that their effect is very much 'second order', i.e. not significant, when compared to the overall weight of the craft and the very large lateral moments of the spars and sponsons. A calculation of the lateral shift of the CG towards the port side shows this to be only 0.25" which is insignificant.[52] Indeed, photographs of the craft at rest (see Ch. 6) illustrate that it is in level trim both fore–aft and laterally, which implies that the centre of buoyancy CB is effectively at the CG (Section 2 v)). If there was an effect, one would expect to see this imbalance manifest itself in a list to port and plainly this is not the case.

viii) Stability

Static stability

In Bluebird K7, it was only possible to achieve a *conditional* static stability condition, as discussed in Section vi) a). In their 1957 paper in *The Engineer*,[2] the Norris brothers confirmed this, as well as the limits to such stability:

'It was not possible to get the C.P. [aerodynamic centre of pressure] acting through or aft of the C.G. However, the lift was of low magnitude and, as will be noted, the craft appeared to have ample margin of safety at 5 deg. pitch angle at speeds up to 250mph.*

It will be appreciated that although the craft would be aerodynamically unstable statically in pitch, i.e. any upward pitching would result in increasing aerodynamic pitching moment, the craft was still aerodynamically-hydrodynamically stable statically, as the same upward pitching would result in much less hydrodynamic lift forward.'

* The lift data shown in this paper indicated that critical pitching angle for take-off 'α' = 8°.

The schematic diagram of lifting forces and moment arm distances to the transom for Bluebird K7 is shown in Fig. 6. As can be seen, the position of L_A lies a long way forward of the CG – nearly 5 feet – and that of L_H is coincident with the CG.[2, 7, 15, 22] The position of the CG is that for K7 on the final run at take-off (see Table 3). The position of L_A was established from the wind-tunnel data.[19]

Fig. 6: Schematic diagram of the principal vertical forces acting on Bluebird K7. Their relative positions in relation to the transom are those pertaining to the final run on 4 January 1967.
© Dr K. Mitchell

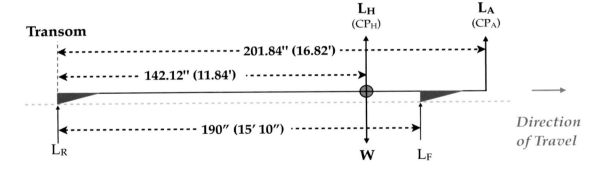

In further discussing stability, it is useful to consider three distinct conditions:

Condition 1:

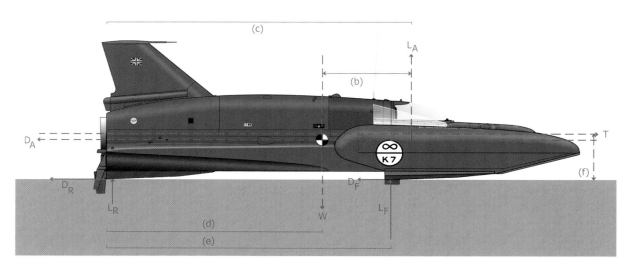

Fig. 7: Side profile of K7 showing the various forces and moment arms impinging on the craft in planing equilibrium (Condition 1 – see text).
© Damien Burke / Sabrina Pennewiss

This is the condition when the craft is planing normally in level trim, as shown in Fig. 7.

The diagram shows the main forces exerted on the craft. Aerodynamic lift L_A is shown acting at the CP_A at the seat position in the cockpit. Hydrodynamic lift is produced at the front and rear planes, L_F and L_R respectively. These upwards forces are balanced by the weight 'W' of the craft acting at the CG. Aerodynamic drag D_A is assumed to act through the horizontal line through K7's CG. Hydrodynamic drag is produced at the planes D_F and D_R respectively. Additionally, there are drag contributions from the wetted areas of the front stabilising fins and the rudder/rear stabilising fin which need to be taken into account in the overall drag assessment. The thrust force generated by the engine 'T' acts some 6" above the line through the CG.

For all these forces, appropriate moments can be calculated. For example, it can be seen that aerodynamic lift L_A produces an upwards moment L_A x b in relation to the CG. However, the convention in hydroplane physics is to relate it – and all other lift and drag moments – to the transom at the rear of the craft, i.e. moment L_A x c (note that this nullifies the moments due to forces acting at the transom, i.e. the rear wedge in contact with the water). By the same token, the hydrodynamic lift moment for a single front plane is L_F x e. For both, it is $2L_F$ x e. When all the contributing aerodynamic and hydrodynamic lift moments equal the restoring moment due to weight, W x d, and thrust T is equal to total aerodynamic plus hydrodynamic drag, equilibrium is achieved and the craft will plane on the water at constant speed.

Now it is important to consider what happens if that equilibrium is altered, e.g. thrust is lost. There has, perhaps, been a general misunderstanding among Bluebird enthusiasts that such an event would cause the craft to overturn. If the throttle is closed suddenly, or fuel flow stops or a flame-out occurs, thrust would be removed completely. The craft's forward inertia force then comes into play. This is initially equal to the lost thrust, but is gradually dissipated by the deceleration due to drag. In the absence of any other disturbing influences, the craft will therefore gradually decelerate in the planing attitude. This is not unlike what happens when driving a car on a level road: if the foot is removed from the accelerator and the gearbox placed in neutral, the momentum continues to carry the car forward but speed gradually decays due to aerodynamic drag and rolling resistance. If the throttle on K7 is partially closed (a realistic scenario considering Campbell's driving technique, see Section 4 iii)), the craft would decelerate due to drag until such drag equalled the new (lower) thrust; equilibrium would then be re-established, albeit at a lower speed.

Condition 2:
If increasing speed or a disturbance causes the craft to pitch up about the transom, a new set of conditions apply. A 'pitching moment' is generated of magnitude L_A x c, see Fig. 7. As this aerodynamic lift moment increases, the bows begin to rise and the forward planes leave the water, see Fig. 8.

This results in a complete loss of hydrodynamic lift at these planes. As 'α' increases, a critical condition is reached whereby the lifting moment, L_A x c, equals the restoring weight moment, W x d. At that point the craft will be on the verge of flying. A further speed increase, or small nose-up disturbance, will render the craft airborne. Accordingly, the craft must be operated within well-defined limits of speed and surface disturbance so that a maximum critical pitching angle is not exceeded.

A graph of pitch angle 'α' versus moment for Bluebird is shown in Fig. 9. Three curves are plotted for speeds of 300mph, 312mph and 328mph – 300mph is close to that at lift-off and was used in retrospective analysis by Ken Norris and associates following the crash,[15] 312mph allows investigation of the planing condition,[15] and 328mph was the peak speed achieved by K7. The progressively increasing moments with 'α' and the effect of speed in producing

Fig. 8: Bluebird K7 with front planes clear, at pitch angle 'α' degrees (Condition 2).
© Damien Burke / Sabrina Pennewiss

higher moments per angle of pitch can be seen. Also shown in the diagram is the limit established by the moment due to the weight of the craft. Where the respective curves cross, a ceiling value defines the critical 'α' at that speed. Exceeding this results in the craft becoming airborne. It can be seen to be 5.8° at 300mph, 5.3° at 312mph and 4.7° at 328mph.

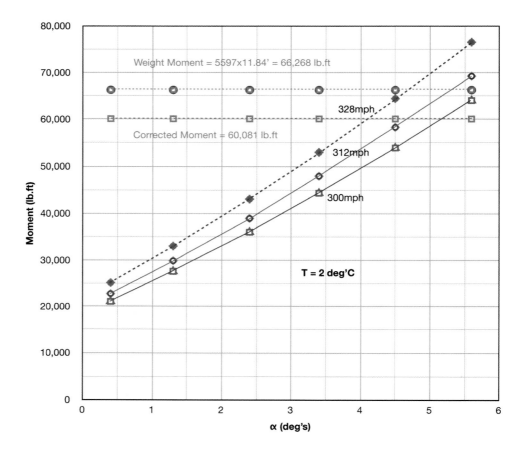

Fig. 9: Aerodynamic lifting moments plotted against pitch angle 'α' at speeds of 300mph, 312mph and 328mph.
© Dr K. Mitchell

However, the ceiling moment referred to above does not quite represent the true value as there were other factors which served to reduce it on the last run. In the retrospective analysis by Ken Norris *et al* referred to above,[15] an attempt was made to determine these factors (see Section 3 viii) d)).

The author has re-evaluated these calculations under the close eye of Tony James, who was involved in related assessments at that time.[35] They indicate that a net correction of 6,187lb.ft moment due to these factors needs to be subtracted from the ceiling figure of 66,268lb.ft, resulting in 60,081lb.ft. This is shown as the corrected moment in Fig. 9 and, of course, indicates that the critical values of 'α' have to be reduced, i.e. to 5.2° at 300mph, 4.7° at 312mph and 4.1° at 328mph. The safe operating envelope of K7 therefore becomes very constrained indeed.

But conventional analysis does not reveal the whole story in relation to the stability of Bluebird K7, and a further condition must be considered:

Condition 3:

Both Neil and I have become progressively intrigued over the last two years or so by photographic and film evidence of episodes in Bluebird's ostensibly normal running trim where it appears that the craft 'hovers' just above the surface with little or no contact of the planes with the water. See Fig. 10, which shows K7 at very high speed on the first run of the record-breaking attempt at Coniston in 1957. Note that Bluebird is running in perfect water conditions – the boat is in level trim – yet the front stabilising fins are visible. The planes are clear of the water and the residual spray is being produced by the only partially immersed fins. The rear shoe, although masked by spray, must be clear too because of the level trim; therefore, the spray must be rudder-generated. It is likely that such an episode was witnessed by Leo Villa:

'. . . *she came by me very fast and tramping badly, the bows higher than usual so I caught an occasional view of the forward port stabilising fin; it was my intention to have warned him that the craft looked very light on the bows. I never got the chance, because he started on his return run without even stopping to re-fuel and came by me much slower . . .*'[3]

Examining Neil's vast archive of photos, we identified more instances of similar behaviour, even as early as the runs at Lake Mead in the USA in 1955. Correlating these pictures with film evidence indicated they were not fortuitous, isolated shots but represented evidence of a hitherto unappreciated phenomenon in Bluebird's running characteristics. It was confirmed in the colour film footage which will be used in later analyses. A frame from that footage is shown in Chapter 8 on page 161.

Fig. 10: K7 on its record-breaking run at Coniston in 1957. Note the exposed stabilising fins as the craft experiences ground effect 'hovering' (Condition 3 – see text).
© G. Campbell

This shot from the final run coincides with K7 entering smoother water conditions north of the area agitated by the water brake on the prior run, but still some 1,000 metres from the start of the measured kilometre. The 'hovering' phenomenon is again evident. The speed of the craft in all these shots is some 270–280mph. Trying to explain this requires analysis of the origins of lift on the craft in this state. The first observation is that hydrodynamic lift cannot be generated in this condition as the planes are clear of the water. Classic analysis as discussed under Condition 2 does not explain this phenomenon, as it predicts that only around 1,000lb of aerodynamic lift exists in these conditions (see Fig. 4). That leaves some 4,600lb of 'latent' lift to be found to balance the weight of the craft.

The explanation appears to lie in what is referred to as 'ground effect'. Just above the surface of land or water, aerodynamic lift is increased quite dramatically by this phenomenon. It is familiar to pilots when they fly close to the ground and is utilised by seabirds as they cruise low over a lake or ocean. The effect has been – and is – exploited in the great Soviet *'Ekranoplans'* and wing-in-ground-effect (WIG) craft which are purpose-designed to maximise this lift.

To further understand the effects of this phenomenon on Bluebird, the writer consulted Dr Robert Englar of Georgia Tech Research Institute (GTRI), Atlanta, Georgia.[36] He is a world authority on the physics of unlimited hydroplane racers and the special conditions applying to the design of hydroplanes operating in ground effect. His specialist wind-tunnel facility at GTRI can test scale hydroplane models – the 1989 Miss Budweiser craft being a particularly well-known example – using both moving-ground and blown-air boundary-layer suppression techniques to simulate the conditions experienced by high-speed craft as they travel close to the surface.[37]

Bluebird's wind-tunnel testing at Imperial College – performed as it was in the 1950s – used the conventional technique of testing a model on the surface of a fixed ground plane positioned in the centre of the tunnel. Specialist wind-tunnel techniques as described above had not then been developed. Lift and drag were measured by sensors attached by wires to the craft. The assumption is made that blowing air down the tunnel and over the ground plane/model arrangement is a true representation of what happens when the full-size craft moves through air which is still in relation to the craft and the ground (with, of course, appropriate numerical corrections to allow for scale).[1, 2, 19, 21]

Research by Robert Englar *et al* (more than 30 years later, it should be noted) shows that the conditions are very different in that there are 'velocity and momentum deficits' due to boundary-layer generation as the air stream passes over the ground plane. There are additional problems due to the free stream flow being split into two above and below the ground plane. Englar's work indicates that lift can be enhanced by '10 to 15 times' when boundary-layer suppression techniques are adopted.[37] There are also increases in drag and nose-up pitching moments.

Notwithstanding the differing configuration of K7 with its less-efficient lift generation compared to unlimited hydroplanes, he was unequivocal in his opinion that Bluebird would be operating in strong ground effect, and lift enhancements of five times or more would be possible at the very high speeds experienced by the craft.* Precise lift figures, of course, can only be established by testing a scale model of K7 in its final 1967 configuration at a facility such as GTRI's. Dr Englar has kindly offered his research facilities and the authors are presently considering this proposal at the time of writing

The rough estimate of lift given above would easily explain the implied lift in our observations of Bluebird's 'hovering' episodes. If, as discussed previously, lift was 1,000lb, then a 5x ground effect enhancement would realise 5,000lb or more – easily enough to overcome weight and support 'hovering', at least for short periods. As the craft is essentially flying, moments are taken about the CG as in an aircraft. The condition is illustrated in Fig. 11.

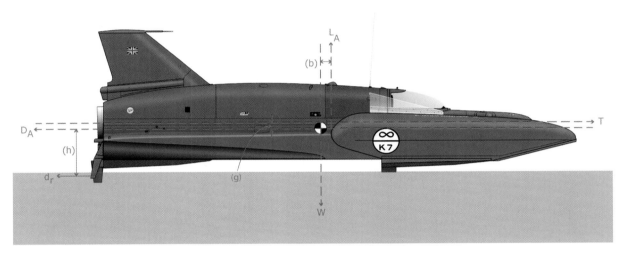

Fig. 11: Side profile of K7 showing the various forces and moment arms impinging on the craft in Condition 3 – see text.
© Damien Burke / Sabrina Pennewiss

Because K7 is 'balanced', it can be inferred that the centre of lift CP_A must be very close to the CG. It is shown in Fig. 11 as a rearwards movement of L_A compared to that in Fig. 7. This still produces a positive (nose-up) pitching moment L_A x b, but of commensurately smaller magnitude.

For equilibrium, this moment is balanced by two negative (nose-down) pitching moments. The first is due to engine thrust, T x 'g', and the second to drag created on the residual wetted area of the rudder and rear fin, d_r x h. The balance is achieved where the moment arm b = 8.40".[38] Therefore, CP_A has moved more than 4' rearwards of that shown in figures 7 and 8. It is of interest to comment that K7's plan form (Fig. 3) and the arguments in relation to 'kite area' (Section 3 v)) result in 'ground effect' lift being centred very close to the CG, which suggests that it is the broad, flat under-belly which is primarily responsible for this lift when K7 is just above the surface.

This condition is not a stable one. Dr Englar has shown that any small disturbance can cause the craft to deviate wildly in pitch, roll and yaw.[36, 37] Also, small height variations can cause huge variations in lift and pitching moments as the craft moves in and out of ground effect. If the nose begins to lift, ground effect is rapidly lost and Condition 3 reverts to that of conventional pitching aerodynamics as described in Condition 2. Engine thrust is critical in Condition 3, since it generates a restoring, nose-down moment. If speed is

* *The evidence of expert witness Dr Happian-Smith at the inquest into the crash in 2002 does not make any reference to the then current understanding of aerodynamic issues pertaining to hydroplanes, including this work, which had been published some 12 years earlier.*

below a certain critical value, throttling back will allow the craft to settle back onto the surface as the inertia force decays, assuming no other extraneous disturbance is experienced. However, if critical speed is exceeded, a reduction in power – for whatever reason – and subsequent decay of inertial energy will lead to a diminishing nose-down moment and the bows beginning to rise. Interestingly, in the course of discussions with Prof John Stollery he alluded to the fact that airflow into the intakes was critically affected by pitch angle, so much so that an engine flame-out could easily be precipitated by a relatively small increase in 'α'.[20]

In addition to this, the intake drag due to the throttled engine discussed earlier[15, 27, 32] introduces a further nose-up moment. The CP_A starts to migrate forward, thus increasing pitching moment. Pitch angle 'α' increases further, increasing moment, and so on. Once the craft exceeds the critical pitch angle (Fig. 9), it then rapidly diverges and 'flips over' backwards. Note in all this that Condition 3 precedes Condition 2, which are both airborne states. Most importantly, they do not require initiation by water disturbance, i.e. they can occur above flat calm.

ix) Yaw stability

Initial wind-tunnel measurements showed that Bluebird K7 was unstable in yaw, i.e. it had little or no 'weathercock' stability.[2] Fink argued that aerodynamic surfaces in the form of a tail plane, i.e. a fin to improve stability in yaw, and an additional horizontal stabiliser to improve stability in pitch should be included. However, the Campbell/Norris team had to reject this on the grounds that the craft needed to comply with the Union Internationale Motonautique (UIM) rules for record-breaking hydroplanes as they existed at the time.[4, 8] These stipulated that controlling methods had to be hydrodynamic, not aerodynamic.[2] In light of this, forward stabilising fins alongside the wedges were fitted which, along with the rudder, were the only directional stabilising elements. As the peak speeds of K7 increased on subsequent record-breaking runs, it was found that additional directional stability was required, and in 1958 a rear, fixed stabilising fin was fitted to the transom of K7.[9] The addition of an aerodynamic fin at around the same time – to house a braking parachute (never used in anger) – enhanced 'weathercocking' and perhaps indicates that the desire to comply strictly with the UIM rules was waning. If this decision was taken accordingly, it was a wise one because the rules were not keeping up with the increase in record-breaking speeds. High-speed hydroplanes may get away without aerodynamic control up to 200mph; those approaching 300mph and beyond will not!

The addition of the cropped Folland Gnat fin on the final version of K7 in 1966 was not just cosmetic; it made a significant difference to yaw stability. In combination with the hydrodynamic fins, the craft was rendered directionally stable.[24] One interesting, and perhaps surprising, benefit was that the enlarged fin had only ⅓ of the drag of its stubby predecessor.[15]

x) Dynamic stability

Fink predicted that the natural frequency of oscillation of K7 would be around 6Hz[4] and it was hoped that the structural rigidity of the craft, plus those elements incorporated in the design to avoid the problems which befell Crusader (see Section 3 i)), would provide sufficient damping up to the speeds then envisaged, i.e. 250mph. A particular resonance of this oscillation was noted at around 150mph.[2] This initiated quite violent tramping, though it quickly dissipated as speed increased beyond that point (Campbell is heard to refer to this on the sound recording of 4 January 1967 as he accelerates towards the kilometre marker on the first run). The problem with such oscillations is that as the energy input into a system or structure increases – and speed provides that energy – the amplitude of the oscillations will increase. The mechanical damping built into a design to combat this may only be effective up to a certain speed; exceeding it may very well further excite the system. In Bluebird, the 'signature' of such oscillation is the characteristic 'rooster-tail' spray pattern emanating mainly from the rear shoe. Analysing the film recordings indicates that this spray modulation is around 4.5–5Hz. As we shall see, it was particularly apparent under the high-speed conditions on the 4th. Perhaps it was this that led to a more detailed retrospective analysis of the phenomenon by Ken Norris after the crash, when he demonstrated that, theoretically, the oscillation in pitch was 5Hz and ~4Hz in roll.[39]

xi) Additional destabilising factors

In the post-crash analysis by Ken Norris *et al* referred to earlier,[15] an attempt was made to determine the potential destabilising effects of three additional factors:

i) Spray shields – these appendages added for the reason described were, nonetheless, aerodynamic lifting surfaces. The magnitude of this lift and the resulting moment was calculated to assess its effect on the overall moment balance equation.

ii) Intake drag – when the engine was throttled – or flamed-out – cessation of airflow into the intakes resulted in drag, which thereby induced a nose-up pitching moment (a condition flagged up by BS's Ken Pearson in his communication to Ken Norris the previous November[31, 32]). This moment and its effect were also calculated.

iii) Damage to the port forward spar fairing – an attempt was made to try and assess the potential lift generated by using a simple approximation of the shape of the damage which was known to have occurred (obviously, there was no physical evidence available). This damage was caused by impact with a duck on the return run of 27 December 1966. It was alluded to by Arthur Knowles – together with his consternation as to its possible effects – but it remained unrepaired apparently, on the instructions of Campbell himself[6] (it is clearly evident in the photo in Chapter 8 where K7 is leaving the water). The telling photograph by Paul Allonby of the extent of this damage can be seen on page 139. It is not known whether this was seen before the accident by those conducting the technical enquiries in the immediate aftermath of the crash. Tony James does not recall seeing it,[18] nor does John Stollery[20]. Like Knowles, on first coming across this picture the writer was aghast to discover that K7 had run like that and appalled by the aerodynamic consequences. Furthermore, the role of this damage in the crash has been almost completely neglected in many accounts and analyses, and not even mentioned in some. Ken Norris refers to it obliquely in his conclusions as to the 'Design and Operation of Future Craft' reported in *The Bluebird Years*[6]:

'Beware of asymmetry due to structural damage (e.g. bird strikes and debris in the lake) as these could aggravate or instigate tramping.'

The issue does not appear to have been raised at the inquest in 2002 and the expert witness, Dr Happian-Smith, makes no mention of it in his deliberations or conclusions.[6] In order to confirm or otherwise this opinion of the damage and its effects, the photograph was sent to three expert aerodynamicists to canvass their opinion. Firstly, Prof John Stollery, who confessed he was as alarmed as the writer to observe the degree of damage and find that Bluebird had run in this condition on the final day.[20] Secondly, my friend David Clarke, one-time aerodynamicist at BAE Warton, whose specialist area was the investigation of aerodynamic effects on military aircraft excrescences, e.g. camera pods, etc.[40] He was equally disturbed by the image and concurred as to its effects. Finally, the specific expertise and opinion of Dr Robert Englar was sought.[36] All three agreed that the predominant effect would be upon drag and that significant disturbance of airflow over that side of the craft would result in loss of lift. This would lead to an asymmetric distribution of lift across the boat, which would worsen with increasing pitch 'α'. The general effect on the trim of the boat would be such as to introduce a yaw–roll couple to port, raising the starboard sponson and effectively increasing 'α'. It would therefore be a destabilising factor.

A close examination of the photo indicates that the spar leading-edge fairing was indented all the way back to the spar itself, as the rivets therein can just be seen impressed into the flattened metal of the fairing (interestingly, secondary damage can be seen to the rear spar inner fairing, and a suggestion that the curvature has been sharpened towards the sponson). Previous damage to the rear port spar by collision with a seagull on 13 December 1966 had been partially repaired. It was decided to attempt a calculation of the differential drag produced by the forward spar damage, to try and get an idea of the inevitable asymmetric moment resulting from it.[41] At the peak speed recorded, the drag force was calculated to be 55.76lb; the moment arm to the centre of the damage (shown as dimension 'a' in Fig. 3) was some 3 ft from the hull axis. The resulting moment was therefore 3 x 55.76 = 167.3lb.ft. Hence the correcting force at the rudder some 12.16ft rearwards of the CG was 167.3lb. ft ÷ 12.16ft = 13.76lb. Such a force would have to be applied through the steering wheel by Campbell, but the effort required cannot be estimated as the gearing between it and the rudder is unknown. Nonetheless, it would have been an added complication in maintaining track, increasing as it would with speed. The consequences of both these effects on the final runs are discussed in Section 4.

Analysis of last runs, 4 January 1967

Preamble

Before one can attempt meaningful analysis of the runs of 4 January 1967, it is imperative that the photographic and film recordings of these events be placed in their correct geographic position. Accordingly, such recordings should show the first north–south run with the craft moving right to left in the frame because the camera positions were located at various points along the eastern shoreline of Coniston Water. The final south–north run should then proceed from left to right. Any recording, photographic or otherwise, which shows the contrary has been 'flipped' retrospectively. A

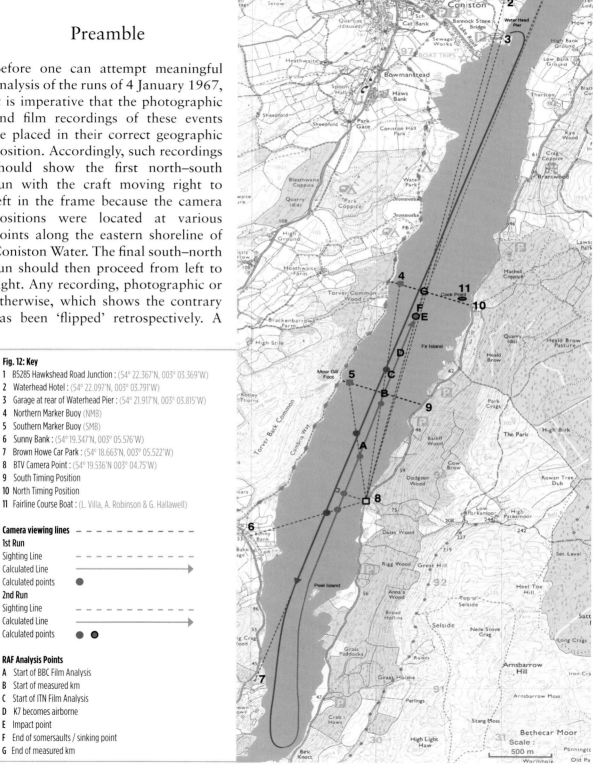

Fig. 12: Key

1 B5285 Hawkshead Road Junction : (54° 22.367'N, 003° 03.369'W)
2 Waterhead Hotel : (54° 22.097'N, 003° 03.791'W)
3 Garage at rear of Waterhead Pier : (54° 21.917'N, 003° 03.815'W)
4 Northern Marker Buoy (NMB)
5 Southern Marker Buoy (SMB)
6 Sunny Bank : (54° 19.347'N, 003° 05.576'W)
7 Brown Howe Car Park : (54° 18.663'N, 003° 05.522'W)
8 BTV Camera Point : (54° 19.536'N 003° 04.75'W)
9 South Timing Position
10 North Timing Position
11 Fairline Course Boat : (L. Villa, A. Robinson & G. Hallawell)

Camera viewing lines – – – – – – – –
1st Run
Sighting Line   – – – – – – – – –
Calculated Line   ⟶
Calculated points   ●
2nd Run
Sighting Line   – – – – – – – – –
Calculated Line   ⟶
Calculated points   ● ◉

RAF Analysis Points
A Start of BBC Film Analysis
B Start of measured km
C Start of ITN Film Analysis
D K7 becomes airborne
E Impact point
F End of somersaults / sinking point
G End of measured km

print of a colour 16mm film resurfaced in early 2010 and became available to the authors. This will be referred to hereafter as 'the film'. It has similar characteristics to the footage produced by Four Companies TV and in all probability are early rushes.

The second problem was to ascertain the exact position of the film camera on the eastern shore. This was not recorded on the RAF's track and timing analysis plot[42] at the time, but it was obvious from the footage that it lay somewhere south of the measured kilometre, a fact confirmed by Tony James's recollections.[18] Extensive frame-by-frame analysis of the 2,000 or so frames of 'the film' was performed and correlated with background topographic features and landmarks, including the north and south marker buoys at the ends of the measured kilometre close to the western shore.

Based on this work, a positional and timing correlation with the RAF analysis diagram and its key event points (see below) plus a direct photographic survey of the various key features around Coniston was undertaken (during January 2011, so that the various features were observed at a similar time of the year to that of the last runs). The landmarks around the lake were confirmed by GPS using Google™ Earth both on-site and remotely. All these findings unequivocally established the camera position on the shoreline immediately adjacent to the car park south-west of Dodgson Wood, see Fig. 12, point '8'.

Establishment of track

With the aid of the aforementioned film (which has been dynamically enhanced with regard to contrast and sharpness[43]), an attempt was made to determine the track of K7 on both runs. In addition, the help of 'Robbie' Robinson in this evaluation has been invaluable.[44] He recalls that Campbell had two sighting targets for his respective runs. On leaving Pier Cottage on the southern run, he focused on a small field immediately behind the car park at Brown Howe, see Fig. 12, point '7'. On the return run, his target was a feature at High Water Head immediately above the T-junction on the B5285 Hawkshead road – point '1' (Donald knew, of course, that he had to position the craft not only in relation to these targets, but in relation to the kilometre markers so that K7 crossed them at as near a right angle as possible, thus minimising errors which would have underestimated his speed). A further revelation resulted from our examination of the sound track, where two previously unintelligible comments were deciphered (see Appendix V). On the first north–south run-up, some 9.5 seconds before the northern marker, Campbell is heard to say '. . . *25 out of the way . . .*', and on the run-down 8.0 seconds beyond the measured kilometre, '. . . *passing through 25 vector off Peel Island . . .*'. Referring to plan-form diagrams of Bluebird (see Fig. 3), it was found that the angle between the boat's axis coincident with Campbell's head and the front of the sponsons was 25°. Correlating run timings with his statements confirmed he was using a sighting line to the Fairline support boat at the northern kilometre marker and beyond the southern end of the measured kilometre to Peel Island.

Key principles in establishing the position of an object from film/photographic recording are 'line of sight', background references, and the geometric method of 'similar triangles'. These were the principles adopted in the RAF analysis. Put simply, the distance from a viewing point to an object of interest can be calculated if one knows or can ascertain the physical dimensions of a feature in the background which, at a point in time, is coincident with the object. If the distance from the viewing point to the background feature can be determined from a map or GPS location, then the distance to the object of interest can be found by scaling its (known) dimensions to that of the background feature using similar triangles.

The film footage was scrutinised for individual frames with such features relative to Bluebird in the foreground. The first, and most obvious, were the marker buoys (see Fig. 12, points '4' and '5') The buoys were rectangular wooden structures 9' wide and rising to 14' above the waterline. They were lashed atop two rowing boats and covered in fluorescent red plastic. Their position was well known, being on the kilometre timing lines, but how far were they out in the lake? Again, Robbie's knowledge was crucial. Having positioned them – and, indeed, having been involved in their construction – he estimated the northern marker buoy (NMB) was about 100 metres from the shore and the southern one (SMB) 75–100 metres. It was thus possible to measure the distance from the camera point at point '8' to these buoys from a large-scale OS map (OL6). The respective distances were 2,016 metres for the NMB and 1,088 metres for the SMB.

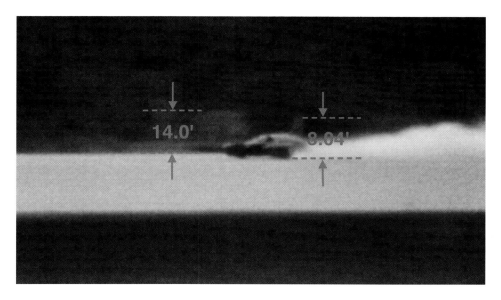

Fig. 13: Bluebird on the first run, one film-frame (1/24sec) before passing the southern marker buoy. Measures used for triangulation method of range-finding, shown in red.
© Dr K. Mitchell / Author's Collection

The relevant line-of-sight frame from the footage for the SMB is shown in Fig. 13. Initially, an attempt was made to apply the similar triangle principle using horizontal measures, but this proved problematic in that it was difficult to assess K7's relative angle to the camera, despite many attempts by Tony James and the writer using small-scale models to mimic it. Also, the blurring of horizontal detail in the background due to camera panning reduced clarity. It was therefore decided to adopt more accurate vertical measures. As it had been established that the height of the buoy(s) from the waterline was 14' and the height of K7 – from the top of the fin to the bottom of the rear wedge – was known (8.04'[55]),*, the distance to the boat could be calculated: 625 metres. The calculated point is shown as a blue dot in Fig. 12 and there is reasonable agreement with the predicted track, considering the errors involved. (*An alternative estimate of this height is 7.75' which is some 3.7% lower than that shown above[54]. However, the effect on the calculation of track is well within the measurement errors inherent in the triangulation method).

Further background references were identified and calculation of tracking points made. Sunny Bank on the south-western shore (point '6') provided good measures of size and elevation and helped enormously in confirming track on both runs at the southern end of the lake. Scaling of K7 in the frames where it was orthogonal to the camera provided further confidence of track on the initial part of the last run.

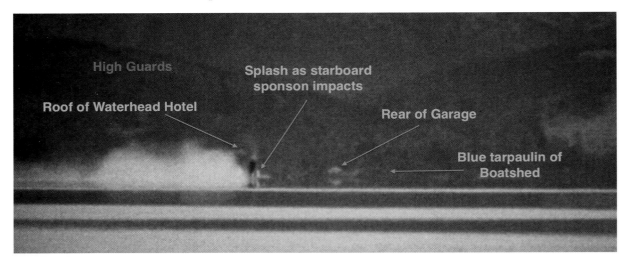

Fig. 14: Film frame coincident with the starboard sponson impacting the water. Annotations indicate other geographic/ structural features.
© Dr K. Mitchell / Author's Collection

Finally, two clear structures were identified in the final part of that run – see Fig. 14. A bright image on this and concluding frames was identified as the concrete garage to the rear of the boat shed at Waterhead Pier – point '3' on Fig. 12 (intriguingly, after very close examination it was possible to perceive a faint royal blue patch to the right of the garage – the tarpaulin of K7's boat shed). Slightly to the left in these frames was the roof and east gable of the Waterhead Hotel – point '2'. The significance of these sighting points becomes evident from Fig. 14, which is coincident in time with K7's starboard sponson impacting the water. This frame is in line of sight of point '2'. The intersection of this line and the track as calculated, and confirmed as coincident with Campbell's targeting on point '1', predicts the position of impact as shown in Fig. 12 (point 'E' on the RAF analysis diagram[42]). A check calculation using the length of the craft in the airborne vertical position to scale length to the line of sight on the garage confirmed the impact point.

This analysis confirms the widely held belief that Bluebird's final run was some way to the east of the first run,[6] passing close to Peel Island and then tracking towards the sighting point ('1') at the northern end of Coniston. This is confirmed by Campbell himself on the soundtrack: '. . . *getting straightened up now on track . . . rather closer to Peel Island . . .*'. Accordingly, it can be seen from Fig. 12 that his direction with regard to the measured kilometre is not quite perfect – 1° off track, to be precise – but the speed error is insignificant, being only 0.05mph at 300mph.

The first run

There has been universal acceptance that the outward run on 4 January 1967 passed off without any problems and in perfect trim.[3-6] This is an understandable view given the observations made by those who were there and were either very experienced, such as Leo Villa, or were otherwise seasoned enthusiasts of Campbell's record-breaking attempts. Much of the photographic and film evidence reinforces this notion. There has, therefore, perhaps been a tendency not to examine this run too closely and to concentrate on events surrounding the final run.

However, the authors have for some time held a view contrary to this, which is based on careful examination of the above evidence. There are two very significant photos of Bluebird in this context. The first is that taken by Geoff Hallawell (see Ch. 8, p. 156), who was stationed in the Fairline with Leo Villa and Robbie Robinson at the northern end of the measured kilometre. The second is the Press Association photograph taken by Eric Shaw as the craft exited the kilometre at the southern end (see Ch. 8, p. 157). The speed of the craft in the former is around 284mph and in the latter around 311mph. On the basis of these images, the craft's trim and running conditions could be taken to be well-nigh perfect. However, closer examination of the latter photo shows the front stabilising fins to be clearly visible and the planes free of the water. The craft has entered 'hovering' mode, Condition 3 (Section 3 viii).

The film footage becomes crucial in the analysis of events from this point onwards. An analysis of the individual frames and their timing was cross-referenced to a similar analysis of the sound recording.[45, 46] The viewing perspective is all-important and the advantage of this footage is that it is shot from a relatively southern camera position, which enables a north-westerly viewing perspective towards the measured kilometre. Events on the starboard (right-hand) side thus become uniquely visible. Some 1.5 seconds after leaving the kilometre, Bluebird develops a significant nose-up trim (perhaps as much as 4° or more) and, at a speed of some 310mph, the starboard sponson leaves the water, see Fig. 15. It remains clear for a period of 15 frames (0.63 seconds), and in that time Bluebird travels some 136 metres before settling back with a series of shorter bounces. It is approximately 2.5 seconds before the craft re-establishes level trim (Fig. 13), having travelled around 300 metres. At no stage of this run is there any evidence of the port sponson behaving in similar manner or of any tramping. The writer believes this to be the result of the port spar damage discussed in Section 3 viii) d). It

Fig. 15: K7 experiences the initial 'bouncing' episode on the first run. Note the 'rooster-tail' spray pattern.
© Author's Collection

is important to recognise that this footage, and the two still photos referred to above, confirm that the state of the lake was very good, indeed perfect in places. There is therefore no evidence of significant disturbance which could have provoked the above condition.

It should also be noted that the timing of the phenomenon coincided with Campbell having backed off the throttle. This is confirmed by his comment on the soundtrack: '. . . *Power off now* . . .' (Appendix IV), which occurs around 1 second prior to the end of the kilometre.[45, 46] Robbie recalls that this was Donald Campbell's usual approach to a run; progressively accelerating into the kilometre (the pilot would experience up to 0.5 g in the run-up at maximum power) then gently easing off towards the end.[44] Bluebird exits the measured kilometre at 311.2mph and speed gradually decays. Under reducing thrust, the craft is now experiencing the 'inertia-loaded' condition as discussed previously, with speed diminishing as aerodynamic and hydrodynamic drag oppose the effect of momentum. The lack of thrust-restoring (nose-down) moment would therefore manifest itself gradually, but eventually critically. Fortuitously for Campbell, the critical moments balancing the craft in this precarious condition were not disturbed and the craft gradually settled back onto the surface.

There is also another striking feature in Fig. 15: the appearance of the spray plume and its striking 'rooster-tail' modulation. As discussed earlier (Section 3 viii) c)), it appears to be the result of K7's natural frequency of oscillation causing the rear shoe to 'hop' across the water surface. The fact that the engine would be backed off during this episode reinforces the idea that engine thrust tended to dampen the oscillation at the shoe and/or jet efflux tended to suppress the spray plume.

Some 13 seconds after leaving the kilometre and at around 200mph, an engine flame-out is indicated as Campbell reports that he is trying to relight the engine[45, 46], see Appendix IV. The engine had obviously cut out as K7 exited the measured kilometre. It is a further 12 seconds and just south of Peel Island

Fig. 16: Initial application of water brake shows little increase in size and form of spray pattern.
© Author's Collection

before Campbell states *'relight made normal'*. Coincident with the start of this relighting episode, he reports *'. . . brake has gone down . . .'*. The authors, in the interests of establishing the time and effect of water-brake deployment on the spray plume, have carefully analysed some 300 or so frames (12 seconds in total) following deployment. Initially little, if any, effect can be seen in the plume, see Fig. 16.

However, over the next 8 seconds the plume gradually changes to that observed in Fig. 17 as K7 passes Peel Island. There appears to be no momentous

Fig. 17: Changing spray pattern as water brake starts to bite; K7 passing Peel Island.

© Author's Collection

cataract of spray conjunctive with the brake being deployed as seen in (albeit slower) runs of late 1966, or as highlighted in the photo of the return run on Christmas Day (see Ch. 7, p. 137). Our speculation here is that the hopping rear shoe tended to reduce the 'bite' of the water brake and thus its effectiveness. As speed decayed, the amplitude of the rear hop decreased and allowed the brake to penetrate the water further.

One other extraordinary revelation came from the soundtrack. We clearly deciphered the phrase *'. . . down at Brown Howe . . .'* some 29 seconds after leaving the kilometre and 8.5 seconds after passing Peel Island. After a further 2.5 seconds, Campbell reports: *'. . . passing through 100 . . .'*. The significance of this is that he must have travelled far deeper into the southern bay than anyone had previously envisaged since he was still doing 100mph beyond Brown Howe (see Fig. 12) before Bluebird finally fell into her taxiing position, off-plane, at around 50mph.

The final run

Campbell was in contact with Leo Villa and base while manoeuvring at the southern end of the lake. For whatever reason, technical or otherwise, there was an interruption in his communication with Leo and no further discussion took place between them. Once he was informed of his speed from the first run, relayed via the base station from the timekeepers, he was on his way back . . .

The film footage commences as Bluebird reappears from behind Peel Island some 27 seconds prior to final impact. On the soundtrack, Campbell confirms he is '. . . *straightening up now on track . . . rather closer to Peel Island . . .*', see Fig. 12. What follows is an 11.5 second episode of the most violent pitching and tramping observed on either run or, indeed, any that the authors have witnessed in previous recordings of Bluebird, see Fig. 17a. Excerpts from Campbell's commentary convey the situation succinctly: '. . . *tramping like mad . . .*', '. . . *tramping like hell . . .*', '. . . *the water's very bad indeed . . .*'. The condition of the lake in this area can be seen to be poor, presumably as a result of the wash from the water brake. However, approximately 16 seconds prior to impact K7 enters very much improved water conditions just north of the coincidence of track and camera line to Sunny Bank, see Fig. 12. The craft then experiences several 'hovering' episodes, the longest lasting some 17 frames (0.71 seconds), (see Ch. 8, p. 161). Its speed is around 270mph. There is no evidence of wash effects from the southern end having migrated northwards. Although there is a suggestion of some disturbance near point 'B',[47] that is not confirmed by Robbie, who recalled that the conditions on the lake that he and Leo Villa were able to survey from the Fairline were very acceptable for both runs and, indeed, long after.[44]

At this point (13.5 seconds to impact), Donald Campbell reports: '. . . *I can't get over the top / I'm galloping over the top . . .*' (there is uncertainty as to the words here). The circumstances at this time are that K7 is accelerating rapidly at nearly 10mph/second (+0.5 g) on a good surface – see Ch. 8, p. 161) – yet is still nearly one kilometre from the start of the measured distance. Campbell would know this and therefore be expecting to arrive at the 'gate' at very high speed – perhaps 320mph or more – and then in customary fashion use his momentum to 'coast' the rest and easily break the record. The context of the aforementioned phrase therefore favours the latter interpretation, i.e. *'I'm galloping over the top'*, as it precisely describes what was happening at that point. This was not to last, however, and in the quickly developing scenario of this unprecedented high-speed run things were about to take a very different course.

To further examine the run, recourse was made to the RAF analysis and the various waypoints defined in it along the craft's track in relation to film recordings made at the time.[42] Very significantly, in this assessment the original velocity–time/frame graphs underpinning the analysis were made available to us by Tony James. These data were re-analysed and the results are shown in Fig. 18. To allow some positional correlation, the reader should view this diagram alongside that in Fig. 12.

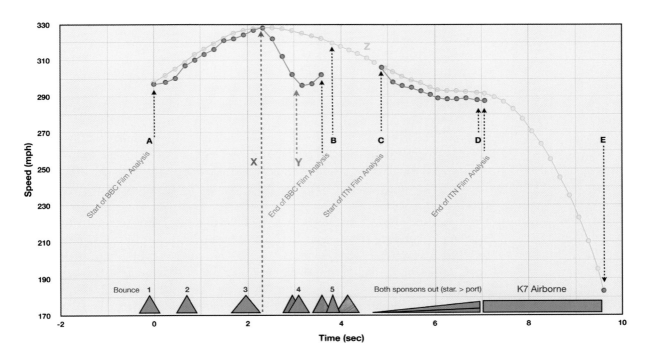

The RAF analysis defined the waypoints as follows:

Point 'A'   Start of BBC film analysis
Point 'B'   Start of measured kilometre
Point 'C'   Start of ITN film analysis
Point 'D'   K7 becomes airborne
Point 'E'   Impact point
Point 'F'   K7 sinking position (not shown on profile)
Point 'G'   End of measured kilometre (not shown on profile)

Fig. 18: Velocity/time graph derived from original RAF analysis data charts.
© Dr K. Mitchell / A.E. James

The diagram is a velocity profile of essentially the last 10 seconds of the run with key features appended. The curves shown in red are those of the original velocity–time/frame graphs determined by the RAF from the raw frames of the BBC and ITN film recordings. Note that the curves are not contiguous and there is a gap in the data between the two recordings of some 1.26 seconds. No analysis exists beyond just over 7 seconds, i.e. the last 2.71 seconds prior to impact (it is important to recognise here that the film recordings themselves covered the entirety of the run; the RAF's analysis is partial because only those frames where a meaningful assessment of speed could be made were analysed).

The curve shown in yellow is the time-honoured profile published following the crash and referred to in many publications and retrospective analyses since. It seems to be an attempt to construct a general speed envelope to explain the circumstances surrounding K7's final few seconds, but it is unclear who produced it.[18] Referring to point 'Z' on that curve, the slope has been used to establish the deceleration figure of -0.6 g commonly quoted in post-hoc analyses and, indeed, in Happian-Smith's assessment at the inquest recorded in *The Bluebird Years*[6]. However, this region lies within the area where there is no RAF analysis so, intriguingly, there are no data to underpin this figure.

Broadly, there is relatively good correlation between the two curves – where source data exist. Bluebird passes point 'A' at just under 297mph and accelerates hard at +0.63 g up to the maximum of 328mph, indicated by 'X'. However, from this point there is a major divergence of the two curves up to the point where the analysis of the BBC recording ceases. The data show a very significant reduction from Bluebird's peak speed of 328mph to 296mph – some 34mph. This represents a deceleration of -1.86 g in the 0.84 second period between points 'X' and 'Y'. Note that this occurs some 0.65 seconds prior to point 'B', the start of the measured kilometre. It is impossible to predict what happens to the speed profile in the interregnum between the BBC footage ending and the ITN material starting. It may swing up towards the other curve before returning to point 'C', but this can only be regarded as conjecture as there are no data.

As for the data derived from the ITN footage, there is relatively good agreement between the two up to the point where K7 is fully airborne and the analysis ceases just beyond point 'D'. Speed decays fairly rapidly from 306mph at 'C' to 289mph, 1.20 seconds later. There then follows a relatively constant speed phase to point 'D' when the craft gets fully airborne at 288mph, 2.70 seconds from impact. Bluebird loses speed very quickly during the somersault phase and impacts the water over 100mph slower, at 183mph.

To assess the events shown in the film footage in relationship to Fig. 18, cross-referencing of the timings therein was performed using the point of impact (9.6 seconds in the RAF analysis) as the reference point and working backwards from there (see Fig. 14).[46] The soundtrack was cross-referenced in like manner.[45] Just prior to point 'A', at around 292mph, Bluebird's starboard sponson is seen to leave the water for some 11 frames (0.46 seconds) in what can only be described as a bounce, see Fig.19.

This is similar to the behaviour observed at the end of the first run. Although the port sponson cannot be seen from this perspective, the spray pattern suggests that it is still in contact with the water. The rear end looks very light, and it is open to conjecture whether the rear shoe is still in contact. This bounce

Fig. 19: First 'bounce' (1) on final run (just prior to point 'A', see Fig. 18).
© Author's Collection

is shown diagrammatically at the bottom of Fig. 18 as a blue triangle, the base of which represents the duration of the bounce (blue – starboard sponson, red – port). The phenomenon coincides with Campbell's comment '. . . *and (she's actually giving) a hell of a bloody row in here . . .*'. A further four bounces of varying duration occur, with the entire episode lasting some 4 seconds.

It would appear that K7, having initiated this cyclic, bouncing condition (mean frequency ≈0.8Hz) and travelling at maximum sustained thrust, is released into a hitherto unprecedented level of acceleration of +0.63 g to speeds never achieved before. Reduced hydrodynamic planing drag experienced during such bouncing would inevitably aid acceleration. Bounce '3' is particularly energetic as it can be seen to last 15 frames (0.62 seconds).

When the starboard sponson re-makes contact with the water it does so with such violence that spray emanates from the whole length of the shoe and perhaps also forward of it. This event coincides with the peak speed of 328mph at point 'X' and therefore appears to initiate the rapid deceleration described previously to point 'Y'. This must be due to the huge reactive loads and concomitant drag experienced by the front shoes. As this happens, Campbell reports: '. . .*I can't see anything . . .*'. One can only conclude that this must have been a pretty brutal event – among several only slightly less so – a fact that can only be fully appreciated by viewing the rolling footage. The fact that Donald Campbell claims his vision is impaired is entirely reasonable given the vertical and horizontal shocks the craft – and its pilot – were experiencing. It must also not be forgotten that the craft was vibrating violently at its natural frequency of around 5Hz (note the spray plume in Fig. 20). Such physiological effects are not unprecedented. Roland Beamont, test pilot of TSR2, experienced 'eyeball oscillation' on one test flight in 1964 caused by one of the Olympus engines violently vibrating at 7Hz.[48]

A further significant revelation was made when studying the film. The increasingly acute angle of view made it possible to see a dull orange glow inside K7's tailpipe – turbine flame! This was clearly evident during bounce '2', 9.04 seconds prior to impact. Further examination of frames during bounce '3', e.g. Fig. 20, confirm the flame and thus engine combustion. However, during bounce '4' and all subsequent frames examined the flame had disappeared, indicating that combustion had ceased, and with it engine thrust. The timing of this is some 0.78 seconds prior to point 'B' and coincident with point 'Y' in Fig. 18, i.e. following the major deceleration associated with bounce '3'. As has already been discussed, engine thrust moment is crucial in exercising some control in the highly unstable hovering and bouncing conditions and this was now lost.

Fig. 20: Second 'bounce' (2) on final run, 9.04 seconds prior to impact. A dull orange turbojet glow can just be seen in the tailpipe.
© Author's Collection

Beyond bounce '4', detail of the craft's behaviour becomes less clear in the film and the viewing perspective favours the BBC and ITN recordings. Analysis of these after the crash was performed not only by the RAF but also by Norris Brothers and associates.[47, 49] Analysis from bounce '4' was possible, but not events prior to that. They confirm bounces '4' and '5' of the starboard sponson, but also three episodes of counter-phase bouncing of the port sponson (red triangles, Fig. 18). The fact that these events overlap indicates that the entire front end is clear of the water for short periods. There is no evidence in any of the recordings or these analyses of any 'tramping'. This is further underscored by the adjunctive notes to the RAF analysis (Note 10): '. . . *there appears to be little evidence of tramping . . .*'.[42]

Bluebird has now entered an extremely dangerous condition. At a speed well in excess of 300mph and perhaps as much as 310mph (sadly indeterminate, as there are no RAF analysis data to confirm it), K7 enters the measured kilometre doubly penalised by lack of engine thrust restoring moment downwards and consequent intake drag moment upwards. The craft experiences strong ground effect and enters the hovering mode, i.e. Condition 3, at point 'C' (see Ch. 8, p. 162). Note the condition of the water; very good, with only the merest undulation. The roll-yaw couple to port due to the damaged spar drag is clearly evident in this photo. So, too, is the fact that all planes are clear, including that on the port side as the stabilising fin is visible. The rear shoe is completely out and the rear fin and rudder are all that retain contact. (Tony James performed a careful geometric analysis of this photo which appears on page 162, picture 1, in late January 1967 and calculated that the starboard sponson was some 7.14" clear, which resulted in a mean pitch angle of $\alpha \approx 1.5°$.[50])

Bluebird then appears to 'glide' for about 2 seconds, albeit with a gradually increasing angle of attack. As ground effect diminishes with increasing 'α', K7 moves into Condition 2 at a speed just under 290mph. With the aerodynamic centre of pressure now advancing forwards, Bluebird's delicate balance is slowly eroded. At 3.5 seconds to impact, Campbell anticipates irrevocable disaster with the cry *'I've got the bows out'*. As he does so, the lift moment approaches the critical 'α' of ~5.2° (Fig. 9), exceeds it, and Bluebird commences its inexorable climb skywards at point 'D'. Donald Malcolm Campbell ushers in his final farewell: *'. . . I'm going . . .'*.

Once airborne, K7's dynamics change dramatically. Because the CG is some way behind the aerodynamic centre of pressure, lift and drag combine to initiate a rotation of the craft about the CG in the vertical plane, i.e. a developing somersault. The rate of rotation is approximately 0.60 revs/sec. The craft's distribution of mass with its large heavy sponsons forwards and significant structure, engine, tailpipe, etc. rearwards – and their inherent momentum – sustains the rotation by virtue of a flywheel effect. The fore–aft plane of the somersault is not in line with the craft's track because it takes off skewed by the roll-yaw to port; a precession in that direction therefore ensues. During this episode, Campbell experiences a 'g' factor varying between +3.6 g (bows vertically upwards) and -0.1 g (bows vertically downwards), due to a combination of the centripetal force of rotation and the rapidly diminishing forward speed (some 40mph/sec).[51] The port sponson impacts the water a fraction of a second before the starboard one ($\approx$40 msec or one frame of the ITN footage) at point 'E' (Fig. 12). The violence of this impact launches K7 into the air for another complete 360° somersault – but in the reverse sense to the first – before impacting the water again. Four somersaults along the surface of the water ensue before the craft comes to rest and ultimately sinks at point 'F'.

Conclusions

The colour film footage referred to extensively in this book presented the authors with a unique opportunity to analyse the last runs of Donald Campbell and Bluebird K7 on Coniston Water on 4 January 1967. Unique because the relatively southern position of the camera provides a perspective denied other recordings. We were also able to assess and analyse much documentation, some of which was already in the public domain (but nonetheless required considerable effort to unearth), and some not. Another key factor was the very generous cooperation of those engaged in the original project and of those still alive who witnessed the events on that fateful day at first hand.

Bluebird was designed in the 1950s to achieve world records, something it did successfully and without challenge for some 11 years. In doing so, K7 raised record speeds from 200mph to approaching 300mph. It was the first craft to achieve this successfully using jet-engine propulsion. In conjunction with its charismatic owner and pilot, Bluebird retains a unique position in the history of speed record-breaking. Within the speed range envisaged for the initial design, i.e. 250mph, and the accrued experience of running beyond that for another nine years, K7 demonstrated an adequate stability margin to cope with those speeds. However, the attempt to take the same basic design into a very different speed and aerodynamic stratum of 300mph+ inevitably reduced stability margins on what was already an 11-year-old craft. Added to this, the aerodynamic precepts underpinning the craft's stability were subject to the hitherto unappreciated complications of ground effect, which would not be fully understood or quantified in relation to hydroplanes for another twenty-five years. It should be emphasised, however, that quantitative verification of this phenomenon requires testing of a scale facsimile of Bluebird in an appropriate wind-tunnel facility, such as that at GTRI. This would not, of course, test the equally vexing question of dynamic stability, and the author's suspicion that the craft's natural frequency was inadequately damped at such high speed remains.

The effect of damage to the port front spar should not be underestimated in any discussion of destabilising factors inherent in the final runs. It created serious disturbance of the airflow over that side of K7, resulting in higher drag and lower lift, and would have further compounded stability problems. Its effect can be clearly seen in the craft's 'hovering' and 'bouncing' episodes, where there is a clear bias in favour of the starboard sponson becoming airborne. It would also have presented additional problems for the pilot as a progressive yaw to port with increasing speed would require proportionate right rudder to maintain track. Although we cannot determine the arm-loads required, at very high speed they could have been considerable.

The modifications to the craft were done within the parameters set by the Campbell/Norris team, which can best be described as part-business, part-promotional, part-social, i.e. quintessentially 'British'. Historical review must therefore pay due homage to such context or it will misrepresent that aspect. The project team was given an inordinately short time to complete the refit of K7 – just seven weeks – but eventually took twice that. There was little opportunity for proper testing due to the financial and time constraints, which must be seen against the complex cocktail of events surrounding Britain's most celebrated post-war record-breaker. That part of the story is not told here, as it has been fully addressed in Chapters 2 and 3. Significant elements in K7's modification were only nominally tested at the factory, e.g. engine runs. High-power running was deferred to that on-site at Coniston, together with substantial replacement tests, modifications and 'fixes' to overcome significant problems. This included engine replacement and issues with the Orpheus's fuel boost pump system, where several tweaks were required to derive the maximum over-rated thrust from the engine as the craft was not performing in line with expectations. It must also be noted that performance would not have been helped by the high wedge angles, with their inherently poorer planing efficiency and increased hydrodynamic drag. Added to this, the advantage of a more forward centre of gravity designed to maintain stability margins was all but lost when lead ballast weight had to be added to allow the craft to 'plane'. Equally frustrating were the vicissitudes of an unusually unsettled and stormy early winter in Coniston, which tested the patience, fortitude and resolve of Bluebird's skipper and his small, yet exceptionally skilled and committed cadre of professionals as they laboured on their charge with little opportunity to savour their work in the form of favourable conditions for a run.

As to the events of the final day, it has been possible to establish the track the craft took on both runs. The first followed that to Campbell's usual sighting target down at Brown Howe. At the bottom end of the lake, it is not possible to verify track, but there must have been some considerable elongation of the run into the southern bay as Bluebird was still at considerable speed beyond Brown Howe. The last run has been thought for many years to be more eastwards than the first, and our study confirms that. It commences much closer to Peel Island and then tracks towards the target at the northern end of the lake.

It has been universally accepted that the first run took place without incident and in perfect trim. This is perhaps understandable because the viewing perspective of TV crews, press photographers and experts such as Leo Villa was remote to events occurring on the starboard side of the craft towards the south-west of the kilometre marker. However, our analysis is such as to challenge that view. The craft passed the southern kilometre marker with a progressively increasing nose-up pitch, followed by a bouncing episode where the starboard sponson left the water. Disaster was only narrowly averted on that run as the highly critical pitching angle for take-off was not quite exceeded. The bouncing episode did not appear to be precipitated by tramping or water conditions; the latter were nearly perfect. An engine flame-out then followed, for which we cannot offer any specific cause. It could have been related to failure of the engine's fuel boost system or its electrical supply trying to sustain the very high levels of fuel pressure demanded by the (over-rated) engine. Equally, fuel agitation/cavitation or starvation effects due to the intense vibration the craft was experiencing, or a breakdown in fuel flow, may have been a factor. Nor can the disturbed airflow into the intakes at higher pitching angles be excluded. It is, of course, quite possible that it was a combination of more than one of these factors. Following this, deployment of the water-brake appears not to have been as efficacious as observed on (slower) previous runs. No vast cataract of spray is evident, only a change in the spray-plume pattern which suggests that the brake was not totally immersed until very late in the run. An oscillating rear shoe could have caused such an effect.

It is our contention that the demise of Bluebird K7 on the final run was caused by the craft entering the highly dangerous hovering state (Condition 3) following a series of violent bouncing episodes. Almost airborne and with a yaw-roll bias to port due to the spar damage, shorn of moderating engine thrust moment the craft proceeded to climb slowly as the aerodynamic centre of pressure moved forwards (Condition 2). Exceeding its critical pitch angle of ~5.2° under these conditions rendered Bluebird fully airborne, then caused the craft to develop a somersault due to inertial flywheel effect. At no time in this critical part of the incident did disturbed water or tramping play a part. The bouncing phenomenon cannot be described as tramping as it is of much lower frequency – around 0.8Hz – whereas true tramping tends to occur at the natural frequency of the craft, i.e. 4–5Hz. Indeed, the only occasion when tramping was observed (to dramatic effect) was on the run-up from Peel Island, when disturbed water was encountered from water-brake deployment on the previous run. Some 1,000 metres prior to the southern kilometre marker this disturbance ceased, and from then on the water surface was very acceptable. This fact is confirmed by expert witness 'Robbie' Robinson, who, along with Leo Villa, was monitoring such conditions in addition to the running of the craft.

This study confirms the long-held view that Bluebird suffered engine failure at a critical stage of the last run. The extinguished turbine flame in the jet-pipe seen some 7 seconds prior to impact bears testimony to that fact. As to why the engine failed on this run, this cannot be specifically identified. It could have been due to a recurrence of the factors discussed with relation to the first run. However, there is one additional and important consideration: K7 was taking a terrible pounding from the bouncing, and following the third and worst it suffered a significant deceleration of 34mph in 0.84 seconds, equivalent to -1.86 g. Although it is impossible to calculate instantaneous vertical loadings as the front plane(s) re-entered the water, they must have been very high as spray is seen to emanate from the whole of the starboard plane and perhaps beyond. Bluebird's overall structure was immensely strong and designed to cope with such exigencies, but it is impossible to completely exclude the possibility that some piece of ancillary equipment – related to engine function, perhaps – may have broken or become dislodged. This, however, can only remain speculative; the true cause of the engine ceasing to produce any meaningful thrust may never be known.

One factor that we might comment on is water-brake deployment. We can find no film or photographic evidence to confirm that deployment occurred. It is important to appreciate that Campbell was very unlikely to use it, as he had received strict instructions from Ken Norris that it was too dangerous at speeds much above 200mph. At the 290mph take-off speed, deployment was therefore not an option and the pilot would have known that. If it had been deployed in the critical hovering phase, it could have introduced a violent destabilising moment with disastrous effects. In the later stages when the transom was well clear of the water, i.e. by ≥ 4", it would have been rendered ineffective in any case.

Once Bluebird left the water and entered its final somersault, Campbell experienced g-forces estimated at -0.1 g to +3.6 g due to a combination of the centripetal force of rotation and the forward deceleration due to drag. Such forces are not – in physiological terms – high enough to produce unconsciousness in the pilot and he would be aware of his situation until final impact.

One question that the writer has often pondered, and perhaps readers might too, is whether Donald Campbell would have been able to regain control of the craft with the aid of a functioning engine. The clue to answering this lies in the first run. Disaster had only just been avoided then, albeit with full throttle control, at some 310mph. Adding a further 18mph to 328mph, plus a diminishing weight moment due to fuel burn, the craft exceeded the bounds of any human control. Campbell and his beloved Bluebird had crossed the

Rubicon and there was no way back. Poignantly, readers might also consider another 'What if . . .' situation. If the measured kilometre had commenced at point 'A', approximately 600 metres south, K7 would have achieved a mean speed of 303–304mph on the final run, which when averaged with the first run of 297.6mph would have just given him the record at a little over 300mph. Sadly, he would not have survived to savour his achievement.

Donald Campbell
Test pilot and master of Coniston Water

Having listened intently to the voice recording of Campbell during those last runs, and spent many hours trying to decipher the problematic phrases buried in the RT crackle, one learns something very profound about the approach that he took to those runs. It resonated with recordings I had heard in a different context; that of the aviation test pilot. The nature of the test pilot's trade is not merely the test-flying of a prototype aircraft. It is to convey – point by point – his observations, data, etc., on the aircraft's status and performance and to do so clearly and succinctly. Why? So that he and those that are listening to – and recording – the comments will not only be informed as events unfold, but will have information to review later, regardless of the outcome. In David Tremayne's book *Donald Campbell – The Man Behind The Mask*, Ken Norris gives a most telling assessment of Campbell in this regard:

'. . . *Donald would tell you all the way through what he was doing. You could hear it: constant; precise; accurate . . . he would simply tell you exactly what was happening . . . He could describe it and tell you about it at the same time. It was natural. He was very test-pilotish . . .*'

During the last six months, while researching, analysing and finally writing this chapter, I have had the uncanny sense that Campbell was not only informing those who were present, but also those who might later wish to review the whole thing – whether the situation ended happily or in disaster.

Allied to this notion, we believe that it is possible to present an argument that Donald Campbell had a strategy when it came to performing these runs. We think it helps the understanding of what happened on that fateful day and is totally consistent with his approach as that of a test pilot. It is important to appreciate that *no* living person had Donald Campbell's knowledge of Coniston Water and the special skills of piloting a craft on it at speeds approaching 300mph and beyond (the only other person had been his father, and even then at half the speed). An excellent example of his mastery of this lake is illustrated in the situation which unfolded following the first run. Approaching Peel Island and still at some 200mph, he had to deal with the relighting issue, the deployment of the water brake and, as he passed Brown Howe still doing over 100mph, to steer to port to avoid the rapidly approaching shoreline (see Fig. 12). One needs no better example than this to understand the remarkable skills and knowledge Campbell brought to bear not only in these runs, but also to the many runs over the years he had negotiated on the same lake.

It is our assertion that Donald Campbell's strategy on that day included a clear intention to return without refuelling after the first run and thereby exploit the advantage of a quick turn-around in the southern bay. There are good reasons that support this theory. Firstly, in relation to water conditions. We know that these were very good and any influence on them would be that generated by K7 itself. The significant water disturbances of Bluebird's runs were generated by two principal effects: a bow-wave at the beginning of the run prior to the craft coming onto the planes, and the application of the water brake following the run. The first of these would spread away from the track at an oblique angle both towards the shore and southwards towards the timing area. It is possible to estimate the velocity of the wave front emanating from K7 to be approximately 2m/sec (this is based on the wave length estimated from the film footage of around 3 metres). The distance it would have had to travel to the northern kilometre marker was around 2,000 metres, so it would start to encroach on the measured distance some 1,000 seconds or approximately 17 minutes later, but very much dissipated in effect.

Beyond the measured kilometre, the disturbance caused by the water-brake would create a wave front travelling southwards and again obliquely towards the shore. Migration northwards would require shoreline reflection mechanisms. Nonetheless, if it were argued that in the worst case a disturbance proceeded northwards at the same velocity as for the northern disturbance, it would arrive at the southern marker around 9 minutes later. Campbell therefore had a window of opportunity to return on the second run without these disturbances having encroached on the critical area, i.e. the measured kilometre. It might also be interpreted that Campbell's RT exchanges in the southern bay which suggest some irritation in trying to obtain the speed of the first run, were an entirely understandable reaction to his wanting to 'get on with things' while this window of opportunity presented itself. A crucial recollection is that of 'Robbie' Robinson who recalls that Campbell often adopted an approach whereby he returned without refuelling and without delay and was entirely confident in it.

There is a further disruptive factor that we have not considered, i.e. that due to planing. This would be relatively second order compared to the effects above, but still needs to be assessed. If the outward and return runs were separated by some distance in terms of track, it is possible to assume that water disturbance in the first would be minimal in the second (see illustrations in Chapter 8). Again, Campbell knew from previous runs on Coniston that this was the case, so he proceeded to make the first run close to the western shore. As well as his aiming point, he cleverly used a sighting line off the front sponsons to confirm his position as he approached the measured kilometre, and beyond it when he entered the southern reaches of the lake. The second run would therefore need to be closer to the eastern shore to maximise the separation, and that is precisely what Campbell did.

We believe that Donald Campbell's narrative clearly accords with this view. He reports the poor water conditions around and beyond Peel Island as he returns, and then, as he enters smoother water (some 1,000 metres before the southern kilometre marker), confirms his status with the report *'I'm galloping over the top'*. The author not only believes this to be the most valid interpretation of that phrase after listening to it *ad nauseam*, but also believes it to be wholly consistent with observations concurrent with it. Firstly, the film footage confirms the water state; secondly, the timing correlations performed on the film and the sound recording locate the comment in time and position, and thirdly, the craft is accelerating so rapidly that Campbell knows he is going to arrive at the southern marker with a record-breaking reserve of speed. Of course, in the drama of this final run he could not, at that stage, have predicted the disaster that was about to unfold only a few seconds later. No strategic forethought or honed skill of a record-breaker could prepare him for that . . .

Much has been written about Campbell's failure to consult with Leo Villa about the water conditions on the lake after the first run. Because of theories built on the presumed poor overall condition of the lake, it has been implied that Leo Villa would have reported this to Donald Campbell and the latter made an error of judgement in not consulting him. This does not fit with the theory set out above or, indeed, with the testimony of an expert witness who sat next to Villa and felt that water conditions were very good. It is therefore equally tenable that if Campbell *had* canvassed Villa's opinion, he would have received a positive response.

Donald Malcolm Campbell addressed himself to the task that cold, dark morning with a full understanding of what he had to do with *his* craft and on *his* lake: to exceed 300mph. What he did not know, was that his beloved Bluebird when pushed to – and beyond – limits never exceeded before became hostage to complex interactions, both aerodynamic and mechanical, some of which could have been predicted and some of which could not.

Summary

1   At speeds in excess of 310mph, Bluebird K7 was only marginally stable. The additive factors of ground effect and port spar damage were such as to reduce the stability margin further to the point where recovery beyond that speed was impossible once moderating engine thrust was lost or reduced. Episodes of 'hovering' on the last runs have been identified and, indeed, confirmed throughout Bluebird's operational life.

2   The hoped-for stability benefits of a further forward CG resulting from the Orpheus conversion were all but lost by the addition of the compensating ballast to facilitate planing.

3   The angle of the wedges incorporated as part of the original design brief to obtain 250mph were sub-optimal for speeds above that and contributed to the additional drag experienced.

4   The strident 'rooster-tail' spray pattern, evident in smooth or rough running conditions implies that Bluebird was near or at its dynamic stability limit.

5   The first run on 4 January was not without incident as has been generally claimed but demonstrated evidence of instability at the climax of that run and catastrophe was only narrowly averted.

6   Application of the water-brake following the first run was less efficacious than that predicted in earlier lower speed runs due to dynamic instability/ rear shoe 'hop'.

7   Campbell used 'sighting lines' off K7's sponsors to aid his positioning on the lake. He also proceeded far deeper into the southern bay of Coniston than has been previously appreciated. The separation/divergence of the tracks on the first and final runs has also been confirmed.

8   The 'bouncing' phenomena observed on the final run are physically distinct to that of 'tramping' as they have a different cyclic frequency and form. Tramping was only observed to occur on the initial run-up from Peel Island and played no part in the critical stages i.e. from point 'A'. The water conditions over the central part of the lake including that of the timed km were good.

9   The speed profile of the latter part of the final run reveals a serious decelerating episode following bounce '3'. There are no data to underpin the '-0.6 g ' deceleration figure used in several post-hoc analyses.

10   Engine failure has been confirmed at around 7 seconds prior to impact.

11   No evidence can be found to indicate that the water brake was deployed in the final seconds.

12   It is asserted that Donald Campbell's strategy on the final runs was to exploit the benefits of a quick turn-round given the good conditions of the water and his knowledge of how K7 itself disturbed the water during such runs. This approach was not unprecedented as he had exploited it on various previous runs.

Epilogue

In 1967, Dad bought me my first car, for £20, a Minivan. Being in the motor trade, he had it repainted for me – in British Racing Green. This was my choice, as it made it look as though it would go faster! So, first run, off to the local (unofficial) 'racetrack', Birtley bypass in Co. Durham, a stretch of dual carriageway with a gentle incline of a mile or so. Foot 'flat to the boards', all 850cc screamed at me as 75 and then 80mph came up on the speedo. I was scared rigid, the front end seemed light and the position of my *derrière* – at most a foot above the road – gave the impression that I was going twice as fast. I pause to reflect on my hero, similarly constrained above Coniston's dark mirror, battling with his vibrating, bouncing jet projectile at more than four times that. We can only admire . . .

'Few are born to skirt the bounds of man's existence; the Many watch and marvel from afar . . .'

Keith William Mitchell, 26 October 2010

References

1   'Naval Document 2392-55', 17 January 1955 (copy courtesy of Fred Blois).

2   'The Hydroplane "Bluebird"', L.H. Norris and K.W. Norris, *The Engineer*,
      29 March 1957, pp. 474–80.

3   *Leo Villa's Bluebird Album*, David de Lara, 2007.

4   Donald Campbell, *The Man Behind The Mask*, David Tremayne, 2004.

5   *Leap into Legend*, Steve Holter, 2002.

6   *The Bluebird Years*, Arthur Knowles and Graham Beech, 2001.

7   'Aerodynamic and hydrodynamic aspects of high-speed water surface craft', R.K. Nangia,
      Aeronautical Journal, pp. 241–68, June/July 1987.

8   *Record Breaking Hydroplanes*, P.T. Fink, 1955.

9   *The Research & Development of Donald Campbell's Bluebird K7 Hydroplane*, F.R. Blois,
      self-published monograph, 2002, final edition, 2007.
      http://www.rainbowcoloured.co.uk

10 'Weight and Centre of Gravity Check', Norris Brothers Report (Job No: D3/323B, KWN,
      7 October 1966) (by kind permission of Tony James).

11 'Orpheus Engine for Mr Donald Campbell' correspondence, J.A. Woodward (MoD),
      1 June 1966.

12 'K7 Weight Revision', personal communication, Tony James to Keith Mitchell,
      2 January 2011.

13 'Hydrodynamic Properties of Planing Surfaces and Flying Boats', N.A. Sokolov, NACA
      Technical Memorandum (TM) 1246, 1950.

14 'Blue-Bird, Some Calculations on Performance of "C" Boat', Norris Brothers Report 18A,
      26 May 1954, K.W. Norris, Norris Brothers Archive, the Science Museum.

15 'Bluebird Boat – Performance on the Last Run', K.W. Norris and J.L. Stollery,
      Norris Brothers Report (Job No: D3/323C), 23 January 1967 (by kind permission of
      Tony James).

16 'A Theoretical and Experimental Study of Planing Surfaces including Effects of Cross
      Section and Plan Form', C.L. Shuford, NACA Technical Note (TN) 3939, 1957.

17 *World's Fastest Coffin on Water – a Biography of Ken Warby*, Bill Tucky,
      Bas Publishing, 2009.

18 Private discussions between Tony James and Keith Mitchell,
      September 2010 – March 2011.

19 'Bluebird Wind Tunnel Model Tests', Series 'D', Sheet '2', 11 May 1955, Norris Brothers
      Archive, the Science Museum.

20 Personal communications with Prof John Stollery, Cranfield University, K.W. Mitchell,
      December 2010.

21 'Take-Off Speed', Norris Brothers Report 18A, 17 July 1958 and 30 July 1958,
      K.W. Norris/J.L. Stollery, Norris Brothers Archive, the Science Museum.

22 Lift assessments re 1958 mods, K.W. Mitchell, 19 January 2011.

23 'Re: Installation of Bristol Siddeley Orpheus Jet Engine in "Bluebird" Hydroplane',
      K.W. Norris, 13 July 1966.

24 'Drag re Bluebird Performance', Norris Brothers Report (Job No: D3/323C),
      15 December 1966, K.W. Norris/J.L. Stollery.

25 Hydrodynamic drag calculations, K.W. Mitchell, 8 February 2011.

26 'Notes re Weight and Centre of Gravity etc.', personal communication, Tony James to
      Ken Norris, 24 October 2001 (by kind permission of Tony James).

27 Correspondence between K.A. Pearson and Norris Brothers Ltd, 8 August and 31 August 1966.
28 'Bluebird' Job No: 323B, minutes of an internal meeting at Norris Brothers, 4 August 1966.
29 Log sheet of engine starts, Orpheus Bluebird, conducted at Haywards Heath by W.R. Vanryne for Rotax Ltd, 28–29 October 1966, Norris Brothers Archive, the Science Museum.
30 Conversation between Bill Vanryne and Keith Mitchell, 23 February 2011.
31 'Recollections and Conclusions of Bluebird K7 and the Water Speed Record Attempt', Ken Wheeler Lecture to RCEA, Sussex, 10 October 2006.
32 'Air Intake Design Points for Orpheus 701 Engine In Bluebird', correspondence from K.A. Pearson to K.W. Norris, 9 November 1966 (courtesy of Steve Holter).
33 With grateful thanks to Steve Holter for helpful comment and discussion.
34 'Notes on visit to Coniston re ballast weights', Job No: D3/323C, K.W. Norris, 25 November 1966.
35 Factors affecting moment balance, K.W. Mitchell, 23 February 2011.
36 Personal discussions with Dr Robert Englar, Georgia Tech Research Institute (GTRI), Atlanta, Georgia, Jan.–Feb. 2011.
37 'Experimental Evaluations of the Aerodynamics of Unlimited Racing Hydroplanes Operating in and out of Ground Effect', R.J. Englar, D.M. Shuster and D.A. Ford, SAE Technical Paper Series 901869, 1990.
38 Condition 3 – moment calculations, K.W. Mitchell, 27 February 2011.
39 'Bluebird Boat – Performance on the Last Run', handwritten notes of Ken Norris (Job No: D3/323C), 23 January 1967, Norris Brothers Archive, the Science Museum.
40 Personal discussions with David Clarke, BAE Warton (retd.), July 2009.
41 Estimation of assymetric drag at damaged spar, K.W. Mitchell, 12 December 2011.
42 'Analysis of Bluebird Crash Run', Fig. 2, RAF analysis, 1967 (courtesy of Tony James).
43 With grateful thanks to Sky TV.
44 Conversation between Robbie Robinson and Keith Mitchell, Coniston Lodge, 27 January 2011.
45 Correlation of soundtrack time with Four Companies TV film frame time, K.W. Mitchell, 7 February 2011.
46 Photo frame timing analysis of Four Companies TV film footage, K.W. Mitchell, 31 January 2011.
47 'Comments on the Two Films (BBC and ITN)', Prof J.L. Stollery, February 1967, Norris Brothers Archive, the Science Museum.
48 *Fighter Test Pilot: From Hurricane to Tornado*, Roland Beaumont, Patrick Stephens Ltd, 1987.
49 Film analysis, Tony James, 11 February 1967, Norris Brothers Archive, the Science Museum.
50 'Calculations of pitch angle from photo', *The Engineer*, 13 January 1967, Tony James Papers.
51 DMC g-factor during somersault, K.W. Mitchell, 21 February 2011.
52 Lateral CG Correction, K.W. Mitchell, 24 April 2011.
53 Private communication from Dr K.J. Wheeler, 20 December 2011.
54 Communications from Bill Smith, October 2011 – July 2012.
55 Paper on ballast weight, tank position, craft height and wedge angle in response to Bill Smith's measurements, K.W. Mitchell, 16 November 2011.

APPENDICES
'WHYS AND WHEREFORES'

APPENDIX I
BLUEBIRD K7 – TECHNICAL SPECIFICATION

Construction:	The hull of Bluebird K7 was stressed to twice the factor of a supersonic aircraft (max. 25g)	
Constructor	Salmesbury Engineering	
Space frame	Chrome-molybdenum seamless square section steel tubing by Accles & Pollock	
Outer skin	Birmabright light aluminium alloy	
Sponsons & spars	Fabricated light alloy angle and plate to form watertight square box section	
Planing shoes	Machined solid alloy castings	
Fasteners	12,000+ rivets, high tensile steel bolts, welding, Dzus fasteners and chromate assembly paste	

Engine:	Bristol Siddeley Orpheus 701 turbojet single-stage turbine, 7-stage axial compressor, 7 flame tubes; turbine inlet temp 640 °C	
	Max. output (nominal) lb thrust / kN	4,500/20.02
	Max. output (boosted) lb thrust / kN	5,277/23.53 (110% of max., 2°C inlet temp)
	Max. output bhp / kW at 328mph	4,623/3,446
	At rpm	10,450
	Max. jet-pipe temperature	720°C
	Fuel	Kerosene (AVTUR DERD 2494)
	Thrust-to-weight ratio	5.78lb/lb or 56.62 N/kg

Weight:	Hull empty (lb/kg)	3,602/1,634
	Orpheus engine (lb/kg)	913/414
	Hull + Orpheus (lb/kg)	4,515/2,048
	Ancillaries and fittings (lb/kg)	375/170
	Buoyancy (floats + aft end) (lb/kg)	120/54.5
	Hull + Orpheus + ancillaries and fittings + buoyancy (lb/kg)	5,010/2,272.5
	Lead ballast (lb/kg)	170/77
	Hull + Orpheus + ancillaries and fittings + buoyancy + lead ballast (lb/kg)	5,180/2349.5
	Fuel boost pump + header tank	(lb/kg) 15/7
	Fuel system – full (51 gallons) (lb/kg)	408/185
	Pilot (lb/kg)	180/81.5
	Radio + Battery (lb/kg)	20/9
	Seat harness + air bottle (lb/kg)	10/4.5
	All up weight (lb/kg)	5,813/2,637

Dimensions:	Length inc. rudder (ft & in/m)	26ft 5.0in/8.05
	Width inc. sponsons (ft & in/m)	10ft 6in/3.20
	Width of main hull (ft & in/m)	5ft 2in/1.58
	Height inc. tail fin & rudder (ft & in/m)	8ft 5.5in/2.58
	Sponson length (ft & in/m)	13ft 4in/4.01

APPENDIX II
BLUEBIRD K7 – PERFORMANCE

Performance:
Maximum speed mph/kph/mps 330/531/147.5
K7 is 1.85 times faster than a contemporary 1966 F1 car (max. speed 180mph)
K7 is 1.50 times faster than a current 2011 F1 car (max. speed 220mph)
K7 would cover the length of a football pitch (105m) in 0.73 seconds at 320mph
K7 would cover 1 km in 6.99 seconds at 320mph

Power-to-weight ratio:
2,000lb of thrust per tonne
8.893 kN of thrust per tonne
1,753bhp per tonne (at 328mph)
1,307 kW per tonne (at 328mph)

Acceleration:

30–70mph	12.0 seconds	(+ 0.15G)
70–150mph	9.0 seconds	(+ 0.42G)
150–200mph	5.7 seconds	(+ 0.40G)
200–250mph	5.7 seconds	(+ 0.40G)
250–300mph	5.7 seconds	(+ 0.40G)
300–328mph	2.0 seconds	(+ 0.63G)

Note: Bluebird's max. acceleration with full power and planing ~0.5G.

Time to accelerate from 70mph to 328mph peak speed on final run: 28.1 seconds

The maximum rate of horizontal acceleration of Bluebird K7 was 0.63G (20.2ft/s/s or 6.09 m/s/s) achieved from 300mph up to 328mph. This meant Donald Campbell was pushed back in his seat with 0.63 times his bodyweight.

Deceleration:
The maximum rate of horizontal deceleration experienced in Bluebird K7 was -1.86G (-59.5ft/s/s or -17.9m/s/s) decelerating from her peak speed of 328mph to 296mph in 0.84 seconds, meaning Campbell was thrown against his safety harness with 1.86 times his bodyweight.

Fuel consumption:
Specific fuel consumption of 1.06lb (1.00lb of thrust for 1 hour per 1.06lb of fuel)
Orpheus thrust, max. = 5277lb at 110% rating, adjusted for 2°C
Consumption ffi 5,277 x 1.06/60 = 93.23lb/min – i.e. ffiffi11.65 gallons per minute, assuming 1 imperial gallon of AVTUR = 8lb.
Fuel tank capacity 46 gallons + 4 gallon low-pressure fuel tank + 1 gallon header tank capacity gives a fuel system capacity of 51 gallons, less 'sump' capacity – 8 gall, gives 43 gallons i.e. sufficient for 3 minutes 41 seconds of full-throttle running.

APPENDIX III
DONALD CAMPBELL'S WORLD SPEED RECORDS

Water Speed Record (Kilometre)

Date	Location	1st Run speed mph	1st Run time seconds	2nd Run speed mph	2nd Run time seconds	Average speed mph
23 Jul 1955	Ullswater	215.080	10.400	189.570	11.800	202.320
16 Nov 1955	Lake Mead	239.500	9.340	192.200	11.639	216.230
19 Sep 1956	Coniston Water	286.780	7.800	164.480	13.600	225.630
7 Nov 1957	Coniston Water	260.100	8.600	218.020	10.263	239.070
10 Nov 1958	Coniston Water	243.410	9.190	253.480	8.825	248.620
14 May 1959	Coniston Water	275.150	8.130	245.550	9.110	260.35
31 Dec 1964	Lake Dumbleyung	283.300	7.896	269.300	8.306	276.300

Land Speed Record (Mile)

Date	Location	1st Run speed speed mph	1st Run time seconds	2nd Run speed mph	2nd Run time seconds	Average speed mph
17 Jul 1964	Lake Eyre	403.100	8.931	403.100	8.931	403.100

1966/67 Water Speed Record Timed Trials (Kilometre)

Date	Location	1st Run speed speed mph	1st Run time seconds	2nd Run speed mph	2nd Run time seconds	Average speed mph
10 Dec 1966	Coniston Water	202.300	11.058	196.100	11.407	199.200
12 Dec 1966	Coniston Water	250.780	8.920	237.720	9.410	244.250
13 Dec 1966	Coniston Water	197.780	11.310	261.330	8.560	229.550
14 Dec 1966	Coniston Water	267.250	8.370	261.850	8.543	264.550
4 Jan 1967	Coniston Water	297.600	7.517	303.600*	7.342*	300.600*

* Final run incomplete. The above speed and time are for the final 1,000 metres covered by K7 as a waterborne craft, 586 m south of the measured kilometre and 414 m inside the measured kilometre, on her final run. The average speed is calculated from the official first run speed and the calculated second run speed. The data for this calculation is taken from the crash analysis in Chapter 10. It is provided for illustration only to show that Bluebird had the performance to achieve a 300mph-plus Water Speed Record.

APPENDIX IV
RADIO TELEPHONE TRANSCRIPT

Donald Campbell's final runs in Bluebird K7 on 4 January 1967
Note: Text in italics is indistinct in the recording and is not certain

Donald Campbell (Call Sign: Skipper)

Leo Villa (Call Sign: Alpha)

Keith Harrison (Call Sign: Kilo)

Stephen Darbishire – Timekeepers (Call Sign: Tango)

Paul Evans (Call Sign: Base)

Louis Goossens (Call Sign: Charlie)

GMT 08.40

Leo, Leo, how's your water? OVER

There appear to be no birds in the way at the moment, and there is a slight down swell on the water, but it could be caused by our own boat. OVER

Kilo, Kilo, Kilo, Kilo, how's the water? OVER

Kilo to Bluebird. The water surface is smooth, but there's a slight ground swell, erm, otherwise conditions are reasonably good, visibility is quite good. OVER

Roger Kilo. We are going to try a slow run. Charlie do you read? OVER

Yes Skipper, read you loud and clear.

Ok . . . all stations . . . rockets fire one . . . NOW!

From Bluebird, Tango, do you read?

Tango, Tango, Tango, do you read? OVER

Base, do you have contact with Tango? OVER

Wait there Skipper, I'll try calling him. Base for Tango, Base for Tango, do you read? OVER

Tango to Base, loud and clear. OVER

Roger. Please listen out on your sets, Skipper has been calling you. OVER

Radio telephone transcript:

Donald Campbell
Call Sign: Skipper

Leo Villa
Call Sign: Alpha

Keith Harrison
Call Sign: Kilo

Timekeepers:
Stephen Darbishire
Call Sign: Tango

Paul Evans
Call Sign: Base

Louis Goossens
Call Sign: Charlie

Tango, you're just ready to build up about runs, how's your . . . are you set?
. . . ready? . . . OVER

Base for Tango, Skipper wishes to know if you are all set, OVER

[Silence]

Base for Tango, Base for Tango, Skipper wishes to know if you are all ready,
OVER

Tango to Base, Tango to Base, yes, we are all ready – we are all ready. Will you
pass that message on to Skipper? – Tango to Base, OVER

Base for Skipper, Tango all ready. OVER

Roger, Paul, assume you'll relay . . . Charlie, Alpha, Charlie and er . . . now Kilo,
have your rockets fired? OVER

Alpha calling Skipper, one rocket fired Skipper, one rocket fired, not
particularly brilliant, we had it too low but it went off. OVER AND OUT

Kilo, Charlie, confirm please. I said fire one, fire one not two. OVER

Kilo . . . confirm.

Base for Kilo, do you read Skipper? OVER

Go!

GMT 08.45

Kilo, we are under way [21-second pause]

OK Leo, do you read me? OVER (Start of first run)

Coming in loud and clear, Skipper . . . Coming in loud and clear

Two bloody swans have just taken off going down the lake . . .

I'm under way, all systems normal; brake swept up, er . . . air pressure warning
light on . . . I'm coming onto track now and er . . . I'll open up just as soon as
I am heading down the lake, er doesn't look too smooth from here, doesn't
matter, here we go . . . Here we go . . . [pause 3 seconds] . . .

. . . Passing through four . . . five coming up . . . a lot of water, nose beginning
to lift, water all over the front of the engine again . . . and the nose is up . . .
low pressure fuel warning light . . . going left . . . OK we're up and away . . . and
passing through er . . . tramping very hard at 150 . . . very hard indeed . . . FULL
POWER . . . Passing through 2 . . . 25 out of the way . . . tramping like hell Leo,
I don't think I can get over the top, but I'll try, FULL HOUSE . . . and I can't see
where I am . . . FULL HOUSE – FULL HOUSE – FULL HOUSE . . . POWER OFF
NOW! . . . I'M THROUGH! . . .

. . . power . . . (garbled) er passing through 25 vector off Peel Island . . . passing
through 2 . . . I'm lighting like mad . . . brake gone down . . . er . . . engine
lighting up now . . . relighting . . . passing Peel Island . . . relight made normal
. . . and now . . . down at Brown Howe . . . passing through 100 . . . er . . . nose
hasn't dropped yet . . . nose down . . .

Leo, do you read me? OVER

Hello . . . read you . . . er, Skipper, come in . . . [16-second-long static]

Base do you read me? OVER

Reading you Skipper, come in . . .

Base, will you get a message from Tango, please? OVER

Base, er . . . Roger, er . . . in actual fact that was Alpha that answered you, Skipper. OVER . . .

Don't worry about Alpha; I want a message from Tango. OVER . . .

Roger, Skipper . . . Tango, Tango, do you read? OVER . . .

Tango to Base, Tango to Base . . . Stand–by . . . [Static]

Tango to Base, Tango to Base . . . Message for Skipper . . . +47 +47 . . . +47 . . . do you copy that? Repeat, OVER . . .

ROGER – ROGER – ROGER . . . Base for Skipper, Base for Skipper, from Tango, +47 +47 OVER . . .

GMT 08.48

Campbell manoeuvring Bluebird ready for return run in the bay south of Brown Howe.

Roger, Paul . . . I'm starting the return run now . . . (3 minutes 18.5 seconds after start of first run)

[20.5-second-long pause including 8 seconds of static. Campbell may have been speaking, but any signal is not being picked up by base, Bluebird's location south of High Peel Near is masking any transmission]

. . . Full nose up . . . Pitching a bit down here . . . coming through our own wash . . . er getting straightened up now on track . . . rather closer to Peel Island . . . and we're tramping like mad . . . and er . . . FULL POWER . . . er tramping like hell OVER. I can't see much and the water's very bad indeed . . . I'm galloping over (I can't get over) the top . . . and she's actually giving a hell of a bloody row in here . . . I can't see anything . . . I've got the bows out . . . I'm going . . . U-hh . . . (31-second transmission)

Hello . . . Tango to Base, Tango to Base, OVER . . .

Base to Tango, OVER . . .

Base to Tango, OVER . . .

Tango to Base . . . Tango To Base . . . Complete accident I'm afraid . . . OVER

Er, roger, er details? OVER

No details as yet, no details . . . STANDBY . . .

APPENDIX V
THE TEAM, THE PRESS AND HANGERS-ON

Donald Malcolm Campbell CBE ('*Skipper*'): Born 1921. Bluebird pilot and team leader. Holder of the WSR seven times and the LSR once. Only person in history to break the LSR and WSR in the same year.

Tonia Bern-Campbell ('*Fred*'): Born 1934. Professional singer and cabaret performer. Donald's third wife, married 24 December 1958.

Leo Villa OBE ('*Unc*'): Born 1899. Chief engineer to Sir Malcolm and Donald Campbell, overseeing 21 world speed records on land and water from 1924 to 1964.

Maurice Parfitt ('*Maurie*'): Born 1916. Technical engineer to Donald Campbell since 1954.

Ken Norris B.Sc., A.C.G.I., F.I.Mech.E., F.R.Ae.S.: Born 1921. Co-designer of Bluebird K7 hydroplane and Bluebird CN7 car. Co-founder of Norris Brothers Ltd, consulting engineers.

Lewis Norris C.Eng., M.I.Mech.E. ('*Lew*'): Born 1924. Co-designer of Bluebird K7 hydroplane and Bluebird CN7 car. Co-founder of Norris Brothers Ltd, consulting engineers.

Tony James C.Eng., M.I.Mech.E.: Born 1933. Project Manager at Norris Brothers R&D Ltd. Manager for Bluebird K7's modifications and refit August – November 1966.

Professor John Stollery CBE F.R.Eng: Born 1930. Professor of Aeronautics, Imperial College, London.

Louis Goossens: Born 1929. Donald Campbell's house manager since 1959. General team assistant.

Clive Glynn: Born 1944. Apprentice mechanic co-opted into Bluebird team in November 1966.

Anthony Robinson ('*Robbie*'): Born 1944. Team assistant and course boat pilot. Son of Connie Robinson, of the Sun Hotel, Bluebird team base in autumn/winter of 1966/67.

Mr Whoppit: Born 1956. Team mascot, accompanied Donald in the cockpit on all his Speed Record attempts from 1958. Today, Mr Whoppit lives in peaceful retirement with Donald's daughter, Gina.

Corporal Paul Evans: Royal Army Signals Corps. Responsible for team radio communications during Bluebird trials.

Bill Jordan: Lancashire RAC. Slipway security and general team assistant.

Ken Pearson: Bristol Siddeley design installation department engineer. Responsible for installation recommendations on the BS Orpheus jet engine.

Jack Lavis: Bristol Siddeley development and service engineer. Responsible for service and development recommendations on the BS Orpheus jet engine.

Bill Vanryne C.Eng., M.I.Mech.E.: Rotax development engineer. Responsible for installation and service recommendations on Bluebird's Rotax engine air start system.

Ted Hamel: Friend of Donald Campbell. Electrical engineer, provided advice and assistance with Bluebird's electrical system.

Raoul Crélerot: Longines' chief timekeeper for the high-speed timed trials.

Norman Buckley: Born 1908. Windermere hotelier and Manchester solicitor. Royal Yachting Association official observer for the timed speed trials. Motorboat record-breaker and friend of Donald Campbell. Chairman of the K7 Club.

Andrew Brown: Kendal businessman and friend of Donald Campbell. Royal Yachting Association official observer for timed speed trials.

Dr Stephen Darbishire: Coniston GP, friend and medical advisor of Donald Campbell. Official observer for timed speed trials.

Connie Robinson: Ran the Sun Hotel, Coniston, team base during the trials and record attempt, and friend of Donald Campbell.

Keith Harrison ('*Keithy*'): Press Association North of England correspondent. Secretary of the K7 Club. Manned the southern course marshal boat during Bluebird's 1966/67 trials.

Geoffrey Mather: *Daily Express* columnist.

David Benson: *Daily Express* motoring correspondent and personal friend of Donald Campbell.

Norman Luck: *Daily Express* from 1964 to 1996 as a staff reporter, foreign correspondent and latterly Chief Investigative Reporter.

Brian Boss: *Daily Sketch* North of England correspondent.

Harry Griffin: *Manchester Guardian* & *Lancashire Evening News* Lakeland correspondent.

Geoff Hallawell: Freelance photographer of the Bluebird trials and friend of Donald Campbell.

Paul Allonby: Freelance photographer of the Bluebird trials for *Lancashire Evening News*.

APPENDIX VI
CONTRIBUTORS TO THE
ORPHEUS BLUEBIRD PROJECT

Accles & Pollock	Technical assistance
Adams & Adams Ltd	Transport of Bluebird
Advel Ltd	Riveting equipment
Air Ministry	Supply of Orpheus engine on loan; supply of Folland Gnat plane at scrap value
Angus, George & Co. Ltd	Washers
APV Crawley	Welding of stainless steel fittings
Avimo Ltd	Pitot static head
Bloctube Controls Ltd	Engine control runs
Bourner, F.H. (Coachworks)	Jet intake modifications and repainting of Bluebird
Bribond Signs Ltd	Supply of nameplates
Bristol Siddeley Engines Ltd	Orpheus engine installation and extensive technical assistance and supplying of equipment
British Aircraft Corporation	Loan of high pressure compressor
British Oxygen Company	Supply of air breathing equipment
British Visqueen Ltd	Buoyancy pillows
Champion Sparking Plug Company	Supply of jet engine igniters
Coley, R.J. & Co.	Transport of engine and equipment
Dennison Deri Ltd	Seals
Dowty Seals Ltd	Seals for air starting system
Dunbar Sheet Metal Works	Intake ducting, stabilising fin parts and body repair
Dunlop Rubber Co. Ltd	Hoses and fittings
Fram Filters Ltd	Supply of fuel and oil filters
Gallay Ltd	Auxiliary fuel tank
Glynn's Garage Ltd	Organisation of external contractors
Hadwins Ltd, Torver	Supply of aviation jet fuel
Hall & Co.	Plastolene cover for Bluebird and boathouse
Hawker Siddeley Aviation Ltd	Technical advice
Horace & Williams Ltd	Paint supplies
Honeywill Atlas Ltd	Rigid polyurethane foam buoyancy
Irving Air Chute Ltd	Safety harness
Lockheed Precision Products Ltd	Hydraulic system fittings and advice
Longines	Timing of high-speed trials
Lucas Electrical Ltd	Wiring and batteries

Macklow Smith & Co.	Welding
Mitchell, R. & Co.	Engine mounting brackets
Neal, John D.	Timing equipment
Norris Brothers (R&D) Ltd	Design and modification of Bluebird K7 inc. engine installation, hydraulic brake; technical organisation
Norris Systems Ltd	Ignition system
Paine Engineering Ltd	Engine mounting blocks
Precision Rubbers	Silicone rubber seals
Protective Materials Ltd	Workshop sealed floor coating
Pyrene Co. Ltd	Fire extinguisher equipment
RAF Non-Destructive Testing	X-raying of mainframe and visual checks
Rapp Metals	Supply of aluminium and carbon steel
Rodell, W.E. & Son	Compressor loan; instruments supply
Rose Brothers Ltd	Engine fitting bearing
Rotax Ltd	Installation/operation advice air start equipment for Bluebird
Seymour Crane Hire	Engine lifting at Coniston
Siebe Gorman Ltd	Air breathing apparatus
Smith & Sons Ltd	Instrumentation supply and technical assistance
Stewart Aeronautical Supply Ltd	Technical advice and supply of Lucas Rotax air start system
Technical Resin Bonders Ltd	Resin bonding for intake and perspex canopy
Tidy Ltd	Crane services
Triplex Safety Glass Ltd	Perspex canopy and spray shield repair
Trist, Hubert Ltd	Supply of hose fittings
Tylers Ltd	High pressure fittings
Ultrasonoscope Co. Ltd	Frame inspection

APPENDIX VII
THE OFFICIAL WORLD WATER SPEED RECORD

Craft	Pilot	Country	mph	km/h	Location	Date
Hydrodome IV	Casey Baldwin	USA	70.86	114.04	Bras d'Or Lake	19 Sep 1919
Miss America	Gar Wood	USA	74.87	120.49	Detroit River	15 Sep 1920
Miss America II	Gar Wood	USA	80.57	129.66	Detroit River	6 Sep 1921
Farman Hydroglider	Jules Fisher	Belgium	87.39	140.64	River Seine	10 Nov 1924
Miss America II	George Wood	USA	92.84	149.41	Detroit River	4 Sep 1928
Miss America VII	Gar Wood	USA	93.12	149.87	Indian Creek	23 Mar 1929
Miss England II	Henry Segrave	GB	98.76	158.94	Windermere	13 Jun 1930
Miss America IX	Gar Wood	USA	102.26	164.57	Indian Creek	20 Mar 1931
Miss England II	Kaye Don	GB	103.49	166.55	Parana River	15 Apr 1931
Miss England II	Kaye Don	GB	110.22	177.39	Lake Garda	31 Jul 1931
Miss America IX	Gar Wood	USA	111.71	179.78	Indian Creek	5 Feb 1932
Miss England III	Kaye Don	GB	117.43	188.99	Loch Lomond	18 Jul 1932
Miss England III	Kaye Don	GB	119.81	192.82	Loch Lomond	18 Jul 1932
Miss America X	Gar Wood	USA	124.86	200.94	St Claire River	20 Sep 1932
Bluebird K3	Malcolm Campbell	GB	126.32	203.29	Lake Maggiore	1 Sep 1937
Bluebird K3	Malcolm Campbell	GB	129.50	208.41	Lake Maggiore	2 Sep 1937
Bluebird K3	Malcolm Campbell	GB	130.91	210.66	Hallwilersee	17 Sep 1938
Bluebird K4	Malcolm Campbell	GB	141.74	228.11	Coniston Water	19 Aug 1939
Slo-Mo-Shun IV	Stanley Sayres	USA	160.32	258.02	Lake Washington	26 Jun 1950
Slo-Mo-Shun IV	Stanley Sayres	USA	178.50	287.26	Lake Washington	7 Jul 1952
Bluebird K7	Donald Campbell	GB	202.32	325.60	Ullswater	23 Jul 1955
Bluebird K7	Donald Campbell	GB	216.20	347.94	Lake Mead	16 Nov 1955
Bluebird K7	Donald Campbell	GB	225.63	363.12	Coniston Water	19 Sep 1956
Bluebird K7	Donald Campbell	GB	239.07	384.75	Coniston Water	7 Nov 1957
Bluebird K7	Donald Campbell	GB	248.62	400.12	Coniston Water	10 Nov 1958
Bluebird K7	Donald Campbell	GB	260.35	418.99	Coniston Water	14 May 1959
Bluebird K7	Donald Campbell	GB	276.33	444.71	Lake Dumbleyung	31 Dec 1964
Hustler	Lee Taylor	USA	285.22	459.02	Lake Guntersville	30 Jun 1967
Spirit of Australia	Ken Warby	AUS	288.18	464.46	Blowering Dam	20 Nov 1977
Spirit of Australia	Ken Warby	AUS	317.60	511.13	Blowering Dam	8 Oct 1978

BIBLIOGRAPHY

The following books, periodicals, and sources have been consulted in the writing of this book. Material from the author's own extensive collection was also used for research purposes, as well as the personal papers of Donald Campbell, Leo Villa, Tony James, Ken Norris, Prof John Stollery and Bill Vanryne.

Books

Blois, Fred, *The Research & Development of Donald Campbell's Bluebird K7 Hydroplane*, self-published, 2003

Campbell, Donald & Mitchell, Alan W., *Into the Water Barrier*, Odhams Press, 1955

Campbell, Gina & Meech, Michael, *Bluebirds: Story of the Campbell Dynasty*, Sidgwick & Jackson, 1988

Campbell, Tonia, *My Speed King: Life with Donald Campbell*, Sutton Publishing, 2001

De Lara, David & Desmond, Kevin, *Leo Villa's Bluebird Album*, Transport Bookman, 2007

Drackett, Phil, *Like Father, Like Son: The Story of Malcolm and Donald Campbell*, Clifton Books, 1969

Holter, Steve, *Leap into Legend: Donald Campbell and the Complete Story of the World Speed Records*, Sigma Leisure, 2002

Knowles, Arthur, *With Campbell at Coniston*, William Kimber, 1969

Knowles, Arthur, & Dorothy, Lady Campbell, *Donald Campbell CBE*, George Allen & Unwin, 1969

Knowles, Arthur, with Beech, Graham, *The Bluebird Years*, Sigma Leisure 2008

Pearson, John, *Bluebird and the Dead Lake*, Collins, 1965, reprinted by Aurum Press in 2002

Stevens, Donald, *Bluebird CN7: The Inside Story of Donald Campbell's Last Land Speed Record Car*, Veloce Publishing, 2010

Tremayne, David, *Racers Apart: Memories of Motor Sport Heroes*, Motor Racing Publications, 1991

Tremayne, David, *Donald Campbell – The Man Behind The Mask*, Bantam Press, 2004

Villa, Leo, with Grey, Tony, *The Record Breakers*, Hamlyn, 1969

Villa, Leo, with Desmond, Kevin, *The World Water Speed Record*, Batsford, 1976

Young-James, Douglas, *Donald Campbell: An Informal Biography*, Neville & Spearman, 1968

Magazines

Car, Classic Speedboats, Cumbria Life, Life Magazine, Men Only, Modern Man, Motorboat & Yachting, Motorsport, Paris Match, Australian Woman's Weekly, Sunday Times Magazine

Newspapers

Daily Express, Daily Mail, Daily Mirror, Daily Sketch, Daily Telegraph, Evening Mail, Evening News, Evening Standard, Manchester Evening News, Lancashire Evening Post, Observer, Sun, Sunday Times

Newsreel, film and TV

How Long A Mile by Donald Campbell, 1965
Movietone and Pathé newsreels
Speed King by Nigel Turner, Castle Video
The Price of a Record by Dougie Hurn, Four Companies TV, 1967
BBC, ITV and Sky News

Websites

www.bluebirdk7.com
www.bluebirdproject.com
http://groups.yahoo.com/group/speedrecordgroup
http://www.acrossthelake.com
www.ruskinmuseum.com

INDEX